EXPORT MARKETING OF MARINE PRODUCTS

EXPORT MARKETING OF MARINE PRODUCTS

By

Dr. K. RAMA MOHANA RAO
M.Com., Ph.D.,
Associate Professor,
Department of Commerce and Management Studies
Andhra University,
Visakhapatnam-530 003.

Dr. D. PRAKASH
M.Com., M.Phil., Ph.D.,
Lecturer in Commerce
Mrs. A.V.N., College
Visakhapatnam-530 001.

DISCOVERY PUBLISHING HOUSE
NEW DELHI-110 002.

First Published-2000
Reprint, 2011
ISBN 81-7141-565-2

Published by
DISCOVERY PUBLISHING HOUSE
4831/24, Ansari Road, Prahlad Street,
Darya Ganj, New Delhi-110002 (India)
Phone: 3279245 • Fax: 91-11-3253475
E-mail:dph@indiatimes.com

Mehra Offset Press
Delhi

This Work is Dedicated to

Sri Lord Venkateswara Tirupati

Preface

Fisheries Sector occupy a prominent place in the Indian Economy for two important reasons- a source of livelihood for millions of fishermen throughout the coastline and an important source of foreign exchange earnings. The development of fisheries has been a focussed area during successive plan periods. Inspite of the developmental activities in providing infrastructural facilities, research, technical and financial support, the industry could not register the progress to the desired level. The vast market potential in foreign countries is not exploited so far. The excessive dependency on a very few markets creating many export marketing problems. The absence of proper vision and strategic approach in exporting marine products is making many markets in accessible to the Indian fish farmers. The efforts of MPEDA in this direction though positive but proved inadequate. The present study makes an attempt to examine the development of fisheries sector in India and the performance of MPEDA's export marketing services.

This book is a research work based on the data from secondary as well as primary resources. The book is divided into X chapters. Chapter 1 presents Introduction and Review of Literature. An overview of the Fisheries Sector in India is presented in Chapter II. The Market-wise and Product-wise exports of Indian Marine Products are analysed in Chapter III. The MPEDA's objectives and organisation structure is studied in Chapter IV. The details of product planning and Quality Control Mechanisms are presented in Chapter V. In Chapter VI the distribution and pricing policies of MPEDA are examined. The promotional strategies of MPEDA are analysed in Chapter VII. Chapter VIII deals with Exporters 'Profile and views, whereas the performance of MPEDA is appraised in

Chapter IX. The conclusions of study and strategies for development are presented in Chapter X.

Dr. K. Rama Mohana Rao

Dr. D. Vijaya Prakash

Contents

1

Introduction

IMPORTANCE OF FISHERIES SECTOR

Fish is one of the important sources of food to human beings since time immemorial. Fish were among the first animals systematically hunted by primitive man[1]. The modern theory of evolution propounded by Charles Darvin is that the life in this universe originated in water, passed through several stages of the acquatic animals viz., Fish, etc., into amphibians and finally through a number of other stages of terrestrial life to the modern man, lends support to the ancient Hindu belief of Dasavathara. The different incarnations of the Lord symbolise the different stages of evolution, 'Matsyavathara' fully acquatic) being the first one.[2]

Long long ago, man discovered fishes as valuable source of food and devised simple weapons like the spear, nets and traps to catch them. The importance of fish in diet lies in the chemical composition of the flesh, which is rich in protein and minerals like calcium, phosphorous and iron. Some fishes, in addition, have varying quantities of fats and oils.[3] Seafood is an excellent food because it is nutrient rich. It has the best and top notch protein which supplies essential amino-acids. It is easily digestable as it has very little connective tissue. It gives many nutrients the human beings need, without worrisome amounts of fats. The small amount of fat present in seafood is of the most favourable kind as it promotes health....

Seafood is also rich in many trace minerals like copper, zinc, cobalt, iodin, floride and selenium. Seafood is nutrient rich and therefore, it is not surprising if any one says that intake of seafood is the nutritional insurance[4] The problem of protein gap in food is much more acute in a populous country like India with chronic food shortage and malnutrition and the diet of a large number of masses constitutes cereals which contains carbohydrates, to a major extent and other inferior type of food[5]. Fish is a good solution to the problem of food.

Fishing is one of the oldest occupations in India. The fishing sector has a place of pride in the national economy. The significance of this sector is of two dimensional i.e., employment potential and export potential. There are 59.59 lakh fishermen in the country by the end of 1994.[6] Out of the total fishermen population, about 24 lakhs are full time fishermen, 14.43 lakhs are part-time fishermen and 21.21 lakhs are occasional fishermen.[7] Apart from the direct employment to fishermen, this sector is responsible for the generation of employment for several millions in seafood and ancillary industries*. Fisheries sector is regarded as a powerful income and employment generator as it stimulates the growth of a number of subsidiary industries[8]

The fisheries sector has been an important source for foreign exchange resources over a period of time in the country. "Although fishing has been a traditional occupation in the coastal villages of India, the recognition that the activity has gained in the economic front is largely due to remarkable achievement on the export front[9]". The exports of marine products increased from a mere 19.7 thousand tonnes in 1950-51 to 296.3 thousand tonnes in 1995-96 recording over 15 times increase. In terms of value, the growth is from Rs. 2,46 crores in 1950-51 to over Rs. 3,500 crores in 1995-96[10]. Out of the total Indian exports, the share of marine products is

* The seafood and ancillary industries are boat building yards, manufacture of fishing gear, synthetic twine, winches, otter boards sinkers, floats, marine diesel engines, refrigerated cabinets, insulated boxes, establishment of service stations for repairs and installation of marine diesel engines in fishing vessels, ice factories, cold storages, construction of carrier vessels and truck establishments of various processing plants and allied infrastructural facilities.

3.32 per cent[11] and this sector is the fourth[12] largest contributor for foreign exchange resources of the country.

REVIEW OF LITERATURE

Several studies have been conducted on fisheries sector. For the purpose of the study, selected research works are reviewed in the areas of fisheries development, economics of fisheries, fisheries management and production and marketing of fish.

Mary Chandy[13], brought out historical perspectives of fisheries, different types of fishes and growth and expansion of trade in fisheries in India. Jhingran, V.G.,[14] in his book on 'Fish and fisheries of India', brought out various facts of the fishing sector in India including, organisation, variety of fish, resource strength, technology and exports of fish. The work stands as a foundation to learn fisheries sector in India Chopra, B.N.,[15] collected the opinions of the researchers in fisheries sector being to various problems and measures for development. Desai, M.B., and Baichwal, P.R.,[16] brought out an economic survey of fishing industry in Thane district of Maharashtra. The study focussed on the role of middlemen and co-operatives in the fishing industry. The scope of the study was restricted to a small geographical area.

Durai Raj, N.,[17] Lukas, H.W.,[18] also conducted studies on fisheries development limiting the scope of the study to a geographical area. Mitra, G.N.,[19] Mohan, K.P.,[20] Silas,E.G.,[21] Prasad, B..,[22] Srivastava., K.R.[23] have contributed significantly to the research on development of fisheries in the country. The proceedings of the National Workshop on "Development of Marine Fisheries for Higher Productivity and Export", organised by Department of Agriculture and Co-operation, Ministry of Agriculture, Government of India from 9th to 10th June, 1992 at Cochin, edited by Verghese, C.P., and Joy, P.S., [24] included the issues like present status, problems and strategy for development of coastal and off-shore fisheries, deepsea fisheries, infrastructure and post harvest facilities, financing, welfare of fishermen and fish marketing - domestic and export. National Council of Applied Economic Research[25] has conducted techno-economic survey of various states and brought out the basic statistics on various aspects of fisheries. Department of Fisheries,[26] Lakshminarayana Ray, M.,[27] Misra., S.N. and Bayer, J.,[28] Perumal, M.C.[29] Subba Rao, N.,[30] have studied various economic aspects of the fishing industry.

Srivastava, U.K., Dharma Reddy, M., and Gupta, V.K.,[31] studied the managerial aspects of marine fishing industry with special reference to Gujarat State. Rao, P.S.,[32] made a comprehensive study on fishing economics and management in India covering aspects such as importance of fisheries in the international scene with special reference to Indian fishery resources, earnings of fishing in India, fish marketing and management.

Babaji, U.,[33] made a study on development of marine fisheries covering socio-economic, production, marketing and consumption characteristics of marine fisheries sector in Visakhapatnam. The National Council of Applied Economic Research[34] attempted to forecast the demand for fishing in three selected cities in India. The study revealed the gaps in data and consequent difficulties in forecasting the demand for fish.

Talwan, P.K., and Kacker, R.K.,[35] in their work on commercial sea fishes of India, highlighted the marketability of the variety of fish available in the country and suggested measures for their development. Sreedharan, V.P.,[36] worked on industrial and commercial prospects of fish and fish products in India with particular reference to Kerala. In his thesis the researcher dealt with the marketability of various fish and fish products in the domestic and international markets and emphasised the need for giving fisheries sector the status of industry. Kulkarni, G.R., and Srivastava, U.K.,[37] studied systems frame work of the marine food industry in India and suggested for an integrated frame work for the development of fisheries sector in the country. The National Council of Applied Economic Research[38] studied the export prospects of fish and fish products from India. Vijaya Prakash, D.,[39] studied the problems and prospects of fishermen including the socio-economic, marketing and financial aspects of marine fishermen. Trivedi, K.K.,[40] brought out an edited volume of the proceedings of an International Conference on fisheries Development : 2000 A.D. held at New Delhi in 1985. The proceedings include various aspects and discussions relating to exclusive economic zone and development strategies for fisheries in India. The Indian Institute of Foreign Trade[41] also conducted a study on India's Export Potential of Marine Products. The studies analysed various factors influencing the markets outside the country and directed the attention for the markets which are not seriously attempted by the Indian producers.

The importance of fisheries sector in the Indian economy cannot be over emphasized. India has a vast coastline and very rich potential for fish catch. The market for fish and fish products is omini present throughout the globe. The fisheries sector in India could not exploit the potential for fish catch in seawaters and also the market potential available outside the country. As a result, India could not earn the much required foreign exchange resources to the extent that is possible. The Government has not neglected this sector but various plans and programmes designed for the development and export promotion has not yielded significant results. The establishment of the Marine Products Exports Development Authority is a right step but the Authority during the last 25 years could not develop adequately the markets abroad for Indian fish and fish products. Several problems are being encountered by the exporters of fish and fish products from India due to political, technological and competitive reasons. Therefore, it is felt that there is a need to undertake a comprehensive study in the area of export marketing of fish and fish products. The study intends to verify the policies and programmes and various facts relating to export of fish and fish products from the country. The findings of the study will be useful to the policy makers to identify various problems that are being confronted on the export of marine products and to develop a strategic approach to accelerate the pace of growth of exports by encouraging the exporters and also by developing markets outside the country.

REFERENCE

1 Babaji, U., 'Development of Marine Fisheries', Department of Commerce and Management Studies, Andhra University, Visakhapatnam, June, 1984 (unpublished thesis).

2. Govindan, T.K. 'Fish and the Nation', *Seafood Export Journal,* Vol. 1, No.7, July 1969, pp. 19-23.

3. Ibid p. 111.

4. S. Rajagopal *et al.*, 'Seafood—The Nutritional Insurance', *Seafood Export Journal,* Vol. XXV, No.8, Cochin, October, 1993, pp.45-46.

5. Gopalan, C., Ramasastri, B.V., and Balasubrahmanian, S.C., 'Nutritive Value of Indian Foods', National Institute of Nutrition, Indian Council of Medical Research, Hyderabad, 1976, p. 40.

6. The Ministry of Agriculture, Handbook on Fisheries Statistics, 1996. Ministry of Agriculture, Department of Agriculture and Co-operation, Fisheries Division, Government of India, New Delhi, 1996,p.1.

7. Ibid.

8. U.K. Srivastava, *et al.,* 'Management of Marine Fishing Industry: An Analysis of Problems in Harvesting and Processing', Oxford and IBH Publishing Co., New Delhi, 1982, p.1.

9. Gharat, N.P. *et al.,* Fisheries in India - A Background Paper', published in National Seminar on Fisheries Development in India, State Bank Staff College, Hyderabad, 1991, p. 48

10. The Ministry of Agriculture, Handbook on Fisheries Statistics, 1996. op. cit, p.77.

11. Economic Intelligence Service, Foreign Trade Statistics of India, May 1996, Centre for Monitoring Indian Economy Pvt. Ltd., Bombay, p.4.

12. Ibid.

13. Mary Chandy, 'Fishes': India the Land and the People, National Book Trust, New Delhi, 1994.

14. Jhingran, V.G., 'Fish and Fisheries of India', Hindustan Publishing Corporation Delhi, 1991.

15. Chopra, B.N., Handbook of Indian Fisheries, Ministry of Agriculture, Government of India, New Delhi, 1951.

16. Desai, M.B., and Baichwal, P.R., 'Economic Survey of Fishing Industry in Thane District, Maharashtra', Part-1, 1960.

17. Durai Raj, N., 'A Study of Marwle Fishing Industry in Thanjavur District', Department of Economics, Madurai Kamaraju University, Tamil Nadu, 1983.

18. Lucas, H.W., 'Fisheries of the Bombay Province', 1908-10, Bombay, 1911.

19. Mitra, G.N., 'Observations on the Development of Fisheries in Orissa', 1961.

20. Mohan, K.P., 'The Situation of Indian Fishing Industry and Indian fishermen', 1950.

21. Silas, E.G., 'Indian Fisheries 1947-1977', The Marine Products Export Development Authority, Cochin, 1977.

22. Prasad, B., 'Post-war Development of Indian Fisheries : Memorandum,' Government of India Press, New Delhi, 1943.

23. Srivastava, K.R., 'Report on the Fishing Industry', Kutch, Government of India, Bhuj Kutch, 1951.

24. Verghese, C.P., and Joy, P.S., 'Development of Marine fisheries for Higher Productivity and Export', Central Institute of Fisheries Nautical and Engineering Training, Cochin, 1993.

25. NCAER, Techno-Economic Survey of Madras, National Council of Applied Economic Research, New Delhi, 1961.

26. NCAER, Techno-Economic Survey of Andhra Pradesh, National Council of Applied Economic Research, New Delhi, 1962.

27. NCAER, Techno-Economic Survey of Kerala, National Council of Applied Economic Research, New Delhi, 1962.

28. NCAER Techno-Economic Survey of Orissa, National Council of Applied Economic Research, New Delhi, 1962.

29. NCAER, Techno-Economic Survey of West Bengal, National Council of Applied Economic Research, New Delhi, 1962.

30. NCAER, Techno-Economic Survey of Gujarat, National Council of Applied Economic Research, New Delhi, 1963.

31. NCAER, Techno-Economic Survey of Maharashtra, National Council of Applied Economic Research, New Delhi, 1963.

32. NCAER, Techno-Economic Survey of Goa, Daman and diu, National Council of Applied Economic Research, New Delhi, 1964.

33. NCAER, Techno-Economic Survey of Mysore, National Council of Applied Economic Research, New Delhi, 1965.

34. Department of Fisheries, 'Report of the Survey to Study to Study the Economics and Mechanisation of Fishing Crafts in Maharashtra State', Government of Maharashtra, Bombay, 1961.

35. Lakshminarayana Ray, M., 'Economics of Boat Building Yard in Mangalore', Central Institute of Fisheries Education, Bombay, 1977 (unpublished).

36. Misra, S.N., and Bayer, J., 'Cost-Benefit Analysis : A Case Study of the Ratnagiri Fisheries Project', Hindustan Publishing Corporation, Delhi, 1976.

37. Perumal, M.C., 'Operation of Taining Vessels, Proc. Symp. on the Need for a Techno-Economic Survey of the Deepsea Fishing Resources', Agricultural Finance Corporation Ltd., Bombay, 1973.

38. Subba Rao, N., 'Economics of Fisheries : A Case Study of Andhra Pradesh', Daya Publishing House, New Delhi, 1986.

39. Srivastava, U.K., Dharma Reddy, M., and Gupta, V.K., 'Management of Marine Fishing Industry', 'An Analysis of Problems in Harvesting and Processing', Oxford and IBH Publishing Co, New Delhi, 1982.

40. Rao, P.S., 'Fishery Economics and Management in India', Pioneers Publishers and Distributors, Bombay, 1983.

41. Babaji, U., 'Development of Marine fisheries', Department of Commerce and Management Studies, Andhra University, Waltair, Visakhapatnam, June 1984 (unpublished thesis).

42. National Council of Applied Economic Research, 'demand for fish and its Transportation and Storage in Selected Cities', Publications Division, National Council of Applied Economic Research, New Delhi, 1980.

43. Talwan, P.K., and Kacker, R.K., 'Commercial Sea Fishes of India', Zological survey of India, Calcutta, 1984.

44. Sreedharan, V.P., 'Industrial and commercial Prospects of Fish and Fish Products in India with Special Reference to Kerala University, 1989 (unpublished thesis).

45. Kulkarni, G.R., and Srivastava, U.K., 'Systems Frame Work of the Marine foods Industry in India', New Delhi, 1986.

46. National Council of Applied Economic Research, 'Export Prospects of Fish and fish Products', National Council of Applied Economic research, New Delhi, 1965.

47. Vijaya Prakash, D., 'Problems and Prospects of Fishermen : A Study of Socio-Economic, Marketing and Financial Aspects of the Marine Fishermen in Visakhapatnam District', Andhra University, 1992 (unpublished M.Phil. thesis).

48. Trivedi, K.K., 'Fisheries Development : 2000 A.D., Oxford and IBH Publishing Co., New Delhi, 1986.

49. Indian Institute of Foreign Trade, 'Survey of India's Export Potential of Marine Products,' Indian Institute of Foreign Trade, New Delhi, March, 1970.

2

Fisheries Sector in India —an Overview

GROWTH AND DEVELOPMENT OF FISHERIES SECTOR IN INDIA

India has a coastline of 8,041 kilometers spread over 10 states and three union territories. The data shown in Table 2.1 reveals, the state of Gujarat has the longest coastline of 1,600 kilometers among the states followed by Tamil Nadu (1,000 kms) and Andhra Pradesh (974 kms). Among the Union Territories, Andaman and Nicobar Islands have the longest coastline of 1,912 kilometers. There are 3,726 fishing villages in the country. Gujarat has the large number of fishing villages (851) followed by West Bengal (652) and Tamil Nadu (442). The number of landing centres in India in the year 1995 is 2,333. Most landing centres are located in Gujarat state (854) followed by Andhra Pradesh (379) and Tamil Nadu (362). The Continental Shelf* of India is 5,06,000 sq. Kilometres. The Gujarat State has the longest continental shelf of 1.64 lakhs sq. kilometres followed by maharashtra with 1.12 lakhs sq. kilometres.

---

* Continental Shelf is the natural extension of land mass into the sea covering the intertidle and littoral zone and the shallow water conventionally accepted as such, till up to a point where the depth of the water increases very fast (continental slope). The extent or width of the continental shelf varies from coast to coast and point to point. However, the extent of the shelf is generally accepted as the area between the base line and a point where the depth of water is about 200 metres.

Besides the rich marine water resources, India is bestowed with inland water resources. The data presented in Table 2.2 shows the state-wise inland water resources in India by the end of the year 1995. The table reveals, the country has 1,71,334 kilometres length of rivers and canals spread over in all the states and union territories with an, exception to Lakshadweep. Uttar Pradesh State occupies first position with 31,200 kilometers length of rivers and canals followed by Jammu and Kashmir with 27,781 kilometres of length and Madhya Pradesh with 20,661 Kilometres of length. Apart from rivers and canals, there are four other inland water resources viz., reservoirs, tanks and ponds, beels*, oxbow** and derelict water*** and brackishwater+. The total size of reservoirs is to the tune of 20.50 lakh hectares. The area under tanks and ponds was 31.30 lakh hectares by the year 1995. The brackshwater is available in 16.32 lakh hectares while beels, oxbow and derelict water is available in 8.27 lakh hectares.

The data relating to the total fish production in the country during 1986-87 to 1995-96 is presented in Table 2.3. The fish production which was 29.42 lakh tonnes in 1986-87 registered a steady increase over the years to reach 49.49 lakh tonnes in 1995-96. In other words, the fish production in the country increased by 68.22 per cent in the span of 10 years. The highest growth in fish production was registered in 1989-90 (16.67 per cent) while the year 1987-88

---

* Beels constitute vitally important fishery resource of Assam. There are wetlands and defined as "Areas of marsh, fen, peatland or water whether natural or artificial, permanent or temporary, with water which is static or flowing, fresh, brackish or salt including areas of marine waters, the depth of which at low tide does not exceed six metres".

** These are one of the beels which are abandoned river courses, oxbow, beels are relatively narrow and long and have either a curved or serpentine shape.

*** Derelict water is the water which is abundant or unused. Such water may be useful in aquaculture practices after treatment and settlement. Usually the stagnet waters of the fresh water ponds and lakes which are inhabituated with weeds come under this category and the water is no longer pure. In case of necessity such water should treated well before use.

\+ Brackishwaters are slightly salty much less than marine waters. They are the mixture of freshwater from rivers and rains and the salt waters of the sea brought by tides.

registered the lowest growth rate (0.58 per cent) during the period. It is to be noted that the growth is positive in all the years during the period.

Table 2.1 : Marine fishery Resources of India

State/Union Territory	Continental Shelf ('000 sq. kms)	Number of Landing Centres	Number of Villages	Approx. Length of Coastline (Kms.)
Andhra Pradesh	31	379	409	974
Goa	10	87	91	104
Gujarat	164	854	851	1600
Karnataka	27	28	204	300
Kerala	40	226	222	590
Maharashtra	112	184	395	720
Orissa	24	63	329	480
Tamil Nadu	41	362	442	1,000
West Bengal	17	47	652	157
Andaman and Nicobar	35	57	45	1,912
Pondicherry	1	28	45	45
Lakshwadeep	4	11	10	132
Daman and Diu	o	7	31	27
Total	506	2,333	3,726	8,041

Source: The Ministry of Agriculture, Handbook on fisheries Statistics, 1996, Department of Agriculture and Co-operation. fisheries Division, Government of India, New Delhi, 1996, p: 127.

Table 2.4 depicts the world fish production during 1985 to 1994. The total fish production in the world which was 863.77 million tonnes in 1985 increased to 1,095.83 million tonnes in 1994 recording an increase of 26.87 per cent during the period. There are 16 major fish producing countries[1] in the world whose contribution in the total fish production varied between 61.08 per cent and 76.03 per cent. Among the major fish producting countries, India occupied either sixth or seventh position during the decade. Its share in the total production varied between 3.08 per cent and 4.25 per cent (Table 2.5). The growth rate in fish production was highest in China with 205.64 per cent followed by Chile (180 per cent) and Indonesia (69.51 per cent). Japan enjoyed the leadership in fish production until 1988 and later due to negative growth rate, its position slided to fourth position by 1994. The country registered

Table 2.2: State-wise Inland Water Resources in India as in 1995

State/ Union Territory	Length of Rivers and Canals (Kilometres)	Area of Reservoirs (Lakh Hactares)	Area Under Tanks and Ponds (Lakh Hactares)	Beels, Oxbow and Derelict water (Lakh Hactares)	Brackishwater Water (Lakh Hactares)
Uttar Pradesh	31,200	1.50	1.62	1.33	-
Jammu & Kashmir	27,781	0.07	0.17	0.06	-
Madhya Pradesh	20,661	2.94	1.19	-	-
Punjab	15,270	Neg.	0.07	-	-
Andhra Pradesh	11,514	2.34	5.17	-	0.64
Karnataka	9,000	2.20	4.14	-	0.08
Tamil Nadu	7,420	0.52	6.91	NA	0.56
Meghalaya	5,600	0.08	0.02	Neg.	-
Haryana	5,000	Neg.	0.10	0.10	-
Assam	4,820	0.02	0.23	1.10	-
Orissa	4,500	2.56	1.14	1.80	4.17
Gujarat	3,865	2.43	0.71	0.12	3.76
Manipur	3,360	0.01	0.05	0.40	-
Bihar	3,200	0.60	0.95	0.05	-
Kerala	3,092	0.30	0.30	2.43	2.43
Himachal Pradesh	3,000	0.42	0.01	-	-
West Bengal	2,526	0.17	2.76	0.42	2.10
Arunachal Pradesh	2,000	-	2.76	0.42	2.10
Maharashtra	1,600	2.79	0.50	-	0.10
Nagland	1,600	0.17	0.50	Neg.	-

(Cont.)...

State/ Union Territory	Length of Rivers and Canals (Kilometres)	Area of Reservoirs (Lakh Hactares)	Area Under Tanks and Ponds (Lakh Hactares)	Beels, Oxbow and Derelict water (Lakh Hactares)	Brackishwater Water (Lakh Hactares)
Mizoram	1,395	-	0.02	-	-
Tripura	1,200	0.05	0.12	-	-
Sikkim	900	-	-	0.03	-
Goa	250	0.03	0.03	-	-
Pondicherry	247	-	Neg.	0.01	0.01
Delhi	150	0.04	-	-	-
Andaman & Nicobar	115	0.01	0.03	-	0.37
Dadra &Nagar Haveli	54	0.05	-	-	-
Daman & Diu	12	-	-	-	-
Chandgarh	2	-	Neg.	Neg	-
Rajasthan	NA	1.20	1.80	-	-
Lakshaddep	-	-	-	-	-
Total	1,71,334	20.50	31.30	8.27	16.32

NA - Not available, Neg - Negligible.

Source : The Ministry of Agriculture, Handbook on Fisheries statistics, 1996, Department of Agriculture and Co-operation, Fisheries Division, Government of India, New Delhi, 1996, p.128.

a negative growth of 35.46 per cent. The other major countries which registered negative growths during the period are Russian Federation, Spain and Iceland.

Table 2.3 : Fish Production During 1986-87 to 1995-96.

Year	Fish Production (in Lakh Tonnes)	Annual Growth Rate (Percentage)
1986-87	29.42	2.29
1987-88	29.59	0.58
1988-89	31.52	6.52
1989-90	36.77	16.67
1990-91	38.36	4.32
1991-92	41.57	8.37
1992-93	43.65	5.00
1993-94	46.44	6.39
1994-95	47.89	3.12
1995-96	49.49	3.34

Source : The Ministry of Agriculture, Handbook on fisheries Statistics, 1996, Department of Agriculture and Co-operation, Fisheries Division, Government of India, New Delhi, 1996, p.19.

The particulars relating to state-wise fish production in India are shown in Table 2.6. The table reveals the West Bengal State is the major contributor in the fish production. This state occupied first position in the country in terms of fish production in all the years during 1986-87 to 1995-96. The Tamil Nadu State which occupied second position in 1986-87 was down to fifth position by 1995-96 due to slow pace of growth. Maharashtra State which occupied third position in 1986-87 became second major producer in 1987-88 and in the following year. But in the year 1989-90 the state was put down to the fourth position and it has been continuing in the same position. Gujarat occupied third position in 1987-88 and has been in the position till 1991-92. In the year 1992-93 the state occupied second position and has been continuing in the same position in 1995-96. The table further reveals, the overall growth rate during the ten year period in fish production in various states and union territories of the country. Assam state registered highest growth rate of 195.86 per cent during the period. This state achieved substantial growth particularly during 1991-92. Next to Assam, Orissa State registered the highest growth of 126.43 per cent followed by Union Territories (123.21 Per cent). It is significant to note that eight major

Table 2.4 World Fish Production During 1985 to 1994

(In '000 Tonnes)

Country	Years									
	1985	1986	1987	1988	1989	1990	1991	1992	1993	1994	Percentage Growth
Japan	11,409.3	11,976.5	11,857.6	11,966.1	11,173.4	10,354.2	9,301.1	8,460.3	8,128.1	7,363.3	(-)35.46
China	6,778.8	8,000.1	9,346.2	10,358.7	11,220.0	11,095.0	13,135.0	15,007.5	17.567.9	20,718.9	205.64
USA	4,950.9	5,186.4	5,992.0	5,956.23	5,778.1	5,870.4	5,488.7	5,602.9	5,948.2	5,940.7	19.99
Chile	4,804.4	5,571.6	4,814.6	5,209.9	6,454.2	5,195.4	6,002.8	6,501.8	6,036.0	7,841.0	63.20
Peru	4,138.1	5,616.2	4,587.4	6,641.7	6,853.8	6,875.1	6,949.4	6,482.7	8,452.4	11,587.3	180.00
India	2,826.1	2,923.2	2,906.6	3.125.4	3,640.3	3,974.2	4,044.2	4,175.1	4,337.7	4,540.1	60.65
Kerea Rep.	2,649.9	3.103.4	2,876.6	2,731.5	2,840.6	2,843.1	2,521.2	2,695.6	2,648.9	2,700.0	1.89
Indonesia	2,332.7	2,457.0	2,583.9	2,795.2	2,948.4	3 ,044.2	3,251.8	3,357.7	3,676.3	3,954.2	69.51
Thailand	2,225.1	2,536.3	2,779.1	2,642.1	2,699.8	2,786.4	2,967.8	2,855.0	3,330.8	3,432.0	54.24
Norway	2,119.0	1.915.0	1,949.5	1,839.9	1,909.8	1,711.3	2,095.9	2,549.1	2,561.7	2,551.4	20.41
Phillipines	1,865.0	1,916.3	1,988.7	2,010.4	2,098.8	2,208.8	2,311.8	2,271.9	2,263.7	2,276.1	22.04

(Cont.)...

Country	Years										
	1985	1986	1987	1988	1989	1990	1991	1992	1993	1994	Percentage Growth
Denmark	1,796.9	1,849.8	1,707.8	1,974.4	1,929.3	1,518.0	1,795.8	1,995.0	1,656.2	1 ,886 .8	5 .00
Korea DPRP	1,700.0	1,700.2	1,700.2	1,700.1	1,750.1	1,700.1	1,700.1	1,700.1	1,780.0	1,800.0	5.88
Ice land	1,680.4	1,658.6	1,632.7	1,757.7	1,502.4	1,508.1	1,050.3	1,577.2	1,718.4	1,560.1	(-) 7.16
Spain	1,482.8	1,489.0	1,525.5	1,593.4	1,560.0	1,400.0	1,320.0	1,330.0	1,290.0	1,380.0	(-) 6.93
Rusian Fed.	0.0	0.0	0.0	0.0	0.0	0.0	6,894.2	5,611.2	40,461.3	3,780.5	(-)45.16
Others	33,618.3	39,945.8	36,154	36,783.0	35,952.1	34,651.8	26,221.6	25,579.7	26,323.9	26.270.3	(-) 21.86
Total	86,377.7	92,845.4	94,402.5	99,085.7	1,00,311.1	97,556.1	97,051.7	98,112.8	1,02,181.5	1,09,582.7	26.86

Source : Compiled from:

1. Handbook on Fisheries Statistics, 1996, The Ministry of Agriculture, Government of India, New Delhi, 1996, p. 179.
2. Seafood Export Journal, vol. XXVII No. 8, August, 1996, Cochin, p. 25.

Table 2.5 : Percentage Distribution of World Fish Production During 1985-1994

Country	Years									
	1985	1986	1987	1988	1989	1990	1991	1992	1993	1994
Japan	13.21	12.90	12.56	12.08	11.14	10.61	9.58	8.62	7.95	6.72
China	7.84	8.62	9.90	10.45	11.19	12.39	13.53	15.30	17.19	18.91
U.S.A	5.73	5.59	6.35	6.01	5.76	6.01	5.66	5.71	5.82	5.42
Chile	5.56	6.00	5.10	5.26	6.43	5.32	6.19	6.63	5.91	7.16
Peru	4.79	6.05	4.86	6.70	6.84	7.04	7.16	6.97	8.27	10.47
India	3.27	3.15	3.08	3.15	3.63	4.06	4.17	4.25	4.25	4.14
Korea Rep.	3.07	3.34	3.05	2.76	2.83	2.91	2.60	2.75	2.59	2.46
Indonesia	2.70	2.65	2.74	2.82	2.94	3.12	3.35	3.42	3.60	3.61
Thailand	2.58	2.73	2.94	2.67	2.69	2.85	3.06	2.91	3.26	3.14
Norway	2.45	2.06	2..06	1.86	1.90	1.75	2.16	2.60	2.51	2.33
Philiphines	2.16	2.06	2.11	2.03	2.09	2.26	2.38	2.32	2.21	2.08
Denmark	2.08	1.99	1.80	1.99	1.92	1.55	1.85	2.03	1.62	1.72
Korea DPRP	1.97	1.83	1.80	1.72	1.74	1.74	1.75	1.73	1.75	1.64
Iceland	1.95	1.79	1.73	1.77	1.50	1.54	1.08	1.61	1.68	1.43
Spain	1.72	1.60	1.62	1.61	1.56	1.43	1.36	1.36	1.26	1.25

(Cont.)...

Country	Years									
	1985	1986	1987	1988	1989	1990	1991	1992	1993	1994
Russian Fed.	-	-	-	-	-	-	7.10	5.72	4.37	3.45
Others	38.92	37.64	38.30	37.12	35.84	35.51	27.02	26.07	25.76	23.97
World Total	100.00	100.00	100.00	100.00	100.00	100.00	100.00	100.00	100.00	100.00

Source : Compiled from:

1. Handbook on Fisheries Statistics, 1996, The Ministry of Agriculture, Government of India, New Delhi, 1996, p. 180.
2. Seefood Export Journal, vol. XXVII No. 8, August, 1996, Cochin, p. 25.

Table 2.6 State-wise Fish Production in India During 1986-87 to 1995-96

(In '000 Tonnes)

State /Union Territory	Years 1986-87	1987-88	1988-89	1989-90	1990-91	1991-92	1992-93	1993-94	1994-95	1995-96	Percentage Growth
Andhra Pradesh	245.50	260.51	217.70	245.78	156.60	264.47	264.55	321.37	345.39	355.96	44.99
Assam	52.41	60.99	65.50	58.43	76.00	130.00	140.00	151.65	153.00	155.06	195.86
Bihar	135.21	152.55	150.10	156.55	159.93	184.97	164.07	200.71	195.37	239.58	7.19
Goa	45.97	36.08	45.70	54.65	56.22	49.55	104.26	105.44	101.90	87.82	91.04
Gujarat	332.63	349.76	381.00	459.51	545.00	556.95	638.00	684.86	715.36	660.00	98.42
Karnataka	187.75	179.30	194.50	241.97	236.83	245.75	239.89	249.15	244.04	304.87	62.38
Kerala	352.93	318.97	364.80	569.02	550.58	565.13	534.40	604.69	596.56	582.14	64.94
Madhya Pradesh	46.89	68.50	54.40	37.96	36.95	40.68	55.71	54.53	80.18	91.28	94.67
Maharashtra	372.78	351.54	384.20	443.00	389.00	455.39	464.74	433.62	446.88	464.00	24.47
Orissa	113.96	117.00	129.90	153.76	161.29	182.91	213.14	232.28	257.66	258.04	126.43
Tamil Nadu	387.35	312.00	368.00	364.00	370.95	385.00	406.00	424.92	438.50	448.00	15.66
Uttar Pradesh	83.79	83.13	90.60	93.47	104.26	113.31	121.43	132.37	139.90	145.70	73.89
West Bengal	470.28	504.59	514.30	601.00	680.00	734.00	757.00	806.00	820.42	893.00	89.89
Other States	71.38	81.44	89.00	84.06	94.97	112.45	92.46	121.04	130.96	138.16	93.56
Union Territories	42.91	40.65	57.30	63.74	67.31	85.85	89.65	91.73	92.45	95.78	123.21

(Cont.)....

State /Union Territory	Years										Percentage Growth
	1986-87	1987-88	1988-89	1989-90	1990-91	1991-92	1992-93	1993-94	1994-95	1995-96	
Chartered Deepsea Fishing vessels	-	42.00	50.00	50.00	50.00	50.00	60.00	30.00	30.00	30.00	(-)28.57
Total	2,941.74	2,959.01	3,157.00	3,676.90	3,845.89	4,325.30	4,644.36	4,788.57	4,949.39	68.25	

Source: The Ministry of Agriculture, Handbook on Fisheries Statistics, 1996, Department of Agriculture and Co-operation, fisheries Division, Government of India, New Delhi, 1996, pp. 24 and 25.

fish producing states have achieved more than 70 per cent growth in fish production during the period.

The fish catch in the country has been disposed in different ways, it is offered as fresh fish in the market for immediate consumption, frozen fish, cured fish, canned fish, reduced fish, miscellaneous purposes and offer reduction. The data presented in Table 2.7 shows how the major share of the fish production is disposed as fresh fish. The share of fresh fish market in the total disposition of fish varied between 64.20 per cent and 68.64 per cent during 1985 and 1994. Cured fish occupy the second position whose share varied between 13.77 per cent and 19.91 per cent. Reduced fish and frozen fish occupy third and fourth position respectively in the disposition of fish. The table further reveals, though there is a growth in all the markets of different fish products, there is a change in proportion. The proportion of fresh fish market increased marginally by 3.38 per cent while the share of cured fish declined by 6.14 per cent. The reduced fish market could improve its share by 2.36 per cent while the frozen fish share was dropped marginally by 0.40 per cent.

DEVELOPMENT UNDER FIVE YEAR PLANS

India's Five Year Plans are milestones in the country's economic progress for intensive and extensive use of the national resources, manpower and skill[2]. From 1951 onwards i.e., after the execution of the Indian constitution, India has adopted the strategy of planned economic development. The First Five Year Plan was launched in April, 1951 and subsequently India completed eight Five Year Plans and five Annual Plans.

During the First Plan the scope and need for increasing the fish production of the feshwater and marine enviornment was identified. The plan, however, noted that the exploitation of the resource was limited by the weaknesses of fish catching methods and inadequacy of the fishing harbour and fish landing facilities. The major thrust areas for marine fisheries development during the First Plan include i) mechanisation of country craft or introduction of new mechanised boats; ii) harbour facilities; iii) supply of requisites to fishermen; iv) development of marketing; v) provision of rice and cold storages and transport facilities vi) introduction of mothership operations; and vii) provision for offshore fishing with large powered vessels such as purse seiners and trawlers.[3]

The Second Five Year Plan (1956-1961) gave importance to the marine fisheries development. Imporvement of fishing methods, development of deep sea fishing, provision of fishing harbours and the integration of fish transport, storage, marketing and utilisation of fish were the major thrust areas of development during the plan[4].

The Third Five Year Plan (1961-1966) objectives for fisheries development includes, increase in fish production, imporvement of the conditions of fishermen, development of export trade, formation and running of fisheries co-operatives and expansion of freezing plants, cold storages and canning facilities[5].

Three Annual Plans (1966-69) followed the Third Plan and they carried forward the objectives of the Third Plan. The Annual Plans sought to consolidate the achievements of the previous plans rather than for further development[6].

In the Fourth Five year Plan (1969-1974) the main objectives for fisheries development were : i) increase in fish production to meet protein requirements, ii) development of export potential, and iii) improvement in the economy of fishermen[7].

Fisheries development programmes till the end of the Third Plan were financed by direct plan outlays. Later, The Agricultural Refinance Corporation and the Industrial Development Bank of India started financing some fisheries development activities.

The Fourth Plan document proposed to introduce 300 fishing travelers to be operated by private companies, co-operatives and state fisheries corporations. The plan also proposed to provide breathing and landing facilities for large vessels at several major and minor ports and for smaller boats at about 48 ports where servicing and repair workshops, ice factories, cold storage and other ancillary facilities would be provided.

Table 2.7 Disposition of Fish Catch During 1985-1994.

('000 Metric Tonnes)

State /Union Territory	Years										Percentage Growth
	1985	1986	1987	1988	1989	1990	1991	1992	1993	1994	
Marketing											
Fresh	1,843.3	1,964.0	1,968.3	2,075.1	2,301.4	2,497.2	2,706.0	2,798.4	3,105.2	3,250.6	76.35
	(65.26)	(67.22)	(67.72)	(67.32)	(64.20)	(65.18)	(66.91)	(67.06)	(68.31)	(68.64)	
Frozen	196.4	209.7	179.0	233.7	261.2	285.7	265.9	284.8	309.5	310.3	57.99
	(6.95)	(7.18)	(6.16)	(7.58)	(7.29)	(7.46)	(6.58)	(6.82)	(6.80)	(6.55)	
Cured	562.2	460.4	526.4	529.0	590.9	598.8	613.8	590.2	644.5	651.9	15.96
	(19.91)	(15.76)	(18.11)	(17.16)	(16.48)	(15.63)	(15.19)	(14.14)	(14.18)	(13.77)	
Canned	9.8	12.1	4.9	20.6	28.7	29.3	30.1	25.9	9.8	12.2	24.49
	(0.35)	(0.41)	(0.17)	(0.67)	(0.80)	(0.76)	(0.74)	(0.62)	(0.22)	(0.26)	
Reduced	170.0	158.3	190.6	174.6	315.2	322.3	333.4	355.8	372.8	397.3	133.71
	(6.02)	(5.42)	(6.56)	(5.66)	(8.79)	(8.41)	(8.24)	(8.53)	(8.20)	(8.38)	
Miscellaneous purpose	28.6	105.8	19.0	25.2	62.0	63.4	47.1	47.4	87.6	74.3	159.79
	(1.01)	(3.62)	(0.65)	(0.82)	(1.74)	(1.65)	(1.16)	(1.14)	(1.93)	(1.57)	

(Cont.)...

State /Union Territory	Years 1985	1986	1987	1988	1989	1990	1991	1992	1993	1994	Percentage Growth
Offer Reduction	14.0 (0.50)	11.5 (0.39)	18.4 (0.63)	24.2 (0.790	25.1 (0.70)	34.8 (0.91)	47.7 (1.18)	70.6 (1.69)	16.3 (0.36)	39.3 (0.83)	180.71
Total	2,824.3 (100.00)	2,921.8 (100.00)	2,906.6 (100.00)	3,082.4 (100.00)	3,584.5 (100.00)	3,831.5 (100.00)	4,044.0 (100.00)	4,173.1 (100.00)	4,545.7 (100.00)	4,735.9 (100.00)	67.68

Source :The Ministry of Agriculture, Handbook on Fisheries Statistics, 1996, Department of Agriculture and Co-operation, Fisheries Division, Government of India, New Delhi, 1996 , p. 38.

In the Fifth Five Year Plan (1974-1979) further efforts were undertaken to explore and exploit fishery resources. Trawlers Development Fund was created to extend financial assistance to promote the introduction of large number of fishing vessels. Through this programme it was decided to import fishing vessels from aboard and also construct indigenously. The state fisheries corporations were provided financial assistance for diversified fishing, processing and marketing. Fish farmers development agencies were introduced in the Fifth Plan to promote intensive aquacutlrure in selected districts. In order to establish the economic advantages of brackishwater fish farming, a pilot project was started in all the coastal states.[8]

The main objectives of fisheries development programmes during the Sixth Plan (1980-85) include: to increase in fish production considerably both in the marine and inland sector; to promote inland fish production on a scientific basis through extension; education and training and provision of inputs with a view to increase the production in the water area; to organise intensive surveys of marine fishery resources assessment and ensure optimum exploitation of marine resources using the traditional country boats; mechanised boats and deep sea fishing vessels; to intensify efforts on processing, storage and transporation of fish; improve marketing, tap the vast potential for export of fish and fish products; and to improve the socio-economic conditions of fishermen.[9]

The Seventh Five year Plan commenced in April, 1984. The Seventh Plan has been set on a fifteen years long term perspective. The investment programmes and the policy envisaged for the seventh and subsequent plans are related to the targets for which the nation has set for the year 2000. The development strategy aims at creating the conditions for self sustaining growth in terms of the capacity to finance and the development of technology by the year 2000.

The Seventh Plan strategy for marine fisheries development was to exploit the Exclusive Economic Zone (EEZ) through higher investments in deep sea fishing, mainly for resources beyond 40 fathoms. For coastal fishing new motorized and mechanised craft and diversified methods of fishing were to be introduced. The traditional sector was to be upgraded by the introduction of new gears and new design of boats. The existing legislations were proposed to be implemented to control the conflict between the mechanised boat operators and traditional fishermen.[10]

The Eighth Five Year Plan was commenced in the year 1992. Two annual plans, 1990-91, 1991-92, preceeded the Eighth Plan with similar objectives set for the Seventh Plan. The Eighth five Year Plan aimed at optimal exploitation of inland and marine fishery resources. Development of infrastructure facilities, improvement of socio-economic status of fishermen, providing technical and financial support to fishermen to increase operational efficiency and to promote direct and indirect employment opportunities are the major tasks envisaged in the plan.[11] Table 2.8 shows the developmental schemes and the proposed outlay for the Eighth Five Year Plan (1992-97). The developmental schemes in the plan are designed as eight central schemes and six centrally sponsored schemes. An outlay of rs. 112.28 crores was provided for central sector schemes and an outlay of Rs. 320.77 crores was provided for centrally sponsored schemes. The total outlay for all the schemes was Rs. 433.05 crores for the period 1992 to 1997.

The data presented in Table 2.9 shows the targets fixed for the Eighth Plan period. The target for fish production was set as 54 lakh tonnes for the plan period and 20,00 0 million fry* as fish seed production. Two major fishery harbours, seven minor fishery harbours, ten fish landing centres, 15 brackishwater fish farmer development agencies, 100 small prawn seed hatcheries, six sea wage fed fish farms and 30 hatcheries under government and private sector are proposed to set up. The targets of the plan include development of 20,000 hectares brackish water area coverage of 40 lakh hectares for intensive fish farming development of 50,000 hectares as reservoir area and providing training facility to four lakh fish farmers throughout the country.

* A developing stage of fish when mouth is open for feeding and yolk present through diminishing fast.

Table 2.8 Developmental Schemes Proposed in Eighth Five Year Plan

(rs. in crores)

Name of the scheme	Proposed outlay Eighth Plan (1992-1997)
Central Schemes :	
Central Institue of Fisheries Nautical and Engineering Training	10.00
Central Institute of Coastal Engineering for fishery	5.00
Integrated fisheries Project	12.00
Fishery Harbour Facilities at Major Ports	55.00
Training and fishery Extension	1.50
Development of Inland Fishery Statistics	3.00
Central Fishery Harbour Authority	1.53
Assistance for Strengthening State Level Organisations for Inland fish Marketing	24.25
All Central Schemes	112.28
Centrally Sponsored Schemes :	
Fresh water Aquaculture	48.97
Open water Fisheries (Development of Reservoir fisheries and Beel Fisheries)	19.70
Development of Coastal Marine Fisheries	137.70
Integrated Brackishwater Fish Farm Development	30.00
Minor Fishery Habours	40.00
Welfare of Fishermen	44.40
All Centrally Sponsored Schemes	320.77
All Eighth Plan Schemes	433.05

Source: Seafood Export Journal, Vol.XXVI, No.5, May, 1995, Cochin, p. 27.

Fisheries is a state subject under Item 21 of the State list of the Seventh Schedule of Article 246 of the Constitution of India. However, fishing and fisheries both in territorial waters and beyond the territorial waters are in the Union list (item 57). Article 257 of the Constitution also gives proprietary rights for anything of value underlying the ocean within the territorial waters, the continental shelf or the exclusive economic zone of India. Hence matters relating to fisheries development, particularly of marine fishing within the territorial waters, are laregely within the purview of the state governments, and fishing beyond the territorial waters comes directly within the ambit of the Central Government. Nevertheless, according to Article 297 of the Constitution, the Central Government exercises a co-ordinating role in respect of fisheries programmes.[12] Table 2.10 presents the state and Central Government's plan-wise outlay and expenditure. The table reveals, the outlay for fisheries development which was Rs. 5.13 crores in First Five year Plan increased to Rs, 1, 265.87 crores in the Eighth Five Year Plan. Particularly from Sixth Plan onwards greater amounts were allocated for the development of fisheries. The share of state government schemes is substantial in the total outlay which varied from 53.19 per cent to 80.51 percent. The table further reveals, the amounts earmarked for the development of the fisheries were not fully utilised during various plan periods. During the first Plan Period the percentage of expenditure to the outlay was one 54.19 per cent. The percentage of expenditure increased to about 74 per cent in the Second Plan and to about 83 per cent in the Third Plan. During Fourth Plan only 65.45 per cent of the funds were spent. However, in the Fifth Plan the funds were utilised to the tune of 92.52 per cent. During the Sixth and the Seventh plans the utilisation of funds were 77.32 per cent and 87.75 per cent respectively. During the subsequent two annual plans the utilisation was more than 90 per cent.

Table 2.9 Targets Fixed for The Eighth Five Year Plan.

Item	Unit	8th Plan (1992-1997)
Fish Production	Lakh Tonnes	54
Fish Seed Production	Million Fry	20,000
Major Fishery Harbours	Number	2
Minor Fishery Harbours	Number	7
Fish Landing Centres	Number	10
Brackishwater Area to be Developed	Hect.	20,000
Brackishwater Fish Farmers Development Agencies to set up	Number	15
Small Prawn Seed Hatcheries to be set up	Number	100
Fish Farmers to be trained by FFDA's	Number	4,00,000
Water area to be covered for intensive Fish Farming	Ha	4,00,000
Hatcheries to be constructed		
i) Government	Number	5
ii) Private	Number	25
Sewage Fed Fish Farms to be Constructed	Number	6
Brackishwater Area to be Surveyed by CICEF	Hect	5,000
Survey of Fishing Harbour Sites	Number	5
Reservoir Area to be Developed	Hect	50,000

Source: Seafood Export Journal, Vol.XXVI, No.5, May, 1997, Cochin, p. 27.

Though there was a substantial growth in the outlay and expenditure from the First Plan to the Eighth Plan in numberical terms, the percentage share allocated for fisheries development in the total outlay of the plans does not reveal the similar picture. The outlay on fisheries by the Central and state governments ranged between 0.26 per cent and 0.38 per cent except for the Fourth Plan when it was 0.58 per cent of the total. Although the allocation to the fisheries sector was raised significantly to 0.58 per cent in the Fourth Plan, it was reduced to 0.38 per cent in the Fifth and the Sixth plans. In the Seventh Plan the share further came down to 0.30 per cent, the lowest for ever since the Third Plan.[13]

It can be noted further that in all the eight five year plans and the intervening annual plans they were significant short falls in the utilisation of plan allocation. Taking into consideration the importance of fisheries development in the development of the national economy there is a need to increase the percentage share in the plan outlay and also to initiate appropriate measures to execute the programmes proposed under various plans. It can be observed further that the export of fish and fish products was not given the importance that it deserves. Fishing export was not a thrust area in any one of the plans envisaged so far. Though the programmes initiated under various five year plans contributed for the development of fisheries and indirectly to the export of fisheries, it is felt that there is a need to direct special focus in the forth coming plans on the export of fish and fish products.

ORGANISATION AND INFRASTRUCTURE

In India, development of fisheries is of great significance both for providing nutritional food for the people in the country and for export trade. A number of national level and state level organisations are established for the development of fisheries sector. The Ministry of Agriculture, Government of India has a separate division for the development of fisheries. The fisheries division looks after the administrative aspects at the national level. It formulates the national development plan strategy for the fisheries sector. It also formulates the policies for resource management and development in fishing industry and provides technical and financial assistance to various

Table 2.10: Outlay and Expenditure During Plan Periods

(Rs. in Crores)

Plan	Outlay				Expenditure				Percentage of utilisation
	Central schemes	Centrally sponsored schemes	State schemes	Total	Central schemes schemes	Centrally sponsored	State schemes	Total	
I Plan (1951-'56)	@ 1.00		4.13	5.13	@0.38		2.40	2.78	54.19
II Plan (1956-'61)	@3.73		8.53	12.26	@1.80		7.26	9.06	73.90
III Plan (1961-'66)	@ 6.72		21.55	28.27	@3.03		20.29	23.37	82.66
Three Annual Plans (1966-67 to 1968-'69)	@15.30		26.91	42.21	@9.04		23.63	31.67	75.03
IV Plan (1969-'74)	28.00	6.00	48.68	82.68	8.11	5.17	40.83	54.11	65.45
V Plan (1974-'79) (Inclusive of Annual Plan 1979-'80)	51.05	17.00	83.19	151.24	54.65	4.06	71.21	139.92	92.52
VI Plan (1980-'85)	137.10	36.00	197.42	371.14	75.54	28.80	182.61	286.95	77.32

(Cont.)....

VII Plan (1985-'90)	156.58$	60.75	329.19	546.52	116.93$	53.26$	307.40	479.59	87.75
1990-'91 (Annual Plan)	11.70	18.91	94.55	125.16	5.85	18.68	94.32	118.85	94.96
1991-'92 (Annual Plan)	13.75	36.25	117.58	167.58	10.63	25.05	117.58*	153.26	91.45
VIII Plan (1992-'97)	112.28	320.77	832.82	1,265.87	NA	NA	NA	NA	

NA = No available

* Provisional

@ Combined figures for central and centrally sponsored schemes

$ Schemes viz., "Fishery Survey of India" and "Trawler Dev. Fund" were transferred to ministry of Food Processing Industries Midway during the VII five year plan. Accordingly the outlay and expenditure of fisheries division during VII plan would be Rs. 99.10 crores and Rs. 88.47 crores respectively.

Source: The Ministry of Agriculture, Handbook on Fisheries Statistics, 1996, Department of Agriculture and co-operation, Fisheries Division, Government of India, New Delhi, 1996, pp. 101 and 102.

states for the development of fisheries. Apart from the Ministry of Agriculture, the Ministry of Finance, the Ministry of Industry, the Ministry of Foreign Trade and the Ministry of Shipping and Transport are directly involved in the development process of fisheries sector in the country (Fig 2.1). Since fisheries is the state subject, all the states on the coastline have their directorates of fisheries. The major activities of the state directorates are planning and development of infrastructure, landing and berthing facilities, distribution and marketing, providing financial assistance and training and improvement of the economic welfare of fishermen.

In order to promote research and technology and to provide education and training facilites to the fishermen and to the entrepreneurs in the fisheries sector, a number of organisations were established in India. They are central Marine Fisheries Research Institute (CMFRI), Central Inland Fisheries Research Institute (CIFRI), Central Inland Capture Fisheries Research Institute (CICFRI), Central Institute of Freshwater Aquaculture (CICFA), Central Institute of Brackishwater Aquaculture (CIBA), Central Institute of Fisheries Technology (CIFT), Cnetral Institute of Fisheries Education (CIFE), National Bureau of Fish Genetic Resources (NBFGR), National Research Centre on Coldwater Fisheries (NRCCF), Central Institute of Fisheries National Bureau of Fish Genetic Resources (NBFGR), National Research Centre on Coldwater Fisheries (NRCCF), Central Institute of Fisheries Nautical and Engineering Training (CIFNET), Central Institute of Coastal Engineering for Fishery (CICEF), Marine Products Export Development Authority (MPEDA), Export Inspection Agency (EIA), Integrated Fisheries Project (IFP) and Fishing Survey of India (FSI).

Inorder to co-ordinate the activities relating to export of fish and fish products and to promote the markets for Indian fish products, the Marine Products Export Development Authority was constituted. This organisation apart from co-ordinating Central and state government establishments, engaged in fishery production and allied activities, formulates exports standards and monitor processing, marketing, extension and training in various aspects of the fisheries that relate to export trade. The establishment of MPEDA proved to be a significant step forward in the development of fisheries sector in the country.

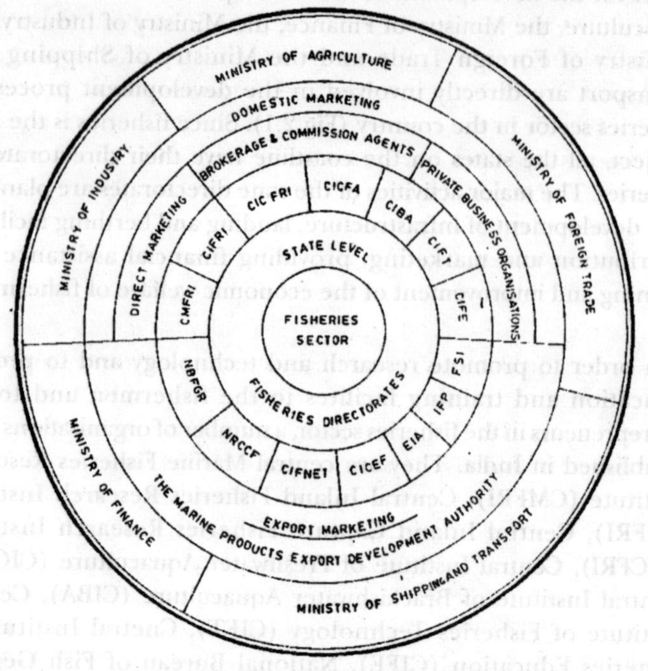

Fig. 2.1 Organisational Set-up for Fisheries Sector

EXCLUSIVE ECONOMIC ZONE (EEZ)

One of the significant land marks in the development of fisheries sector in India is the declaration of exclusive economic zone in 1977. Through the 41st Amendment to the Indian Constitution (article 298), which provided an opportunity to enforce the Maritime Zone Act 1976, relating to territorial waters to twelve nautical miles, a contiguous zone of the same dimension of the continental shelf, and the two hundred nautical mile exclusive economic zone (EEZ). Figure 2.2 shows the details of EEZ of India. Without the exclusive economic zone, the perspective of India's marine fisheries development would probably have been different. This exclusive jurisdiction has provided development, a boost and a sense of confidence about the future[14]

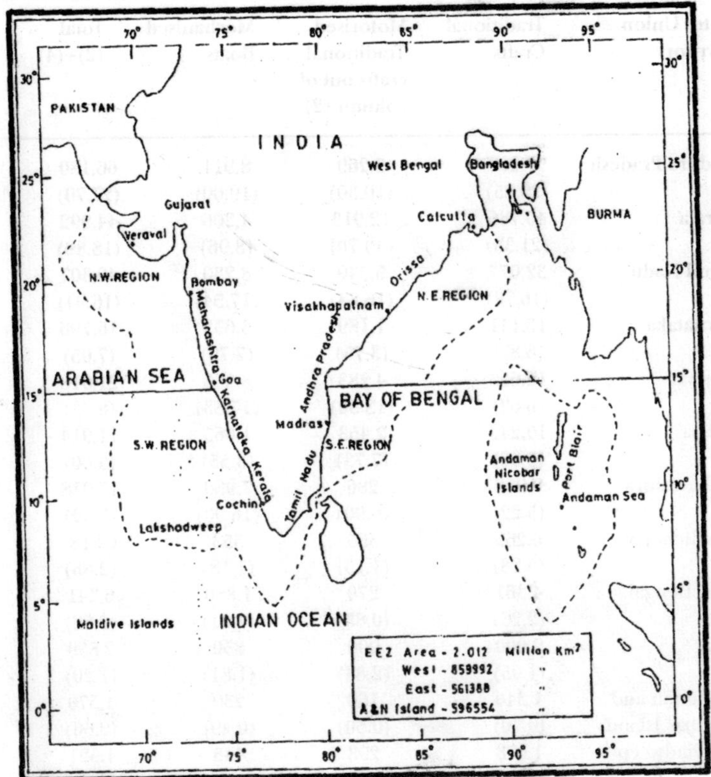

* The outer martin of the EEZ in only provisional and without prejudice to agreements reached or to be reached with the concerned countries.

Fig. 2.2 Exclusive Economic zone of India

The EEZ has 2.02 million sq. kilometres of water spread area along the 8,041 kilometres of coastline in the country. About one lakh tonnes of Tuna and allied fish are estimated to be present in Andaman and Nicobar Islands alone. Another 50,000 tonnes of potential resources are available around the lakshadweep island. About 0.18 million tonnes of squid and cuttlefish are estimated to be available within the EEZ. As per the survey reports, the annual harvestible marine fishery potential within India's EEZ is estimated at 4.5 million tonnes, while the present production is only about 2.2 million tonnes. Deep sea pelagic tuna and skip jack can be mentioned as examples of under-exploited sea fish species[15].

Table 2.11 : Fishing Crafts in Maritime States?union Territories as in 1994-95

State/Union Territory	Traditional Crafts	Motorised Traditional crafts out of column (2)	Mechanised Boats	Total (2)+(4)
Andhra Pradesh	57,269 (29.95)	3,269 (10.30)	8,911 (19.00)	66,180 (27.79)
Kerala	40,786 (21.33)	12,913 (40.70)	4,206 (8.96)	44,992 (18.89)
Tamil Nadu	32,077 (16.78)	5,340 (16.84)	8,230 (17.54)	40,307 (16.94)
Karnataka	13,141 (6.87)	1,189 (3.75)	3,655 (7.79)	16,796 (7.05)
Gujarat	12,653 (6.62)	4,283 (13.50)	8,365 (17.83)	21,018 (8.83)
Orissa	10,249 (5.36)	2,453 (7.73)	1,665 (3.55)	11,914 (5.00)
Maharashtra	9,988 (5.22)	286 (0.90)	7,930 (16.90)	17,918 (7.52)
Pondicherry	6,265 (3.28)	365 (1.15)	553 (1.18)	6,818' (2.86)
West Bengal	4,361 (2.28)	270 (0.85)	1,880 (4,01)	6,241 (2.62)
Goa	2,000 (1.05)	900 (2.84)	850 (1.81)	2,850 (1.20)
Andaman and Nicobar Islands	1,340 (0.70)	160 (0.50)	230 (0.49)	1,570 (0.66)
Lakshadweep	1,078 (0.56)	298 (0.94)	443 (0.94)	1,521 (0.64)
Total	1,91,207 (100.00)	31,726 (100.00)	46,918 (100.00)	2,38,125 (100.00)

Source: The Ministry of Agriculture, Handbook on Fisheries Statistics, Department of Agriculture and Co-operation, Fisheries Division 1996, Government of India, New Delhi, 1996, p. 138.

OTHER INFRASTRUCTURE FACILITIES

There are over 2.38 lakh fishing crafts in the country by the end of 1994-1995. The data presented in Table 2.11 shows that out of the total fishing crafts, 1.91 lakh crafts representing 80.30 percent are traditional crafts and 0.47 lakh crafts are mechanised. However, out of the total traditional crafts 0.32 lakh crafts are motorised. The largest number of fishing crafts representing about 28 per cent of the total are located in the Andhra Pradesh State. The Kerala State occupies second position in terms of having a number of fishing crafts (19 per cent) and Tamil Nadu is in the third place with about 17 per cent of total fishing crafts.

The data relating to fish seed hatcheries established in public and private sector undertakings in the country is shown in Table 2.12. The table reveals, there are 334 hatcheries with a total capacity of 3.401 million fry in the Government sector and 575 hatcheries with a production capacity of 12,267 million fry in the private sector by the end of 1994-95. The largest number of Government sector hatcheries are located in Andhra Pradesh (92 hatcheries representing about 28 per cent of the total). In terms of production capacity Gujarat occupies the first position (about 34 per cent of the total). The largest number of private sector hatcheries (360 hatcheries representing about 63 per cent of the total) were located in West Bengal and 92.12 per cent of the total capacity under private sector was also from the state.

There are 414 Fish Farmers Development Agencies (FFDAs) established in various states and union territories in the country (Table 2.13). The FFDAs had a coverage of 3.87 lakh Mt's. Over five lakh fish farmers were trained by the end of 1995-96. The total beneficiaries of the FFDAs are over 7.3 lakhs. The Government also encouraged for the establishment of primary fisheries co-operatives to bring the unorgaised farming activities into organisational fold. As a result, a number of primary fisheries co-operative societies established in the country over a period of time and the number of co-operative societies reached to 11,440 by the end of 1994-1995 (Table 2.14). The membership of the societies was to the tune of 12.50 lakhs. Out of the total membership, over 1.1 lakh are from scheduled tribes and about 95,000 are from scheduled caste.

Table 2.12: Hatcheries in Public and Private Sector

(Capacity in Million Fry)

State/Union Territory	Government Sector Number of Hatcheries	Total Capacity	Private Sector Number of Hatcheries	Total Capacity
1	2	3	4	5
Andhra Pradesh	92 (27.54)	180 (5.92)	80 (13.91)	400 (3.26)
Madhya Pradesh	35 (10.47)	313 (10.29)	9 (1.56)	200 (1.63)
Orissa	34 (10.18)	384 (12.62)	10 (1.74)	11 (0.09)
Karnataka	25 (7.48)	220 (7.23)	4 (0.70)	24 (0.20)
Haryana	21 (6.29)	40 (1.32)	-	-
Tamil Nadu	20 (5.99)	-	26 (4.52)	-
Maharashtra	18 (5.39)	-	-	-
Uttar Pradesh	16 (4.79)	255 (8.39)	25 (4.35)	75 (0.61)
Rajasthan	13 (3.89)	70 (2.30)	3 (0.52)	10 (0.08)
Assam	13 (3.89)	-	48 (8.35)	- -
Gujarat	10 (2.99)	1,020 (33.54)	- -	- -
Himachal Pradesh	8 (2.40)	15 (0.49)	-	-
West Bengal	7 (2.10)	300 (9.87)	360 (62.61)	11,300 (92.12)
Bihar	5 (1.50)	208 (6.84)	4 (0.70)	225 (1.83)
Arunachal Pradesh	4 (1.20)	20 (0.66)	-	-
Kerala	3 (0.90)	6 (0.20)	1 (0.17)	6 (0.05)
Manipur	3 (0.90)	-	-	-
Punjab	2 (0.60)	9 (0.30)	3 (0.52)	15 (0.12)
Meghalaya	2 (0.60)	1 (0.30)	-	-

(Cont.)...

1	2	3	4	5
Tripura	2 (0.60)	Neg.	2 (0.35)	1 (0.01)
Chandigarh	1 (0.30)	Neg.	-	
Total	334 (100.00)	3,041 (100.00)	575 (100.00)	12,267 (100.00)

Neg. Negligible
Source: The Ministry of Agriculture, Handbook on Fisheries Statistics, 1996, Department of Agriculture and Co-operation, Fisheries Division, Government of India, New Delhi, 1996, p. 142.

Table 2.13 Fish Farmers Development Agencies by the Year 1995-1996

State/ Union Teritory	F.F.D.As.	Water Area Covered (Ha)	Fish Farmers Trained Number	Beneficiaries Number
1	2	3	4	5
Uttar Pradesh	56	74,738	71,811	67,896
Bihar	49	22,795	22,790	15,242
Madhya Pradesh	45	62,877	27,195	61,325
Maharashtra	29	12,531	8,398	55,030
Orissa	27	24,743	39,743	1,05,669
Assam	23	2,874	14,260	8,356
Andhra Pradesh	22	4,052	11,843	5,805
West Bengal	18	98,735	1,81,321	3,26,283
Karnaaka	18	24,699	8,537	5,330
Gujarat	17	30,401	11,816	12,794
Tamil Nadu	17	4,893	7,263	9,422
Haryana	16	5,933	8,506	8,691
Rajasthan	15	2,020	7,857	1,566
Punjab	14	1,663	6,665	9,643
Manipur	8	1,831	3,026	5,050
Nagland	8	1,324	1,871	4,893
Mizoram	5	208	536	733
Tripura	3	1,820	53,585	17,389
Jammu and Kashmir	2	2,323	1,183	1,413
Himachal Pradesh	2	271	1,839	903
Arunachal Pradesh	2	237	1,100	1,308
Meghalaya	1	169	489	489

(Cont.)..

1	2	3	4	5
Pondicherry	1	72	454	506
Sikkim	1	12	687	679
Goa	1	0	0	0
Total	414	3,87,548	5,04,493	7,34,531

Source: Ministry of Agriculture, Handbook on Fisheries Statistics, 1996 Department of Agriculture and Co-operation, Fisheries Division, Government of India, New Delhi, 1996, p. 143.

Table 2.14 Primary Fisheries Co-operatives as on 31st March, 1995

State/Union Territory	Number of Societies	Total	Membership of which SC	ST
1	2	3	4	5
Andhra Pradesh	3646	3,59,021	-	-
Assam	456	-	-	-
Bihar	532	66,835	5,450	1,136
Goa	10	971	-	-
Gujarat	385	43,631	4,313	10,799
Haryana	59	1,005	-	-
Himachal Pradesh	28	3,369	1,277	-
Jammu and Kashmir	-	-	-	-
Karnataka	296	76,136	7,448	3,357
Kerala	-	-	-	-
Madhya Pradesh	1,001	44,100	-	-
Maharashtra	2,024	2,08,273	23,285	80,546
Manipur	181	9,182	200	850
Meghalaya	58	2,569	55	2,414
Nagaland	168	4,285	-	4,255
Orissa	482	73,752	30,419	1,951
Punjab	4	60	-	-
Rajasthan	107	4,624	546	2,462
Sikkim	-	-	-	-
Tamil Nadu	675	2,31,224	-	-
Tripura	129	14,225	13,000	1,120
Uttar Pradesh	-	-	-	-
West Bengal	1,072	85,895	8,980	1,000
Andaman and Nicobar	43	1,433	-	130

(Cont.)..

1	2	3	4	5
Arunachal Pradesh	4	300	-	-
Chandigarh	-	-	-	-
Dadra and Nagar Haveli	-	-	-	-
Daman and Diu	6	1,993	-	34
Delhi	2	239	-	-
Lakshadweep	-	-	-	-
Mizoram	36	808	-	808
Pondicherry	36	16,449	-	-
Total	11,440	12,50,379	94,973	1,10,892

Source: The Ministry of Agriculture, Handbook on fisheries Statistics, 1996, Department of Agriculture and co-operation, fisheries Division, government of India, New Delhi, 1996, p. 153.

ORGANISATIONS PROMOTING RESEARCH AND TECHNOLOGY TRAINING IN FISHERIES SECTOR

To provide a strong based for the development of fishery sector in India, several research institutions have been set up over the years.

1. Central Marine Fisheries Research Institute (CMFRI):

The Central Marine Fisheries Research Institute (CMFRI) was established in 1947. The objectives of the Institute are : assessment of the marine living resources, their distribution and abundance, study of their life histories and habits and development of techniques for culture of fish, shell fish and sea weeds. The work is spread over five divisions viz., fishery resources, fishery biology, crustaceans, molluscs and marine biology and oceanography. The institute has one regional centre at Mandapam camp, six sub-stations, one each at Bombay, Karwar, Mangalore, Calicut, Vizihinjam, Tuticorin, Madras and Waltair. It has six research units and 28 survey centres distributed along the east and west coasts. This set up provides adequate coverage to the extensive coastline and fishing areas.

2. Central Inland fisheries Research Institute (CIFRI):

The Central Inland Fisheries Research Institute was located at Barrackpore on the left bank of river Hoogly. This institute was established in 1947. Its objectives broadly cover scientific investigations for an appraisal of the inland fishery resources of the country; development of suitable methods for their management and conservation with an emphasis on culture fisheries. This institute has several sub-station units and research projects spread over the country.

3. Central Inland Capure Fisheries Research Institute (CICFRI):

The Central Inland Capture Fisheries Research Institute had a pond culture division in Cuttak, a riverline and lacustrine division in Allahabad, estuaries division and a training unit in Barrackpore. This institute is engaged in research on capture fisheries in the rivers, reservoirs and estuaries, and on investigations related to conservation and management of fisheries in the river systems, reservoirs and the estuaries.

4. Central Institute of Freshwater Aquaculture (CICFA):

The CIFRI pond culture division was located at Cuttack, Orissa, in 1985. It has established nine research divisions at the headquarters. Besides, it has seven additional centres viz., frog culture centre and sewage-fed fish culture prawn breeding centre; tank fisheries centre, Paddy-cum-fish culture unit, training centre; and Krishi vigyan kendra (farm science centre) located at important centres on the coastline.

The major objectives of the institute are to conduct researches in the areas of nutrition, physiology, genetics, pathology, pond environmental monitoring and aquaculture engineering for commercially important species of both finfish and shell fish, and to conduct specialised training and extension courses to increase fish production by private fish farmers. Through its research programmes, the institute has significantly contributed to the development of freshwater aquaculture in India.

5. Central Institute of Brackishwater Aquaculture (CIBA):

The CIBA was established in April 1985 under the Indian Council of Agricultural Research. CIBA has a major and an important role to play in conducting research and development activities in brackishwater aquaculture.

The headquarters of CIBA are presently located at Madras with regional centres at 1) Kakdwip (West Bengal), 2) Puri (Orissa), 3) Madras and 4) Narakkal (Kerala). The objectives are : a) breeding and seed production of important cultivable candidate species to evolve suitable and better hatchery techniques for mass-scale production of seed; b) studies on nutritional aspects of prawn and finfish in hatchery; c) monitoring the health of cultured animals and to conduct pathe biological studies; d) studies on genetic engineering to improve the stock; e) culture and breeding of the horse-shoe crab for biomedical research; f) evolve suitable soil and water quality criteria for brackishwater aquaculture; g) conduct micro-level surveys to locate suitable areas for brackishwater aquaculture; h) studies on the coastal zone management and land use planning; studies on mangrove ecology and ecosystems to evolve suitable and right technologies for development of brackishwater acquaculture. The institute has separate divisions at its headquarters: 1) finfish culture, 2) crustacean culture, 3) fish farm survey and engineering, 4) resources and technology improvement, 5) nutrition and pathology, 6) training and extension and 7) technical and monitoring cell.

6. Central Institute of Fisheries Technology (CIFT):

The Central Institute of Fisheries Technology was Established in 1957 with the objective of carrying out need based research investigations on various aspects of fishing and fish processing methodology and equipment. This institute has its headquarters in Cochin. An integral part of the functions of the institute is the training of personnel required by fisheries sector. The scientific programmes of the institute distributed under six division are 1) Processing, 2) Chemistry and Microbiology, 3) Craft, 4) Gear, 5) Engineering and 6) Extension, Information and Statistics.

7. Central Institute of Fisheries Education (CIFE):

This institute was established in Bombay in 1961 by the Government of India, largely as a facility to train in-service personnel. The courses offered by the institute are 1) a two year Post Graduate diploma course in fishery science at Bombay, 2) a one year post-graduate Certificate course in inland fisheries development and administration at the Inland fisheries Training Unit. Barrackpore, 3) a nine-month training course for inland fisheries operatives at the Regional Training Centre for Inland Operatives, Agra, with specialisation in induced breeding of carps in bundhs, techniques of nursery pond management, spawn collection and fish seed transport, reservoir fisheries development, weed control techniques, intensive fish culture and culture of common carps and 4) a ten month post-graduate training in extension techniques and methods in fish culture practice at the Central Fisheries Extension Training Centre, Hyderabad.

8. National Bureau of Fish Genetic Resources (NBFGR):

The National Bureau of Fish Genetic research (NBFGR) was established under the ICAR in 1983. The objectives of the bureau are:

1) collection, classification and evaluation of information on fish genetic resources of the country, 2) cataloguing of genotypes, 3) maintenance and preservation of fish genetic material 4) introduction of exotic species in Indian waters; and 5) conservation of endangered species. It has four centres, namely freshwater resource centre at Allahabad; brackishwater resource centre at Madras, marine resource centre at Cochin, and coldwater resource centre at Haldwani (to be shifted to Pithoragarh) in Uttar Pradesh.

The Bureau has initiated a survey for the identification and genetic evaluation of fish resources of the Ganga river system for preparation of an annotated catalogue of the genotypes.

9. National Research Centre on coldwater Fisheries (NRCCF):

To conduct investigations on coldwater fisheries of the rivers and lakes, a national research centre on coldwater fisheries was established in 1985. The centre will conduct research on the indigenous coldwater species such as the mahseer and schizothorax species and the exotic trout.

10. The Central Institute of Fisheries Nautical And Engineering Training (CIFNET):

The Central Institute of Fisheries, Nautical and Engineering Training was established in the year 1963 at Cochin by the Government of India. Subsequently, to meet the increased demand of the trained manpower to units of the institute were started at Madras (1968) and Visakhapatnam (1981). The institute trains operatives of different skills in both theoretical and practical fields to conduct fishing in high seas with modern large fishing vessels. Skippers, fishing mates, marine engineers, electronic engineers, gear technicians, boat building foreman, shore mechanics and radio telephone operators required for manning the high sea fishing vessels are trained by the institute. An operative institute was later started in Madras in 1969.

11. Central Institute of Coastal Engineering for Fishery (CICEF):

The Central Institute of Coastal Engineering for fishery is involved in the development of brackishwater aquculture to produce fish and prawns. the objectives are : 1) carrying out feasibility studies for selection of suitable sites and conducting site surveys, 2) developing suitable engineering designs for coastal aquaculture farms and shrimp hatcheries and operational procedures for the types of sites commonly found in the country, 3) testing the suitability of designs, their operational procedures and economic viability through the establishment of representative pilot projects, 4) establishing guidelines for designing and operation of small and large coastal farms and shrimp hatcheries in different types of sites, and 5) training adequate number of personnel to undertake feasibility studies, site surveys, preparation of farm designs, economic viability, establishment and operation of farms and hatcheries. The institutions total target in the Seventh plan is to cover 2,500 ha of brackishwater area by survey investigation. therefore, each year it is expected to take up 500 ha of brackishwater area for survey investigation.

12. Export Inspection Agency (EIA):

The Export Inspection Agency (EIA) was established in, 1969. Under Export (Quality Control and Inspection) Act. The prominent exportable fish products including : a) forzen shrimps, b) canned shrimps (wet pack), c) frozen froglegs, d) dried fish and dried shrimps, e) dried shark fins and fish maws, f) frozen lobster tails, g) dried Bombay duch and laminated Bombay duch, h) canned crab meat (wet pack), i) frozen pomfrets, j) frozen cuttle fish and squids, K) beehe-de-mer, l) frozen lobsters and m) frozen fish were brought under the control of the Agency.

13. Integrated Fisheries Project (IFP):

The Indo-Norwegian Project was set up in 1953 under an agreement between Norway, India and UN at neondakara in Kerala. The project envisaged mechanisation of fishing boats, provision of repair facilities, construction of ice plants, supply of insulated vans for transport of fish, organisation of fisheries co-operatives, improvement of environmental sanitation with emphasis on supply of drinking water and establishment of a health centre. Under a new agreement in 1956 the project site in Cochin came into being. The international agreement having come to an end in 1972, the project was renamed as 'Integrated Fisheries Project'. The Integrated Fisheries Project engages in the survey of fishery resources, fish processing, product diversification and marketing, training in mechanised fishing and in fish processing techniques.

14. Fishery Survey of India (FSI):

Fishery Survey of India with its headquarters at Bombay has at present 10 operational bases, established at Porbandar, Bombay, Goa, Mangalore, cochin, Tuticorin, Madras, Visakhapatnam,

Roychowk and Port Blair for survey assessment and monitoring of the marine fishery resources in the Indian Exclusive Economic Zone.

15. The Marine Products Export Development Authority (MPEDA):

It was found necessary to bring this industry under a unified and centralised control of a statutory agency on the lines of similar organisation in other maritime countries. The Marine Products Export Development Authority was constituted under an Act of Parliament in 1972. The authority is a statutory body with an executive committee, technical committee and market promotion committee, under the Ministry of Commerce. It is a nodal agency for joint venture in deep sea fishing and has taken up export promotion by providing financial support and encouraging brackishwater farming.

It was entrusted with registration and licensing, export production, marketing, in-plant inspection, infrastructure and related facilities, R and D manpower and financial assistance.

REFERENCE

1 The countries are Japan, China, U.S.A., Chile, Peru, India, Korean Republic, Indonesia, Thailand, Norway, Phillipines, Denmar, Korean DPRP, Iceland, Spain and Russian Fed.

2 The Marine Products Export Development Authority, 'Indian Fisheries 1947-1977', the Author, Cochin, 1977, p. 4.

3 Planning Commission, 'First Five Year Plan', Ministry of Information and Broadcasting, Government of India, Delhi, 1952, pp 138-41.

4 Planning Commission, 'Second Five Year Plan', Government of India, New Delhi, 1956, pp 292-97.

5 Planning Commission, 'Third Five Year Plan', Government of India, New Delhi, 1961, pp 357-61.

6 Planning Commission, 'Third Five Year Plan', A Draft Outline, Government of India, New Delhi, 1960, oo 171-72.

7 Planning Commission, 'Fourth Five Year Plan', Government of India, New Delhi, 1969, pp. 201-05.

8 Planning Commission, 'Fifth Five Year Plan', Government of India, New Delhi, 1976, pp 57-58.

9 Planning Commission, 'Sixth Five Year Plan', Government of India, New Delhi, 1981. pp 133-35.

10. Planning Commission, 'Seventh Five Year Plan', Government of India, New Delhi, 1985, pp 34-36.

11 Planning Commission, 'Eighth Five Year Plan', Government of India, New Delhi, 1993, pp 146-47.

12 U.K. Srivastava, et al., 'Fishery Sector of India', Oxford and IBH Publishing co. New Delhi, 1991, p. 24.

13 Ajith Thomas John and Shahul Hameed, M., 'Fisheries Development in India During the Plan periods - Part-1, Objectives, Outlays and Achievements till the end of Seventh Five Year Plan', Seafood Export Journal, Vol. XXVI No. 3, March 1995, p. 32.

14 P.V. Dehadrai, 'Creation of EEZ and Development of Marine Fisheries in India', Published in Trivedi, K.K., Fisheries Development 2000 A.d. Proceedings of an International conference held at New Delhi, February 4-6, 1985, Oxford and IBH Publishing Co. New Delhi, 1986, p. 63.

15 Singh, S.B., Hon. Minister for Agriculture and Rural Development - At International Conference- 'Fisheries Development : 2000 A.D.' held at New Delhi, February 4-6, 1985 (Memio).

3

Export of Indian Marine Products

Fish and fish products are the important food items for the larger population spread throughout the world. Several fish producing countries, apart from meeting the demand in the domestic market, are exporting fish products to many countries to meet the demand in the international market and also to earn foreign exchange. The data presented in Table 3.1 shows the quantity-wise export growth of marine products in the world during 1986-87 to 1995-96. The table reveals, the total exports of marine products to various markets in the world which was 85,843 tonnes in 1986-87 increased to as high as 3.07 lakh tonnes in 1994-95. However, in the subsequent year the exports declined to 2.96 lakh tonnes. The growth of exports of marine products shows an erratic trend during the period. The growth over the previous year varied between 2.62 per cent and 25.98 per cent during 1986-87 and 1994-95 . During 1995-96 the quantity exported was declined by 3.60 per cent. The table also reveals the annual growth rate of the exports of marine products was more than 20 per cent during 1990-91 to 1992-93 and during 1994-95. The quantity-wise growth of export of marine products is also shown in Figure 3.1.

The data relating to the value-wise export growth of marine products in the world during 1986-87 to 1995-96 is presented in Table 3.2. The value of exports which was Rs. 460.76 crores in 1986-87 tremendously increased to Rs. 3,501.11 crores in 1995-96 recording an enviable increase of 760 per cent. The growth rate over the previous year varied between (-) 2.07 per cent and 54.01

per cent. There was continuous growth with varied growth rates during the first nine years and in the last year, there was a negative growth. The years 1990-91, 1991-92, 1993-94 and 1994-95 registered a growth rate of more than 40 per cent over the previous years. The unit value of the fish in the international market has been on the increase year by year, except in 1989-90. During the period, starting from Rs. 53.66 per Kg. at the beginning of the decade, the unit value increased to Rs. 118.17 by 1995-96. The value-wise growth in export has been presented in Figure 3.2.

Table 3.1: Quantity -wise Export Growth of Marine Products in the World During 1986-87 to 1995-96

(Quantity in Tonnes)

Year	Export quantity	Variation over previous year	Export Growth per centage
1986-87	85,843	2,192	2.62
1987-88	97,179	11,336	13.21
1988-89	99,777	2,598	2.67
1989-90	1,10,843	11,066	11.09
1990-91	1,39,419	28,576	25.78
1991-92	1,71,820	32,401	23.24
1992-93	2,09,025	37,205	21.65
1993-94	2,43,960	34,935	16.71
1994-95	3,07,337	63,377	25.98
1995-96	2,96,277	(-) 11,060	(-)3.60

Source: Compiled from the Marine Products Export Reviews of The Marine Products Export Development Authority, Cochin.

The year 1995-96 did not witness any major calamities in the seafood sector in India. But the export of seafood from the country during the year has been showing a trend of decline mainly due to market conditions of overseas. The reasons attributed for this decline in export of seafood from the country are: a) restrictions and embargoes imposed by the FDA authorities in US from time to time with regard to Table 3.2 Value-wise Export Growth of Marine Products in the World During 1986-7 6to 1995-96 import of shrimp from India. b) restrictions imposed by the French, Italian and Spanish authorities with regard to import of seafood from India including the recent incidents of detention of seafood at the Italian ports for alleged salmonella contamination and c) sluggish market

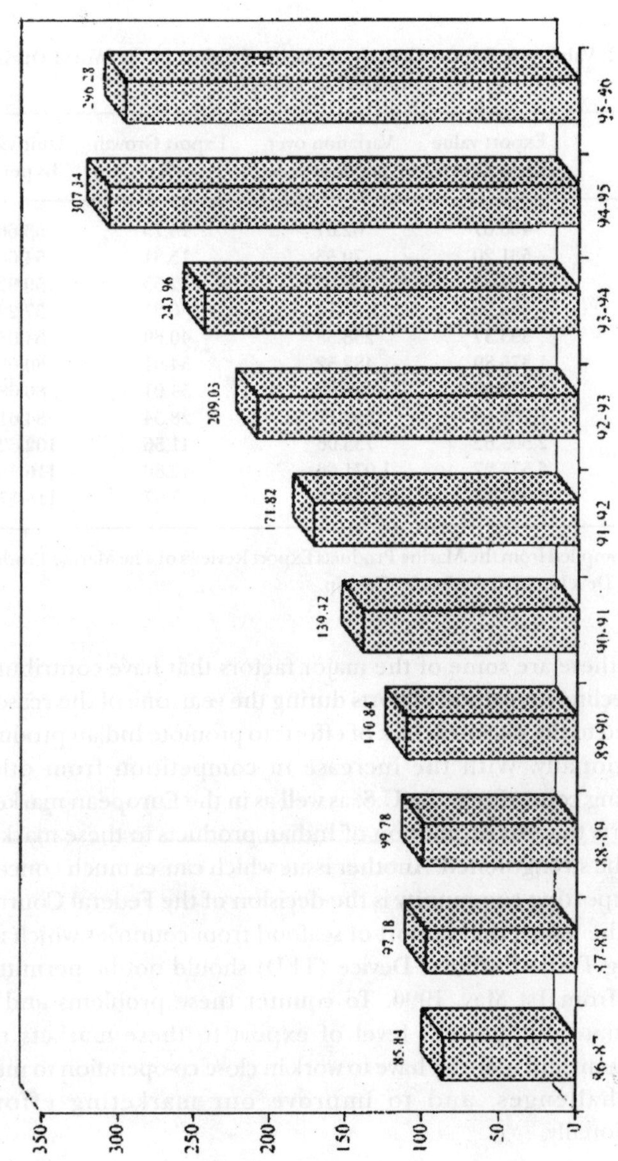

Fig. 3.1. Export Growth Of Marine Products During 1986-87 to 1995-96 Baded On Quantity ('000 Tons)

conditions in Japan as a result of the appreciation of yen vis-a-vis U.S. dollar and the after effect of the Kobe earth-quake.

Table 3.2: Value-wise Export Growth of Marine Product in the World During 1986-87 to 1995-96

Year	Export value (Rs. in Crores)	Variation over previous year	Export Growth (%)	Unit Value Rs per Kg
1986-87	460.67	62.67	15.75	53.66
1987-88	531.20	70.53	15.31	54.66
1988-89	597.85	66.65	12.55	59.92
1989-90	634.99	37.14	6.21	57.29
1990-91	893.37	258.38	40.69	64.08
1991-92	1,375.89	482.52	54.01	80.08
1991-92	1,375.89	482.52	54.01	80.08
1992-93	1,768.56	392.17	28.54	84.61
1993-94	2,503.62	735.06	41.56	102.62
1994-95	3,575.27	1,071.66	42.80	116.33
1995-96	3,501.11	(-) 74.16	(-) 2.07	118.17

Source: Compiled from the Marine Products Export Reviews of The Marine Products Export Development Authority, Cochin.

While these are some of the major factors that have contributed to the decline in seafood exports during the year, one of the reasons attributed to the decline is lack of efforts to promote Indian products internationally. With the increase in competition from other developing countries in the U.S. as well as in the European markets, our efforts towards promotion of Indian products to these markets need to be strengthened. Another issue which causes much concern to the exporting community is the decision of the Federal Court of USA to the effect that import of seafood from countries which are not using Turtle Excluder Device (TED) should not be permitted to USA from 1st May, 1996. To counter these problems and to substantiate our present level of export to these markets the Government and industry have to work in close co-operation to meet these challenges, and to improve our marketing efforts internationally.

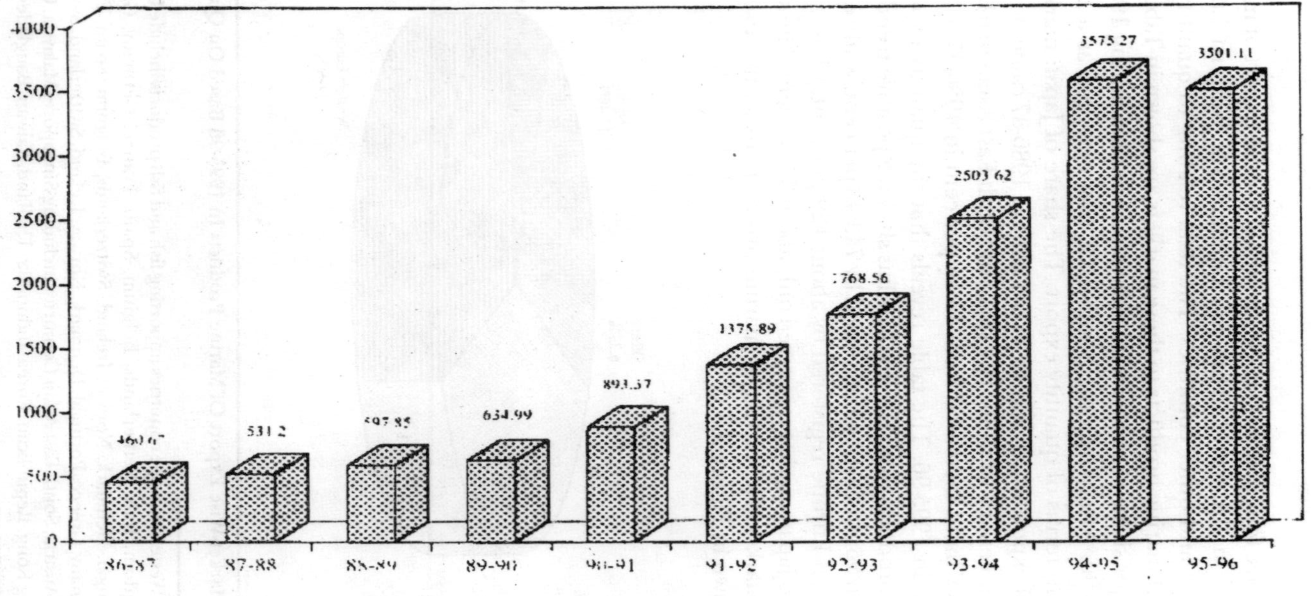

Fig. 3.2. Export Growth Of Marine Products During 1986-87 to 1995-96 Based On Value (Rs. in Crores)

MARKET-WISE EXPORTS

There are four major markets identified for the export of marine products in the world. They are Japan, USA, Western Europe countries, and other countries. The data relating to quantity-wise export of marine products to these markets are shown in Table 3.3. The major share of export was to the Japan market during 1986-87 to 1989-90. Afterwards the South East Asia emerged as a major market in terms of quantity export. The share of Japan market in the total export which was 43.44 per cent in 1986-87 came down to 17.48 per cent in 1995-96. The share of South East Asian market on the other hand increased from 15.54 per cent in 1986-87 to 37.97 per cent in 1995-96. The table reveals that the quantity export of marine products to all the markets has shown a positive trend. The export to South East Asia increased by 743.48 per cent, while export to Western Europe registered by about 129 per cent, whereas, the export to Japan market registered only about 39 per cent. The shares of the markets for export of marine products (quantity-wise) are also shown in Figure 3.3.

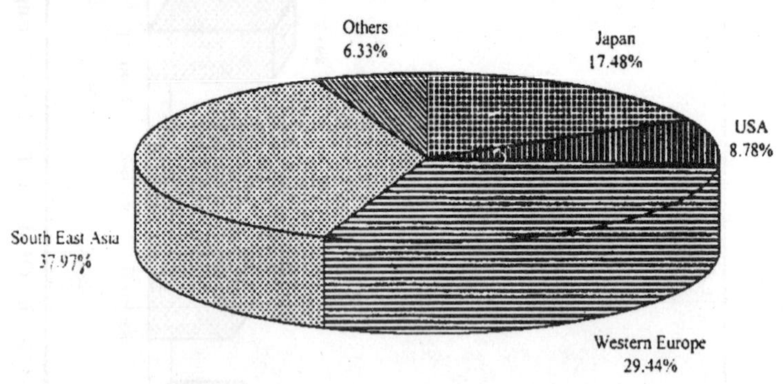

Fig 3.3. Market-Wise Export Of Marine Products In 1995-96 Based On Quantity

* The Western Europe countries importing fish and fish products include United Kingdom, Italy, Netherlands, Belgium, Spain, France, Germany, Greece, Portugal, Denmark, Norway, Ireland, Switzerlands, Belgium, Spain, France, Germany, Greece, Portugal, Denmark, Norway, Ireland, Switzerland, Sweeden and Austria, South East Asian Countries including Singapore, Malaysia, China, Hong Kong, Republican. Korea. Indonesia, Thailand, Taiwan, Bangladesh and Philippines.

Table 3.3: Market-wise Export of Marine Products During 1986-87 to 1995-96 (Based on Quantity)

(Quantity in Tonnes)

Country	Years										Percentage Growth
	1986-87	1987-88	1988-89	1989-90	1990-91	1991-92	1992-93	1993-94	1994-95	1995-96	
Japan	37,287	38,738	35,811	38,742	38,092	39,480	41,240	4,985	53,500	51,789	38.89
	(43.44)	(39.86)	(35.89)	(34.89)	(27.32)	(22.98)	(19.73)	(18.45)	(17.41)	(17.48)	
U.S.A.	11,374	14.444	13,531	13,802	16,155	20,844	20,141	26,152	32,102	26,008	128.66
	(13.25)	(14.86)	(13.56)	(12.42)	(11.59)	(12.13)	(9.64)	(10.72)	(10.45)	(8.78)	
Western Europe	17,555	22,310	32,347	35,240	42,964	55,605	67,582	71,857	71,224	87,212	396.79
	(20.45)	(22.96)	(32.42)	(31.74)	(30.82)	(32.36)	(32.33)	(29.45)	(23.17)	(29.44)	
South East Asia	13,338	14,885	12,387	9,480	36,925	44,585	64,465	87,099	1,35,567	1,12,504	743.48
	(15.54)	(15.32)	(12.41)	(8.54)	(26.48)	(25.95)	(30.84)	(35.70)	(44.11)	(37.97)]	
Others	6,289	6,802	5,701	13,779	5,283	11,306	15,597	13,867	14,994	18,764	198.36
	(7.32)	(7.00)	(5.72)	(12.41)	(3.79)	(6.58)	(7.46)	(5.68)	(4.86)	(6.33)	
Total	85,843	97,179	99,777	1,11,043	1,39,419	1,71,820	2,09,025	2,43,960	3,07,337	2,96,277	245.14
	(100.00)	(100.00)	(100.00)	(100.00)	(100.00)	(100.00)	(100.00)	(100.00)	(100.00)	(100.00)	

Source: Compiled from the Marine Products Export Reviews of The Marine Products Export Development Authority, Cochin.

Table 3.4 reveals value-wise data relating to export markets for marine products. In terms of value in rupees, Japan is an undisputed leader in all the years- during 1986-87 to 1995-96. However, the share of Japan has been on the declined during the period. In the year 1986-87, as much as 67.42 per cent of the total exports were made to Japan, while in the year 1995-96 the share of the market fell to 45.03 per cent. Western Europe and South East Asia improved their share significantly during the period. While the share of Western Europe increased from 12.70 per cent in 1986-87 to 26.05 per cent in 1995-96, the South East Asia increased its share from 5.26 per cent in 1986-87 14.31 per cent in 1995-96. The share of USA which was 12.22 per cent in 1986-87 declined marginally to 10.46 per cent in 1995-96. The table further reveals, the South East Asia registered highest growth (1,969 per cent) followed by Western Europe (1,458 per cent) during the period. USA registered the growth of 550.55 per cent while Japan registered 407.66 per cent growth. The share positions of the markets in terms of value are shown in Figure 3.4.

Since very early times, India was an exporter of processed fish products particularly dry prawn pulp and cured fish to some of her immediate neighbours[1]. Over a period of time India achieved a substantial progress in exporting fish and fish products to various countries. In the year 1995-96, India exported marine products to 61 countries in the world[2]. The quantity-wise export of Indian marine products to various countries during 1986-87 to 1995-96 are shown in Table 3.5. The table reveals, the quantity of export which was 85,843 tonnes in 1986-87 increased to over 2.96 lakh tonnes in 1995-96 recording an increase of 245 per cent. The highest growth over previous year was recorded in 1994-95 followed by 1990-91 and 1991-92. The year 1995-96 registered a decline by about four per cent over previous year. The table further reveals, the share of export of marine products in the total fish production which was 2.89 per cent in 1986-87 increased to 6.43 per cent in 1994-95 and in the subsequent year registered a marginal decline to reach 5.98 per cent. In other words, out of the total fish production in the country about 94 per cent has been consumed in the domestic market.

The data relating to the export of marine products in terms of value in rupees are shown in Table 3.6. The table reveals the foreign exchange earned by the country through the export of marine

Table 3.4 Market-wise Export of Marine Products During 1986-87 to 1995-96 (Based on Value)

(Rupees in Crores)

Country	Years										Percentage
	1986-87	1987-88	1988-89	1989-90	1990-91	1991-92	1992-93	1993-94	1994-95	1995-96	Growth
Japan	310.58	326.18	356.84	345.51	458.27	633.45	801.90	1,185.67	1,643.82	1,576.69	407.66
	(67.42)	(61.40)	(59.69)	(54.41)	(51.30)	(46.04)	(45.35)	(47.36)	(45.98)	(45.03)	
U.S.A.	56.30	75.15	70.12	78.33	109.31	154.64	190.48	306.17	490.23	366.26	550.55
	(12.22)	(14.15)	(11.72)	(12.34)	(12.24)	(11.25)	(10.77)	(12.23)	(13.71)	(10.46)	
Western Europe	58.52	82.59	119.75	149.68	231.86	395.87	511.52	645.29	726.30	911.87	1,458.22
	(12.70)	(15.55)	(20.03)	(23.57)	(25.95)	(28.77)	(28.92)	(25.77)	(20.31)	(26.05)	
South East Asia	24.22	31.09	30.72	25.16	71.78	130.50	185.05	288.40	602.32	501.03	1,968.66
	(5.26)	(5.85)	(5.14)	(3.96)	(8.03)	(9.48)	(10.46)	(11.52)	(16.85)	(14.31)	
Others	11.05	16.19	20.42	36.31	22.15	61.43	79.61	78.09	112.60	145.26	1,214.57
	(2.40)	(3.05)	(3.42)	(5.72)	(2.48)	(4.46)	(4.50)	(3.12)	(3.15)	(4.15)	
Total	460.67	531.10	597.85	634.99	893.37	1,375.89	1,768.56	2,503.62	3,575.27	3,501.11	660.00
	(100.00)	(100.00)	(100.00)	(100.00)	(100.00)	(100.00)	(100.00)	(100.00)	(100.00)	(100.00)	

Source: compiled from the Marine Products Export Reviews of the Marine Products Export Development Authority, Cochin.

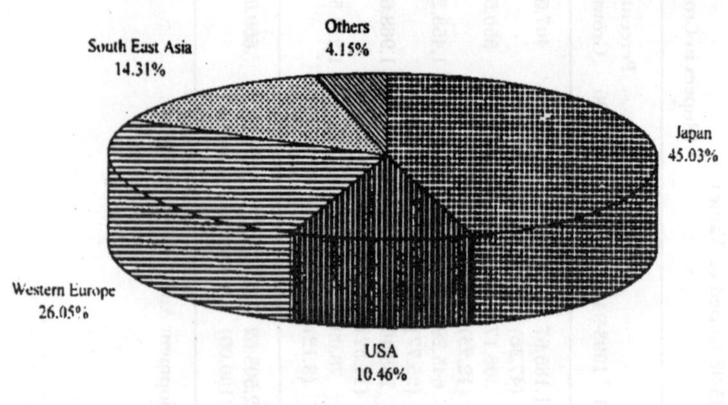

Fig 3.4 Market-Wise Export of Marine Products in 1995-96 Based on Value

products increased from Rs. 460.67 crores in 1986-87 to Rs. 3,501.11 crores in 1995-96 recording an increase of 660 per cent. The growth rate is erratic during the period ranging from 6.21 per cent to 54.01 per cent on the positive side. The year 1991-92 registered highest growth rate over previous year followed by 1994-95 with 42.83 per cent, 1993-94 with 41.56 per cent and 1990-91 with 40.69 per cent.

Port-Wise Exports

The export of the Indian marine products is routed through seaways to reach the markets in various countries. In India there are 11 major ports and a large number of minor ports. The major ports are Cochin, Bombay, Madras, Vizag, Calcutta, Paradeep, Tuticorin, Goa, Kandla, Mangalore and Jawaharlal Nehru Port (Bombay). The data presented in Table 3.7 reveals the Port-wise export of marine products (quantity-wise) during 1986-87 to 1995-96. The table reveals that the marine export were routed through only Cochin and madras ports in the year 1986-87. The share of Cochin Port in the total export during the year was 73.26 per cent. From the subsequent year the exports are routed through all the major ports and also through minor ports. The Cochin Port occupies the first position in terms of quantity export during all the years in the decade. The share of this port in the total marine products export varied between 23.53 per cent and 73.21 per cent. Bombay Port occupies the second position, the share of which in the total marine products export varied between 10.54 per cent and 29.22 per cent. Madras Port occupies third position from 1985-86 to 1992-93 and later relegated its position to Kandala Port. The Kandla Port was in the third position during 1993-94 and 1994-95 and in the year 1995-96 Jawaharlal Nehru Port of Bombay has occupied third position. The share of minor ports in the export of the total marine products increased from 3.28 per cent in 1987-88 to 20.02 per cent in 1995-96, while the percentage share of Cochin, Bombay, Madras, Calcutta, Tuticorin, Mangalore Ports have shown a declining trend. The major ports of Vizag, Goa, Kandla and Jawaharlal Nehru Port have shown an increasing trend. The exports from Paradeep Port were stopped from the year 1992-93 due to economic reasons. The table further reveals, the growth rates of quantity-wise marine products export in different ports. The highest growth rate was registered in minor ports (1,758 per cent increase). Among the major ports Jawaharlal Nehru Port registered 538 per cent growth in just six years in the export of marine products. Kandla Port registered 510 per cent increase, whereas Vizag Port registered about 478 per cent increase. Mangalore Port registered a negative growth rate of about 78 per cent while Bombay and Madras Ports registered a marginal growth of about 10 per cent and 47.54 per cent respectively.

Table 3.5: Export of Indian Marine Products During 1986-87 to 1995-96 (Based on Quantity)

(Quantity in Tonnes)

Year	Quantity	Increase/decrease over previous year	Increase/ decrease over previous year (%)	Percentage in total production
1986-87	85,843	2,192	2.62	2.89
1987-88	97,179	11,336	13.21	3.28
1988-89	99,777	2,598	2.67	3.14
1989-90	1,11,043	11,266	11.29	3.02
1990-91	1,39.419	28,376	25.55	3.62
1991-92	1,71,820	32,401	23.24	4.14
1992-93	1,99,025	27,205	15.83	4.56
1993-94	2.43,960	44,935	22.57	5.25
1994-95	3.08,368	64,408	26.40	6.43
1995-96	2,96,259	(-)12,109	(-) 3.93	5.98

Source: compiled from the Annual Reports of The Marine Products Export Development Authority, Cochin.

Table 3.6: Export of Indian Marine Products During 1986-87 to 1995-96 (Based on Value)

(Rupees in Crores)

Year	Value	Increase/decrease over previous year	Increase/ decrease over previous year (%)
1986-87	460.67	62.68	15.75
1987-88	531.20	70.53	15.31
1988-89	597.85	66.65	12.55
1989-90	634.99	37.14	6.21
1990-91	893.37	258.38	40.69
1991-92	1,375.89	482.52	54.01
1992-93	1,768.56	392.67	28.54
1993-94	2,503.62	735.06	41.56
1994-95	3,575.91	1,072.29	42.83
1995-96	3,501.11	(-) 74.8	(-) 2.09

Source: Compiled from the Annual Reports of The Marine Products Export Development Authority, Cochin.

The port-wise exports of marine products in terms of value are presented in Table 3.8. The table reveals, the Cochin Port leads in export value though there is a declining trend in percentage share which was down from 72.93 per cent in 1986-87 to 24.39 per cent in 1995-96. The Jawaharlal Nehru Port occupied second position in 1987-88 and continued in the position upto 1989-90. The Madras Port occupied the second position in 1990-91 and since 1991-90 and since 1991-92, Vizag Port occupied the second position. The table reveals the Tuticorin Port registered a substantial growth (3,460 per cent). The percentage share of this port out of the total exports also increased from 1.01 per cent in 1987-88 to 5.47 per cent in 1995-96. Vizag Port registered 1,519 per cent increase over the period and the share in total export increased from 7.08 per cent in 1987-88 to 17.39 per cent in 1995-96. Goa Port and Jawaharlal Nehru Port and minor ports shares also increased during the period. In the other ports, though there is a positive growth during the period the percentage share in the total export have shown a declining trend.

Table 3.7: Port-wise Exports of Indian Marine Products During 1986-87 to 1995-96 (Based on Quantity)

(Quantity in Tonnes)

Country	1986-87	1987-88	1988-89	1989-90	1990-91	1991-92	1992-93	1993-94	1994-95	1995-96	Percentage Growth
Major Ports											
Cochin	3,906	35,576	45,614	47,194	50,997	58,743	49,094	63,809	74,576	78,682	132.06
	(73.21)	(36.61)	(45.71)	(42.60)	(36.58)	(34.19)	(23.53)	(26.18)	(24.27)	(26.56)	
Bombay	-	28,400	18,978	22,167	16,781	26,454	38.614	38,890	46,006	31,213	9.90
	(29.22)	(19.02)	(20.01)	(12.04)	(15.40)	(18.50)	(15.95)	(14.97)	(10.54)		
Madras	12,405	9,219	11,034	15,761	22,699	17,988	18,444	11,602	18,876	18,302	47.54
	(26.79)	(9.49)	(11.06)	(14.23)	(16.28)	(10.47)	(8.84)	(4.76)	(6.14)	(6.18)	
Vizag	-	3,465	2,955	5,238	8,562	10,349	12,844	16,018	19,811	20,017	477.69
	(3.57)	(2.96)	(4.73)	(6.14)	(6.02)	(6.16)	(6.57)	(6.45)	(6.76)		
Calcutta	-	4,707	6,381	7,404	6,001	7,921	9,956	11,993	12,914	14,044	198.36
	(4.84)	(6.40)	(6.68)	(4.30)	(4.61)	(4.77)	(4.92)	(4.20)	94.74)		
Paradeep	-	1,422	1,097	429	163	438	-	-	-		
	(1.46)	(1.10)	(0.39)	(0.12)	(0.25)	(-)	(-)	(-)	(-)	-	214.53
Tuticorin	-	4,142	3,931	2,739	4,641	7,060	12,914	14,044	198.36		
	(4.27)	(3.94)	(2.47)	(3.33)	(4.10)	(6.00)	(3.63)	(3.24)	(4.40)		
Goa	-	2,586	1,093	691	1,966	4,236	5,647	13,693	13,334	13,938	438.98
	(2.66)	(1.10)	(0.62)	(1.41)	(2.47)	(2.72)	(5.62)	(4.34)	(4.70)		
Kandla-	3,848	6,416	7,617	10,927	11,704	17,304	27,304	27,087	32,582	23,462	509.72
	(3.96)	(6.43)	(6.88)	(7.84)	(6.81)	(8.30)	(11.10)	(10.60)	(7.92)		

(Cont.)...

Country	1986-87	1987-88	1988-89	1989-90	1990-91	1991-92	1992-93	1993-94	1994-95	1995-96	Percentage Growth
					Years						
Mangalore	-	622	500	344	846	1,474	-	179	148	.37	(-) 77.97
	(0.64)	(0.50)	(0.31)	(0.61)	(0.86)	(-)	(0.08)	(0.05)	(0.04)		
JNP	-	-	-	-	3,784	5,973	15,851	18,949	24,653	24,144	538.05
(Bombay)	(-)	(-)	(-)	(2.71)	(3.48)	(7.60)	(7.77)	(8.02)	(8.14)		
Minor Ports	-	3,192	1,778	1,203	12,052	19,480	28,329	32,745	54,481	59,310	1,758.08
		(3.28)	(1.78)	(1.08)	(8.64)	(11.34)	(13.58)	(13.42)	(17.72)	(20.02)	
Total	46,311	97,179	99,777	1,10,788	1,39,419	1,71,820	2,08,602	2,43,960	3,07,337	2,96,277	539.76
	(100.00)	(100.00)	(100.00)	(100.00)	(100.00)	(100.00)	(100.00)	(100.00)	(100.00)	(100.00)	

Source: Compiled from the Annual Reports of the Marine Products Export Development Authority, Cochin.

Table 3.8: Port-wise Exports of Indian Marine Products During 1986-87 to 995-96 (Based on Value)

(Rs. in Crores)

Country	Years										Percentage
	1986-87	1987-88	1988-89	1989-90	1990-91	1991-92	1992-93	1993-94	1994-95	1995-96	Growth
Major Ports											
Cochin	164.56	183.94	221.31	240.82	313.79	44.47	414.25	621.53	814.96	853.76	418.81
	(72.93)	(34.63)	(37.02)	(37.94)	(35.12)	(32.30)	(23.44)	(24.83)	(22.79)	(24.39)	
Bombay	-	132.37	95.78	105.53	88.04	165.03	209.82	228.35	312.22	272.48	105.85
	(-)	(24.92)	(16.02)	(16.63)	(9.85)	(11.98)	(11.87)	(9.12)	(8.73)	(7.78)	
Madras	61.09	60.82	96.79	88.96	134.47	175.02	228.18	338.13	592.78	527.65	763.73
	(27.07)	(11.45)	(16.19)	(14.01)	(15.05)	(12.72)	(12.91)	(13.51)	(16.58)	(15.07)	
Vizag	-	37.60	38.95	60.21	125.95	202.19	289.88	454.11	637.29	608.88	1,519.36
	(7.08)	(6.52)	(9.49)	(14.10)	(16.40)	(18.16)	(17.83)	(17.39)			
Calcutta	-	55.33	84.65	84.33	86.62	130.72	195.15	266.26	321.11	354.60	540.88
	(10.42)	(14.16)	(13.29)	(9.70)	(9.50)	(11.04)	(10.66)	(8.98)	(10.13)		
Paradeep	-	15.11	12.70	4.01	2.86	6.81	-		-	-	-
	(2.85)	(2.12)	(0.63)	(0.32)	(0.50)	(-)	(-)	(-)	(-)		
Tuticorin	-	5.38	6.16	10.57	31.41	55.51	109.27	123.75	187.34	191.54	3,460.22
	(1.01)	(1.03)	(1.67)	(3.52)	(4.04)	(6.18)	(4.95)	(5.24)	(5.47)		
Goa	-	5.23	4.19	1.17	3.38	8.16	27.00	54.07	59.20	70.36	1,245.32
	(0.98)	(0.70)	(0.18)	(0.38)	(0.59)	(1.54)	(2.16)	(1.66)	(2.01)		
Kandla	-	10.57	21.86	31.75	40.53	55.47	76.91	134.63	174.17	131.96	1,148.44
	(1.99)	(3.66)	(5.00)	(4.54)	(4.03)	(4.35)	(5.30)	(4.87)	(3.77)		

(Cont.)...

Country	1986-87	1987-88	1988-89	1989-90	Years 1990-91	1991-92	1992-93	1993-94	1994-95	1995-96	Percentage Growth
Mangalore	-	3.69	2.92	1.54	5.93	14.99	-	1.32	8.70	11.54	212.74
(0.69)	(0.48)	(0.24)	(0.66)	(1.09)	(-)	(0.05)	(0.24)	(0.33)			
JNP	-	-	-	-	19.31	38.20	96.75	145.78	221.71	211.88	997.26
(Bombay)	(-)	(-)	(-)	(2.16)	(2.78)	(5.47)	(5.84)	(6.20)	(6.05)		
Minor Ports	-	21.16	12.54	5.87	41.07	79.33	120.22	135.42	245.80	266.46	1,159.26
(3.98)	(2.10)	(0.92)	(4.60)	(5.77)	(6.80)	(5.42)	(6.88)	(7.61)			
Total	225.65	531.20	597.85	634.76	893.36	1,375.90	1,767.43	2,503.62	3,575.28	3501.11	1451.57
	(100.00)	(100.00)	(100.00)	(100.00)	(100.00)	(100.00)	(100.00)	(100.00)	(100.00)	(100.00)	

Source: Compiled from the Annual Reports of the Marine products Export Development Authority, Cochin.

PRODUCT-WISE EXPORTS

There are four major marine products exported from India. They are frozen shrimp, frozen fish, frozen squid and frozen cuttle fish. The data on quantity-wise export of marine products reveals that the frozen shrimp and frozen fish put together account for 66 per cent to 73 per cent out of the total export during the period (Table 3.9). The share of the frozen shrimp which was 57.32 per cent in 1986-87 declined to 32.30 per cent in 1995-96, inspite of increase in quantity terms by about 95 per cent. The share of frozen fish registered a substantial increase, from 15.30 per cent in 1986-87 to 33.78 per cent in 1995-96. The percentage share of frozen squid increased from 11.35 per cent to 15.20 per cent during the period. The frozen cuttle fish exports also have shown an increasing trend, the share of which increased from 5.47 per cent in 1986-87 to 11.42 per cent in 1995-96. The substantial increase in quantity terms was registered in the case of frozen fish (662 per cent) followed by frozen cuttle fish (621 per cent). The item-wise export of marine products in 1995-96 based on quantity is shown in Figure 3.5.

In terms of value of marine products export, the share of frozen shrimp varied between 82.04 per cent and 66.78 per cent during the period 1986-87 to 1995-96 (Table 3.10). The foreign exchange earnings by the export of frozen shrimp which was Rs. 377.93 crores in 1986-87 increased to Rs. 2,356.43 crores in 1995-96 recording an increase of 524 per cent. Frozen fish occupies second position in contribution to the foreign exchange resource with a contribution ranging from Rs. 22.29 crores in 1986-87 to Rs. 446.57 crores in 1994-95 and Rs. 372.26 crores in 1995-96. This product registered the growth of 1,570 per cent in terms of value during the period. The contribution from frozen squid which was Rs. 17.27 cores in 1986-87 increased to Rs. 319.58 crores in 1995-96 recording an increase of 1,750 per cent during the period. The frozen cuttle fish, on the other hand, increased its contribution from Rs. 13.96 crores in 1986-87 to Rs. 260.86 crores in 1995-96 recording an increase of 1,769 per cent. The contribution from other fish items increased from Rs. 29.22 crores in 1986-87 to Rs. 191.98 crores in 1995-96 recording an increase of 557 per cent. It can be inferred from the above that though frozen shrimp was the major product item in the Indian marine products export during the last decade, the other

Table 3.9: Item-wise Export of Indian Marine Products During 1986-87 to 1995-96 (Based on Quantity)

(Quantity in Tonnes)

Year	Frozen Shrimp	Frozen Fish	Frozen Squid	Frozen Cuttle Fish	Others	Total
1986-87	49,203	13,138	9,739	4,694	9,069	85,843
	(57.32)	(15.30)	(11.35)	(5.47)	(10.56)	(100.00)
1987-88	55,736	14,904	7,621	9,195	9,723	97,179
	(57.35)	(15.34)	(7.84)	(9.46)	(10.01)	(100.00)
1988-89	56,835	11,234	16,374	8,262	7,072	99,777
	(56.96)	(11.26)	(16.41)	(8.28)	(7.09)	(100.00)
1989-90	57,846	21,128	11,846	14,140	5,828	1,10,788
	(52.21)	(19.07)	(10.69)	(12.77)	(5.26)	(100.00)
1990-91	62,395	42,340	16,667	11,596	8,660	1,39,419
	(44.75)	30.37)	(11.95)	(8.32)	(6.21)	(100.00)
1991-92	76,080	49,119	25,529	12,437	8,655	1,71,820
	(44.28)	(28.59)	(14.86)	(7.23)	(5.04)	(100.00)
1992-93	74,393	75,376	30,364	18,981	9,488	2,08,602
	(35.66)	(36.13)	(14.86)	(9.10)	(4.55)	(100.00)
1993-94	86,541	94,002	34,741	18,998	9,618	2,43,900
	(35.48)	(38.54)	(14.25)	(7.79)	(3.94)	(100.00)
1994-95	1,01,751	1,22,529	37,194	28,145	17,718	3,07,337
	(33.10)	(39.87)	(12.10)	(9.16)	(5.77)	(100.00)
1995-96	95,697	1,00,093	45,025	33,845	21,617	2,96,277
	(32.30)	(33.78)	(15.20)	(11.42)	(7.30)	(100.00)
Percentage growth	94.49	661.86	362.32	621.03	138.45	245.14

Source: Compiled from the Annual Reports of The Marine Products Export Development Authority, Cochin.

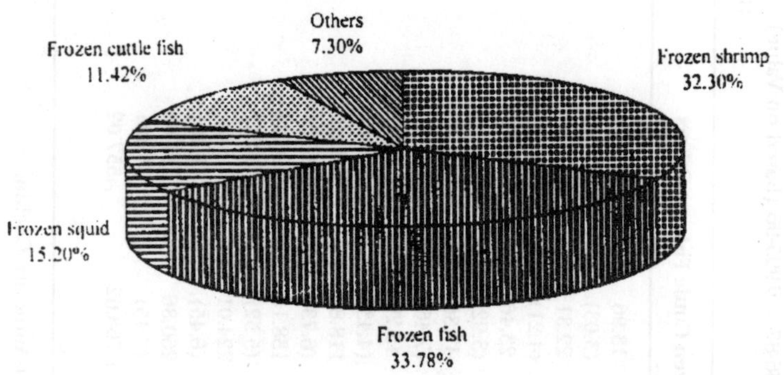

Fig.3.5. Item-Wise Export of Marine Products In 1995-96 Based On Quantity

fish products such as frozen cuttle fish, frozen squid and frozen fish registered substantial growth during the period and only reduced the share of the frozen shrimp in the total exports significantly. The item-wise export of marine products during 1995-96 based on value is shown in Figure. 3.6.

The Indian frozen shrimp has been exported to Japan, European Union, USA, South East Asian countries and other countries for several years. Table 3.11 shows the quantity-wise export of Indian frozen shrimp to various markets. Japan is the major importing country of the Indian frozen shrimp. The export to this country which was 30,961 tonnes in 1986-87 increased to 41,955 tonnes in 1995-96 recording an increase of 35.51 per cent during the decade. Though there is an increase in absolute terms, the share of Japan in the total frozen shrimp export was declined from 62.93 per cent in 1986-87 to 43.83 per cent in 1995-96. Inspite of the decline in the

Table 3.10: Item-wise Export of Indian Marine Products During 1986-87 to 1995-96 (Based on Value)

(Rupees in Crores)

Year	Frozen Shrimp	Frozen Fish	Frozen Squid	Frozen Cuttle Fish	Others	Total
1986-87	377.93	22.29	17.27	13.96	29.22	460.67
	(82.04)	(4.84)	(3.75)	(3.03)	(6.34)	(100.00)
1987-88	425.78	30.23	13.73	22.31	39.15	531.20
	(80.15)	(5.69)	(2.58)	(4.21)	(7.37)	(100.00)
1988-89	470.33	28.44	38.09	23.46	37.54	597.83
	(78.67)	(4.76)	(6.37)	(3.92)	(6.28)	(100.00)
1989-90	463.44	48.06	28.25	47.30	47.71	634.76
	(73.00)	(7.57)	(4.45)	(7.46)	(7.52)	(100.00)
1990-91	663.33	90.82	44.99	45.29	56.07	893.37
	(74.25)	(10.17)	(7.95)	(4.43)	(6.36)	(100.00)
1992-93	1,180.26	232.41	151.90	118.88	83.98	1,767.43
	(66.78)	(13.15)	(8.59)	(6.73)	(4.75)	(100.00)
1993-94	1,770.73	296.00	192.47	138.18	106.24	2,503.62
	(70.73)	(11.82)	(7.69)	(5.52)	(4.24)	(100.00)
1994-95	2,510.94	446.57	245.10	224.01	48.65	3,475.27
	(72.25)	(12.85)	(7.05)	(6.45)	(1.40)	(100.00)
1995-96	2,356.43	372.26	319.58	260.86	191.98	3,501.11
	(67.31)	(10.63)	(9.13)	(7.45)	(5.48)	(100.00)
Percentage growth	523.51	1,570.08	1,750.49	1,768.62	557.02	660.00

Source: Compiled from the Annual Reports of The Marine Products Export Development Authority, Cochin.

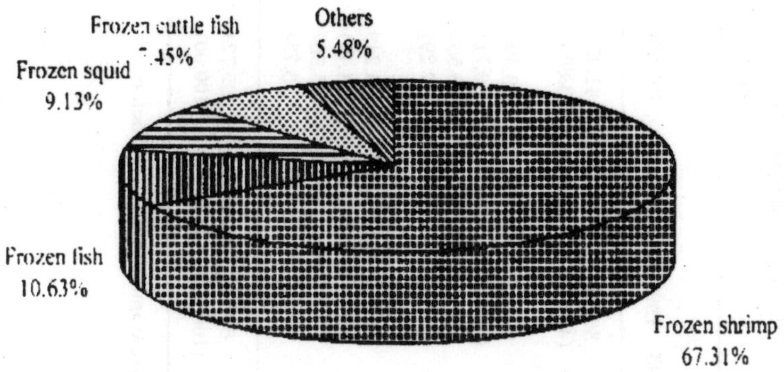

Fig. 3.6. Item-Wise Export of Marine Products In 1995-96 based on Value

percentage share, Japan continues to be the major market during the period.

USA was the second major importing country of frozen shrimp during 1986-87 to 1989-90. During the period the share of export to this country varied between 21.60 per cent and 23.71 per cent, while export increased quantitatively by 53.62 per cent. However, the share in the total exports declined to 17.29 per cent in 1995-96. The export to European Union registered a significant growth from 6,466 tonnes in 1986-87 to 29,397 tonnes in 1995-96 recording an increase of about 355 per cent. The share of the European Union in the total export increased from 13.14 per cent to 30.71 per cent. The export to South East Asian countries started in 1992-93 and since then there was a marginal increase in the export to these countries.

In terms of value also Japan occupies first position in importing Indian frozen shrimp. Through frozen shrimp export to this country, the foreign exchange earnings which was Rs. 282.53 crores in 1986-87 increased to Rs. 1,426.04 crores in 1995-96 recording an increase of over 400 per cent (Table 3.12). The share of this country

Table 3.11: Major Markets for Indian Frozen Shrimp during 1986-87 to 1995-96 (Based on Quantity)

(Quantity in Tonnes)

Market	Years										Percentage
	1986-87	1987-88	1988-89	1989-90	1990-91	1991-92	1992-93	1993-94	1994-95	1995-96	Growth
Japan	30,961	32,514	31,696	31,344	29,751	31,787	34,258	36,564	43,856	41,955	35.51
	(62.93)	(58.34)	(55.77)	(54.21)	(47.68)	(41.77)	(46.26)	(42.25)	(43.10)	(43.863)	
European Union	6,466	8,463	10,366	11,988	16,540	21,308	20,757	28,417	24,653	29,397	354.63
	(13.14)	(15.18)	(18.24)	(10.73)	(26.51)	(28.00)	(28.03)	(32.84)	(24.23)	(30.71)	
UAS	12,898	10,777	13,214	12,488	14,009	17,893	14,045	16,891	22,842	16,556	53.62
	(21.90)	(23.71)	(22.69)	(21.60)	(22.45)	(23.51)	(18.97)	(19.52)	(22.45)	(17.29)	
South East Asia	-	-	-	-	-	-	2,625	2,916	7,081	4,249	61.87
	(-)	(-)	(-)	(-)	(-)	(-)	(3.54)	(3.37)	(4.09)	(4.44)	
Others	999	1,545	1,875	1,999	2,095	5,119	2,366	1,753	3,319	3,567	257.06
	(2.03)	(2.77)	(3.30)	(3.46)	(3.36)	(6.72)	(3.20)	(2.02)	(3.26)	(3.73)	
Total	49.203	55.736	56,835	57,819	62,395	76,107	74,051	86,541	1,01,751	95,724	94.55
	(100.00)	(100.00)	(100.00)	(100.00)	(100.00)	(100.00)	(100.00)	(100.00)	(100.00)	(100.00)	

Source: Compiled from the Marine Products Export Reviews of The Marine Products Export Development Authority, Cochin.

Table 3.12 Major Markets for Indian Frozen Shrimp During 1986-87 to 1995-96 (Based on Value)

(Value in Rs. Crores)

Market	Years 1986-87	1987-88	1988-89	1989-90	1990-91	1991-92	1992-93	1993-94	1994-95	1995-96	Percentage Growth
Japan	282.53	292.45	329.23	294.75	391.77	545.77	718.31	1,062.70	1,481.38	1,426.04	404.74
	(74.76)	(68.69)	(70.00)	(63.62)	(59.06)	(55.91)	(61.04)	(60.01)	(59.01)	(60.51)	
European Union	37.16	54.60	65.17 86.41	153.26	244.14	257.24	399.35	416.68	495.28	1,232.83	
	(9.83)	(12.82)	(13.86)	(18.65)	(23.12)	(25.00)	(21.86)	(22.55)	(16.60)	(21.01)	
UAA	52.55	69.03	64.59	70.43	100.79	137.69	145.17	235.62	421.88	290.12	452.08
	(13.90)	(16.21)	(13.73)	(15.20)	(15.19)	(14.11)	(12.33)	(12.31)	(16.81)	(12.31)	
South East Asia	-	-	-	-	-	-	19.51	42.50	125.44	75.11	284.98
	(-)	(-)	(-)	(-)	(-)	(-)	(1.66)	(2.40)	(5.00)	(3.18)	
Others	5.69	9.70	11.34	11.72	17.51	48.62	36.60	30.56	64.89	70.26	1,134.80
	(1.51)	(2.28)	(2.41)	(2.53)	(2.36)	(4.98)	(3.11)	(1.73)	(2.58)	(2.98)	
Total	377.93	425.78	470.33	463.31	663.33	496.17	1,176.83	1,770.73	2,510.27	2,356.81	602.99
	(100.00)	(100.00)	(100.00)	(100.00)	(100.00)	(100.00)	(100.00)	(100.00)	(100.00)	(100.00)	

Source: Compiled from the Marine Products Export Reviews of The Marine Products Export Development Authority, Cochin.

in the total value of export of frozen shrimp varied between 59.01 per cent and 74.76 per cent. The share of European Union increased from 9.83 per cent to 21.01 per cent, while the share of USA declined from 13.90 per cent to 12.31 per cent.

Out of the total frozen shrimp imports to Japan, India occupies third position, the first and second positions being occupied by Indonesia and Thailand respectively. A part from these two countries India face competition in Japan market for this product from China, Vietnam, Philippines, Green Land, Australia, Bangladesh, Iceland, Norway and Canada[3]. The United States of America import shrimp mostly from ten countries. India occupies fourth position in the total shrimp imports of this country, while Thailand, Ecuador and Mexico occupy the first three positions respectively, China, Bangladesh, Panama, Handuras, Indonesia and Brazil occupy fifth to tenth positions respectively[4]. The European Union is importing frozen shrimp mostly from Ecuador, Thailand, India, Bangladesh, Argentina, Greenland and Mozambique. India occupies fourth position in the import. Indian frozen shrimp is exported to different countries in varied product forms. The details of product forms exported to various countries are shown in Annexure 3.1.

The data relating to quantity-wise export of frozen fish during 1986-87 to 1995-96 are presented in Table 3.13. The table reveals that South East Asia is the major importer of Indian frozen fish. The export to this group of countries increased from 9,664 tonnes to 83,429 tonnes during the period. The share in the total export of frozen fish to South East Asia also increased from 73.56 per cent in 1986-87 to 83.35 per cent in 1995-96. Though Japan was the second the major importer upto 1989-90, the share of this market was declined to reach 1.88 per cent in 1995-96. The export of this product to USA market has shown a positive trend as the quantity exported increased from a mere 152 tonnes in 1986-87 to 6,177 tonnes in 1995-96. Its share also increased from 1.16 per cent to 6.18 per cent. The export to European Union started in 1992-93 and the product is still at the introductory stage in the market.

In value terms the foreign exchange earnings of India from South East Asia through frozen fish export increased from Rs. 13.76 crores in 1986-87 to Rs. 252.62 crores in 1995-96 recording an increase of over 1,700 per cent (Table 3.14). The earnings from USA increased from Rs. 0.35 crores in 1986-87 to Rs. 41.05 crores in 1995-96. The earnings of this product increased from Rs. 6.91 crores in 1986-87 to Rs. 25.51 crores in 1995-96 from Japan market.

The European Union is the major market for Indian frozen squid outside the country. The data presented in Table 3.15 reveals, the export to this Union which was 9,211 tonnes in 1986-87 increased to 29,288 tonnes in 1995-96 recording an increase of 218 per cent. The share of this market in the total frozen squid export varied between 65.05 per cent and 94.58 per cent during the period. Though the share of the European Union is on down trend, its leadership is unchallenged. The share of South East Asia increased from 1.22 per cent in 1986-87 to 13.17 per cent in 1995-96. The share of Japan which was below one percent in 1986-87 increased to 5.36 per cent in 1995-96. The share of USA increased from 0.31 per cent to 3.64 per cent during the period. In terms of value of export of Indian frozen squid, the earnings from European Union which was Rs. 16.17 crores in 1986-87 increased to Rs. 199.44 crores in 1995-96. The earnings from Japan increased from Rs. 0.28 crores to Rs. 40.02 crores while the earnings from South East Asia increased from Rs. 0.21 crores to Rs. 29.04 crores during the period. The share of South East Asia in the total frozen squid export increased from 1.22 per cent in 1986-87 to 9.09 per cent in 1995-96 in value terms (Table 3.16).

Among the markets for frozen cuttle fish outside India, European Union emerged as the major market since 1987-88. The data shown in Table 3.17 reveals there was a sudden increase in quantity exports from 1,825 tonnes in 1986-87 to 6,618 tonnes in 1987-88 and since then, the exports were increased to European Union to reach 17,899 tonnes in 1995-96. The share of European Union in the total, which was 38.88 per cent in 1986-87 increased to about 72 per cent in the subsequent year and since then there was a facultative trend. In 1995-96 the share of the European Union was a fluctuative trend. In 1995-96 the share of the European Union was about 53 per cent. The Japan market which was the leader in 1986-87 with 45.53 per

Table 3.13: Major Markets for Indian Frozen Fish During 1986-87 to 1995-96 (Based on Quantity)

(Quantity in Tonnes)

Market	Years										Percentage
	1986-87	1987-88	1988-89	1989-90	1990-91	1991-92	1992-93	1993-94	1994-95	1995-96	Growth
Japan	2,699	2,918	2,184	3,439	3,739	2,913	2,852	3,154	2,841	1,886	(-) 30.12
	(20.54)	(19.58)	(19.44)	(16.20)	(8.83)	(5.90)	(3.76)	(3.35)	(2.32)	(1.88)	
European Union	-	-	-	-	-	-	696	748	714	630	(-) 948
	(-)	(-)	(-)	(-)	(-)	(-)	(0.92)	(0.80)	(0.58)	(0.62)	
USA	152	716	243	801	1,811	2,236	4,273	6,608	5,175	6,177	3,963.81
	(1.16)	(4.80)	(2.16)	(3.77)	(4.28)	(4.54)	(5.68)	(7.03)	(4.22)	(6.18)	
South East Asia	9,664	10,624	8,030	12.360	32,826	37.646	60.749	75.967	1,09,051	83.429	763.30
	(73.56)	(71.28)	(71.48)	(58.23)	(77.53)	(76.31)	(80.60)	(80.79)	(89.00)	(83.35)	
Others	623	646	777	4,627	3,964	6,538	7,224	7,545	4,748	7,971	1,179.45
	(4.74)	(4.34)	(6.92)	(21.80)	(9.36)	(13.25)	(9.54)	(8.03)	(3.88)	(7.97)	
Total	13,138	14,904	11.234	21,227	42,340	49,333	75,370	94,022	1,22,529	1,00,093	661.86
	(100.00)	(100.00)	(100.00)	(100.00)	(100,00)	(100.00)	(100.00)	(100.00)	(100.00)	(100.00)	

Source: Compiled from the Marine Products Export Reviews of The Marine Products Export Development Authority, Cochin.

Table 3.14: Major Markets for Indian Frozen Fish During 1986-87 to 1995-96 (Based on Value)

(Value in Rs. Crores)

Market	Years										Percentage
	1986-87	1987-88	1988-89	1989-90	1990-91	1991-92	1992-93	1993-94	1994-95	1995-96	Growth
Japan	6.91	9.27	9.26	14.11	20.39	22.48	29.75	41.86	54.05	25.51	269.18
	(21.81)	(30.68)	(33.65)	(29.29)	(22.08)	(15.86)	(12.75)	(11.24)	(12.10)	(6.85)	
European Union	-	-	-	-	-	-	3.23	4.16	4.07	5.31	64.40
	(-)	(-)	(-)	(-)	(-)	(-)	(1.38)	(1.12)	(0.91)	(1.43)	
USA	0.35	1.16	044	1.82	5.58	7.44	21.74	35.83	24.95	41.05	11,628.57
	(1.51)	(3.84)	(1.60)	(3.78)	(6.04)	(5.26)	(9.30)	(9.62)	(5.59)	(11.03)	
South East Asia	13.76	18.58	16.57	22.57	56.00	87.37	146.62	176.10	335.79	252.62	1,735.90
	(59.36)	(61.50)	(60.21)	(46.85)	(60.63)	(61.70)	(62.79)	(47.30)	(75.19)	(67.86)	
Others	2.16	1.20	1.25	9.67	10.39	24.31	32.20	38.05	27.71	47.77	2,111.57
	(9.32)	(3.98)	(4.54)	(20.08)	(11.25)	(17.18)	(13.78)	(10.22)	(6.21)	(12.83)	
Total	23.18	30.21	27.52	48.17	92.36	141.60	233.54	372.26	446.57	372.26	1,505.95
	(100.00)	(100.00)	(100.00)	(100.00)	(100.00)	(100.00)	(100.00)	(100.00)	(100.00)	(100.00)	

Source: Compiled from the Marine Products Export Reviews of The Marine Products Export Development Authority, Cochin.

Table 3.15: Major Markets for Indian Frozen Squid During 1986-87 to 1995-96 (Based on Quantity)

(Quantity in Tonnes)

Market	Years										Percentage Growth
	1986-87	1987-88	1988-89	1989-90	1990-91	1991-92	1992-93	1993-94	1994-95	1995-96	
Japan	82	251	92	-	1,077	1,574	1,285	1,798	1,521	2,415	2,845
	(0.84)	(3.29)	(0.56)	(-)	(6.46)	(6.12)	(4.23)	(5.18)	(4.09)	(5.36)	
European Union	9,211	6,830	15,101	-	12,779	19,620	23,533	24,303	25,177	29,288	217.97
	(94.58)	(89.62)	(92.12)	(-)	(76.67)	(76.32)	(77.50)	(69.95)	(67.69)	(65.05)	
USA	30	85	43	-	87	436	808	1,294	2,125	1,636	5,353.33
	(0.31)	(1.12)	(0.26)	(-)	(0.52)	(1.70)	(2.66)	(3.72)	(5.71)	(3.64)	
South East Asia	118	161	-	-	82	146	1,708	3,851	3,277	5,932	4,927.12
	(1.22)	(2.11)	(-)	(-)	(0.49)	(0.57)	(5.63)	(11.08)	(8.81)	(13.17)	
Others	298	294	1,156	-	2,642	3,933	3,030	3,495	5,097	5,754	1,830.87
	(3.05)	(3.86)	(7.06)	(-)	(15.86)	(15.29)	(9.98)	(10.07)	(13.70)	(12.78)	
Total	9,739	7,621	16,392	-	16,667	25,709	30,364	34,741	37,197	45,025	362.32
	(100.00)	(100.00)	(100.00)	(100.00)	(100.00)	(100.00)	(100.00)	(100.00)	(100.00)	(100.00)	

Source: compiled from the Marine Products Export Reviews of the Marine Products Export Development Authority, Cochin.

Table 3.16: Major Markets for Indian Frozen Squid During 1986-87 to 1995-96 (Based on Value)

(Value in Rs. Crores)

Market	1986-87	1987-88	1988-89	1989-90	1990-91	1991-92	1992-93	1993-94	1994-95	1995-96	Percentage Growth
	Years										
Japan	0.28	0.96	0.50	-	5.31	11.77	15.16	22.82	21.03	40.02	14,192.86
	(1.63)	(6.54)	(1.31)	(-)	(11.80)	(10.76)	(10.00)	(11.86)	(8.58)	(12.52)	
European Union	16.17	12.61	34.36	-	31.90	77.27	109.96	123.09	152.16	199.44	1,133.40
	(93.84)	(85.90)	(90.30)	(-)	(70.94)	(70.65)	(72.56)	(63.95)	(62.08)	(62.41)	
USA	0.05	0.12	0.09	-	0.35	2.09	4.24	7.80	16.77	12.94	25,780.00
South East Asia	0.21	0.33	-	-	0.19	0.65	0.67	19.60	17.44	29.04	13,728.57
	(0.29)	(0.82)	(0.24)	(-)	(0.78)	(1.92)	(2.80)	(4.05)	(6.84)	(4.05)	
	(1.22)	(2.25)	(-)	(-)	(0.42)	(0.59)	(0.44)	(10.18)	(7.12)	(9.09)	
Others	0.52	0.66	3.10	-	7.22	17.59	21.51	19.16	37.70	38.14	7,234.61
	(3.02)	(4.49)	(8.15)	(-)	(16.06)	(16.08)	(14.19)	(9.96)	(15.38)	(11.93)	
Total	17.23	14.68	38.05	-	44.97	109.37	151.54	192.47	245.10	319.58	1,754.79
	(100.00)	(100.00)	(100.00)	(100.00)	(100.00)	(100.00)	(100.00)	(100.00)	(100.00)	(100.00)	

Soruce: Compiled from the Marine Products Export Reviews of The Marine Products Export Development Authority, Cochin.

Table 3.17 : Major Markets for Indian Frozen Cuttle Fish During 1986-87 to 1995-96 (Based on Quantity)

(Quantity in Tonnes)

Market	1986-87	1987-88	1988-89	1989-90	1990-91	1991-92	1992-93	1993-94	1994-95	1995-96	Percentage Growth
Japan	2,137	1,491	645	1,606	1,612	1,415	823	1,075	1,974	2,657	25.73
	(45.13)	(16.22)	(7.80)	(11.34)	(13.91)	(11.38)	(4.34)	(5.66)	(7.01)	(7.85)	
European Union	1,825	8,618	6,749	10,285	8,426	7,455	16,320	11,798	12,389	17,899	880.77
	(38.88)	(71.97)	(81.68)	(72.64)	(72.66)	(59.94)	(85.98)	(62.10)	(44.02)	(52.89)	
USA	-	-	-	-	-	-	-	-	-	-	
	(-)	(-)	(-)	(-)	(-)	(-)	(-)	(-)	(-)	(-)	
South East Asia	499	725	441	298	435	408	737	4,316	10,408	6,966	1,295.99
	(10.63)	(7.88)	(5.35)	(2.10)	(3.75)	(3.28)	(3.88)	(22.72)	(36.98)	(20.58)	
Others	233	361	427	1,969	1,123	3,159	1,101	1,809	3,374	6,323	2,613.73
	(4.96)	(3.93)	(5.17)	(13.92)	(9.68)	(25.40)	(5.80)	(9.52)	(11.99)	(18.68)	
Total	4,694	9,195	8,262	14,158	11,596	12,437	18,981	18,998	28,145	33,845	621.03
	(100.00)	(100.00)	(100.00)	(100.00)	(100.00)	(100.00)	(100.00)	(100.00)	(100.00)	(100.00)	

Source : Compiled from the Marine Products Export Reviews of The Marine Products Export Development Authority, Cochin.

cent share in the total export of frozen cuttle fish from India, fell to second position with a substantial decline in share to 16.22 per cent in the subsequent year. During the period the export of frozen cuttle fish to this country has undergone fluctuative trend and in 1995-96 the country secured 7.85 per cent share. The export to South East Asia received a boost in 1993-94 and reached the peak position in 1994-95 with as high as 10,408 tonnes of frozen cuttle fish securing about 37 per cent share in the total export. However, in 1995-96 the export declined to 6,966 tonnes with 20.58 per cent share in total export. The Indian frozen cuttle fish could not make an entry to the USA market.

The data presented in Table 3.18 shows the foreign exchange earnings through the export of frozen cuttle fish during 1986-87 to 1995-96. The foreign exchange earnings from European Union increased from Rs. 3.16 crores in 1995-96. The earnings from Japan market which was Rs. 9.23 crores in 1986-87 suffered major fluctuations during 1987-88 to 1993-94. The earnings were more than doubled in 1994-95 over previous year to reach Rs. 35.53 crores and it further increased to Rs. 37.67 crores in 1995-96. The earnings from South East Asia were marginal upto 1992-93. In 1993-94, the earnings were about Rs. 33 crores and in the subsequent year the earnings increased to Rs. 70.79 crores from South East Asia. However, in 1995-96 the earnings from this market declined to Rs. 39.81 crores.

The export of Indian marine products registered a steady growth during 1982-83 to 1993-94 and registered a marginal decline to an extent of 11,060 mt.tonnes in quantity (-3.6 per cent of the total) and Rs. 74.6 crores in value (-2.07 per cent of the total). Despite the decline, the foreign exchange realised crossed the one billion US doller mark as in 1994-95. The Unit value realisation increased from Rs. 116.30 per Kg. in 1994-95 to Rs. 118.17 per Kg. in 1995-96.[5] The decline in export in 1995-96 could be attributed to the disease outbreak in shrimp farms which lead to crop holiday and consequent fall in production of cultured shrimps. The other reasons being non-addition of new areas to fish farming due to the litigation against aquaculture projects and reluctance of the commercial banks to support aquaculture projects due to poor landing of fin fish along the west coast of the country.

Table 3.18 :Major Markets for Indian Frozen Cuttle Fish During 1986-87 to 1995-96 (Based on Value)

(Value in Rs. Crores)

Market	1986-87	1987-88	1988-89	1989-90	1990-91	1991-92	1992-93	1993-94	1994-95	1995-96	Percentage Growth
Japan	9.23 (66.30)	5.17 (23.33)	3.66 (15.62)	12.27 (25.95)	11.08 (24.47)	12.86 (21.11)	8.22 (6.91)	14.53 (10.52)	30.53 (13.63)	37.67 (14.44)	308.13
European Union	3.16 (22.70)	13.99 (63.13)	17.06 (72.81)	27.02 (57.14)	29.19 (64.47)	35.02 (57.49)	100.98 (84.94)	78.23 (56.61)	96.14 (42.92)	135.56 (51.97)	3,873.42
USA	- (-)	- (-)	- (-)	- (-)	- (-)	- (-)	- (-)	- (-)	- (-)	- (-)	
South East Asia	1.07 (7.70)	1.88 (8.49)	1.33 (5.68)	0.95 (2.01)	1.44 (3.18)	2.05 (3.37)	3.70 (3.12)	32.97 (23.86)	70.79 (31.60)	39.81 (15.26)	3,620.56
Others	0.46 (3.30)	1.12 (5.05)	1.38 (5.89)	7.05 (14.90)	3.57 (7.88)	10.98 (18.03)	5.98 (5.03)	12.45 (9.01)	26.55 (11.85)	47.82 (18.33)	10,295.65
Total	13.92 (100.00)	22.16 (100.00)	23.43 (100.00)	47.29 (100.000)	45.28 (100.00)	60.91 (100.00)	118.88 (100.00)	138.18 (100.00)	224.01 (100.00)	260.86 (100.00)	1,773.99

Source: Compiled from the Marine Products Export Review of The Marine Products Export Development Authority, Cochin.

EXPORT PROBLEMS

The world seafood trade is expanding very fast due to increase in per capita consumption of seafood in many industrialised nations. The gap between supply and demand is widening and it is projected by FAO that the gap will be to the tune of 20 million tonnes by the turn of the century. India's marine fish production has touched 2.0 million tonnes as against the estimated potential of 3.9 million tonnes. Since the fish production from capture fisheries is stagnating due to over exploitation and spiralling fuel cost, culture fisheries is picking up very fast to augment fish production. When countries like China, Taiwan, Thailand, Indonesia, Philippines and Vietnam have made rapid strides in coastal aquaculture during eighties and the fist half of nineties, India's progress is very slow, despite rich potentials in terms of cultivable fishery resources, material wealth and large human capital of the country.

India depends heavily on capture fisheries for fish production. The fishery resources of inshore seas are over-exploited and the resources of off-shore and deepsea areas, await exploitation. Therefore, a major thrust in the Eighth five Year Plan scheme, was given for development of deep-sea fishing and coastal aquaculture for augmenting export production of seafood.

The seafood industry in many countries is undergoing a rapid change to process more and more ready to cook and ready to eat in convenient packs. Indian seafood industry, by and large, remains still as a supplier of raw-material to the re-processors in foreign countries and 90 per cent of export goes in bulk packs. Because of the effort taken by The Marine Products Export Development Authority, only 10 per cent of our seafood export has started moving in as value-added individually quick frozen packs. The export more quantity in value added form, the industry has to be modernised with induction of new technology.

India depends heavily on one product (Shrimp) and one market (japan) for its marine products exports. Therefore, there is a need for diversification in products and markets. India's predominant position in shrimp market is being eroded due to sudden spurt in farmed shrimp production in China, Thailand, Indonesia, Vietnam etc. The export of these countries has gone up in recent years each earning around US$ 1,000 to 3,000 million and India is trailing behind because of slow growth in production of exportable varieties. West Europe is emerging as a promising market for individually quick frozen seafood products from India . Indian frozen fish has opened new markets in South East Asia, japan and USA and the export is in rising trend. Dried fish export is declining due to ethnic problem in Sri Lanka. Southern Europe and Japan are emerging as important markets for squids and cuttle fish.

The trend in the marine products exports during the last five years is quite encouraging. The market for Indian frozen shrimp expanded significantly to European Union emerged as a major market for Indian frozen fish, European Union emerged as a major market for Indian frozen squid and the frozen cuttle fish. New markets were opened for Indian marine products throughout the year. There is a need to accelerate the efforts to promote the export of marine products. The experience of 1995-96 should be a lesson to be policy makers to safeguard the industry from such shocking diseases and other problems.

In July, 1997 the European Union announced ban on the import of Indian seafood with effect from August 15, 1997. According to reports from Brussels, the ban follows the discovery by several European Union States of salmonella and vibiro bacteria in import of frozen and conserved fish or seafood. European Union inspectors who visited India in June also reported widespread hygiene problems in local production and processing facilities.[6] The Indian exporters feared that the ban would cost around Rs. 1,500 crores annually. The Indian exporting community disputed the reasons expressed by European Union and suspected some vested European business interests behind the move mainly to tarnish the image of Indian seafood and bring down the prices in the highly competitive international market.[7]

The Indian Government quickly reacted to the situation and held discussions with the officials of European Union and could convince them to lift the ban. The Commerce Ministry revamped the export inspection procedures and systems besides gearing up the Export Inspection Council.

An Inter-Departmental Panel (IDPP consisting of officials of export inspection agencies, Marine Products Export Development Authority (MPEDA) and Central Institute of Fisheries Technology (CIFT) was set up to inspect and recommend the units which could be permitted to export to the European Union. This was also cross checked by another Supervisory audit Team consisting of officials senior to the members of Inter-departmental Panel.[8] The European Union has there by lifted the ban on marine products in December, 1997.

The incidents of this kind will effect the image of the marine products of India in the international market. India occupies seventh position in the world in terms of fish production and emerged as one of the major fishery products exporter. As our fishery products are exported mainly to sophisticated and fastidious markets such as USA, Japan, Australia, UK, etc., the quality control will play definitely a leading role in the exciting saga of Indian fish export trade in future too. The Indian Government has brought out number of legislations to ensure quality control and brought fish and fish products under the purview of compulsory quality and control preshipment inspection scheme. The establishment of export inspection councils in the year 1963 is a major development in the export trade of fish and fish products from India. The export inspection councils vital role as an impartial third party guarantee to the overseas buyers has been to assure the quality of Indian fish products to the ultimate consumers, thereby to improve the image of our products in international market.[9] Although the task is extremely hard and challenging, the export inspection agencies with a net work of 24 inspectorate and micro biological laboratories manned by well trained and experienced personnel have been able to accomplish the same with a reasonable degree of competence. As the importing countries have started stimpulating stringent quality standards for the different fish products they import, the future of seafood export appears to depend largely on the capability of the regulatory authority to meet such requirements. The challenging role of the export inspection agencies to safeguard the country's image by certifying the quality of fish and fish products will continue to remain significant. Therefore, efficient execution of statutes, orders, Policies and procedrures is necessary to prevent the possible damage in the international market in matter of quality.

REFERENCE

1 Gopakumar, K., Seafood Processing, 'Product Development for Value Addition with reference to Employment Opportunities in marine Fisheries Sector', article published in verghese, C.P., and Joy, P.S., 'Development of Marine fisheries for Higher Productivity and Export', Op. cit p. 226.

2 The Marine Products Export Development Authority, Marine Product Export Review 1995-96, the Author, Cochin 1997, p. 8.

3 The Marine Products Export Development Authority, Marine Products Export Review 1995-96, Op. cit p. 15.

4 Ibid p. 28.

5 The Marine Products Export Development Authority, Marine Products Export Review 1995-96, Op. cit. p. 7.

6 The Economic Times, "EU ban on Indian Seafood exports comes into effect, Saturday, 2 August, 1977, p.1.

7 The Economic times, 'EU bans Indian Seafood exports from August 15,' Thursday 31, July, 1997, p. 1.

8 The Hindu, 'European Union lifts ban on marine products', Friday, December 19, 1997 p. 1.

9 Mujumdar, D.C. 'Managing Marine Products Quality, Productivity', New Delhi, 1987, p. 365.

Annexure 3.1
Product Forms of Indian Frozen Shrimp Exported During 1995-96

Item	Country		
	Japan	Western Europe	USA
Head on:			
White	√	√	√
Tiger	√	√	√
Sea Tiger	–	√	–
Brown	√	√	√
Flower	√	√	√
Scampy	–	√	√
Deepsea Shrimp	√	√	√
Cooked	–	–	–
Head less shell on:			
White	√	√	√
Tiger	√	√	√
Sea Tiger	√	√	√
Brown	√	√	√
Flower	√	√	√
Scampy	√	√	√
Karikadi	√	√	√
Deepsea Shrimp	–	√	√
Pealed :			
PUD	√	√	√
Tailon	√	√	√
CP	√	√	√
PDC	√	√	√
PD	√	√	√
PC	√	√	√
PD Tailon	√	√	√
AFD Shrimp	√	√	√
Cooked salad shrimp	–	–	√
Un-classified	√	√	√

Source : Compiled from the Marine Products Export Review of The Marine Products Export Development Authority, 1995-96, Cochin.

4

The Organisation of the Marine Products Export Development Authority

The Marine Products Export Development Authority (MPEDA) was constituted in the year 1972 under the Marine Products Export Development Authority Act, 1972. The MPEDA replaced the erstwhile Marine Products Export Promotion Council which was till then looking after the promotion of export of marine products from India. The role envisaged for the MPEDA under the statute was comprehensive covering fisheries of all kinds, export standards, processing, marketing, extension and training in various aspects of the fisheries sector. According to the MPEDA Act, the "marine products" include all varieties of fishery products known commercially as shrimp, prawn, lobster, crab, fish, shell-fish, other aquatic animals or plants or part there of and any other products which the authority may, be notification in Gazette of India, declare to be marine products for the purposes of this Act.[1]

MPEDA OBJECTIVES

The objectives of Marine Products Export Development Authority are: a) regulating marine products export; b) laying down standards and specifications; c) rendering financial assistance to processors and export; d) helping the industry in relation to market intelligence, export promotion, trade enquiries and the import of essential items; e) providing training in different aspects of the marine products industry, with special reference to quality control, processing and marketing; and f) promotion of prawn farming for export production[2].

The MPEDA Act specified that the duty of the Authority is to promote by such measures as it thinks fit for the development of the marine products industry with special reference to export. The Act further referred to the functions to be performed by MPEDA without prejudice to the generality of the provisions. The functions referred in the Act[3] are a) developing regulating off-shore and deepsea fishing and undertaking measures for the conservation and management off-shore and deepsea fisheries; b) registering fishing vessels, processing plants or storage premises for marine products and conveyances used for the transport of marine products; c) fixing standards and specifications for marine products for purposes of export; d) rendering financial or other assistance to owners of fishing vessels engaged in off-storage premises for marine products and for conveyances used for the transport of marine products, and further acts as an agency for such relief and subsidy schemes as may be entrusted to the Authority; e) carrying out inspection of marine products in any fishing vessel, processing plant, storage premises, conveyance or other place where such products are kept or handled, for the purpose of ensuring the quality of such products; f) regulating the export of marine products; g) improving the marketing of marine products outside India; h) registering of exporters of marine products on payment of such fees as may be prescribed; i) collecting statistics from persons engaged in the catching of fish or other marine products, owners of processing plants of storage premises for marine products, owners of processing plants of storage premises for marine products or conveyances used for the transport of marine products, exporters of such products and such other persons as may be prescribed on any matter relating to the marine products industry and the publishing of statistics so collected, or portions there of or extracts therefrom; j) training in various aspects of the marine products industry; and k) such other matters as may be prescribed.

The MPEDA has developed a work programme towards the achievement of the said objectives. The work programme of MPEDA includes :

i. registration of infrastructural facilities for seafood export trade;
ii. collection and dissemination of trade information;
iii. projection of Indian marine products in overseas markets by participation in overseas fairs and organising international seafood fairs in India;
iv. implementation of development measures vital to the industry like distribution of insulated fish boxes, putting up fish landing platforms, improvement of peeling sheds, financial assistance for modernisation of industry such as installation of plate freezers, IQF machinery, generator sets, ice making machinaries, quality control laboratory, etc;
v. promotion of brackishwater aquaculture for production of prawn for export;
vi. promotion of deepsea fishing projects through test fishing, joint venture and equity participation; and
vii. financial support to the industry through equity participation in setting up of integrated aquaculture projects, seafood processing units and deepsea fishing projects.[4]

The central office of the MPEDA is located at Cochin, Kerala State. The MPEDA functions under the Ministry of commerce, Government of India and acts as a co-ordinating agency with different Central and State Government establishments engaged in fishery production and allied activities. The developmental schemes of MPEDA are implemented under four major heads. they are : i) export production-capture fisheries; ii) export production-culture fisheries; iii) induction of new technology and modernisation of processing plants; and iv) market promotion.

ORGANISATION STRUCTURE

Organisation is relating to the efforts and capacities of individuals and groups engaged upon a common task in such a way as to secure the desired objectives with least friction and to with utmost satisfaction to those for whom the task is done and those engaged in the enterprise[5]. It is the systematic bringing together of inter-dependent parts for a unified whole through which authority, co-ordination and control may be exercised to achieve the given purpose. Organisation is for structure and human relations.[6] The structure contributes to the successful implementation of plans by formally allocating people and resources to the tasks which have to be done and by providing mechanisms for the coordination.[7] The method of dividing activities, delegating authority for performance of activities, fixing responsibility for the quality of performance and co-ordinating the work of all, determine the organisation structure of a business or industry.[8]

The MPEDA's managing body comprises of a Chairman, the director of marine products export development, three members of parliament, five members to represent one each from Ministry of Agriculture, Ministry of Finance, Ministry of Foreign Trade, Ministry of Agriculture, Ministry of Finance, Ministry of Foreign Trade, Minister of Industry and Ministry of Shipping and Transport, Government of India. The Central Government can also nominate other members not exceeding 20 who are in its opinion capable of representing: i) the state governments or union territories having a sea coast; ii) the interests of owners of fishing vessels, processing plants or storage premises for marine products and conveyances used for the transport of marine products; iii) the interest of dealers; iv) the interest of persons employed in research institutions engaged in the researches connected with the said industry; and vi) such other persons or class of persons who, in the opinion of the Central Government ought to be represented on the authority.

The Chairman of the MPEDA will be appointed by the Central Government. The Director of Marine Products Export Development Authority is an ex-officio and shall be nominated by the Central Government. All the positions of the managing body are on term basis. The term of the managing body is five years. The Chairman is the Convener of the body and is responsible for all the activities of MPEDA. The Chairman has a defined organisation structure to design and execute various operations. The Figure 4.1 shows the organisation structure of the Marine Products Export Development Authority. The figure reveals the chairman is assisted by two directors and one secretary. The Secretary takes the responsibility of the functions relating to Accounts and Audit Cell, Publicity, Administration of Hindi and Vigilance Cell, Co-ordination and

Registration, Art and Photographic Section. The Director, Appraisal and Investment, is supported by the Joint Director and he will be responsible for appraisal of various project proposals and offer suggestions on investment projects. The other Director takes the major responsibility of organising the activities of MPEDA. He will be assisted by three Joint Directors, one Project Director at the Central Office and Joint Director/Deputy director incharge of regional Centres and the Resident Directors at overseas trade promotion offices and he Trade Promotion Office established in New Delhi. The Project Director under him was assigned the function of organising the prawn farm project complex.

The Joint Director, prawn farming, is responsible for undertaking farming activities at various regional and sub-regional centres, established at Alibag, Valsad, machilipatnam, Cochin, Thanjavur, Bhubanewar, Karwar and Calcutta and also co-ordinating the activities of these centres. The Joint Director of marketing is responsible for collection, analysis and interpretation of statistics relating to fisheries sector, and also delivers the functions relating to economics and marketing services. The Joint Director, Development, takes care of developmental activities, extension activities, frozen storage, quality control and laboratory and research and product development.

The MPEDA has two overseas trade promotion offices one at Tokyo (Japan) and the other at New York (USA) and each office is headed by a resident director. The objectives of the overseas trade promotion offices are; to promote seafood imports in the respective countries by assisting both Indian exporters as well as overseas importers; developing contact with the government agencies; to promote the image of Indian products through publicity campaigns; identify markets for new products; create awareness on the capability of Indian processing, packaging, quality inspection procedures and also to identify suitable joint venture partners for deep-sea fishing projects, aquaculture projects, processing and marketing value-added products, etc. The aquaculture marine products division of the Indian Trade Centre, Brussels, assists MPEDA in its trade promotion activities in Europe and liaisons with the European countries. The Trade Promotion Office at New Delhi acts as liaison office with central ministries connected with fisheries sector.

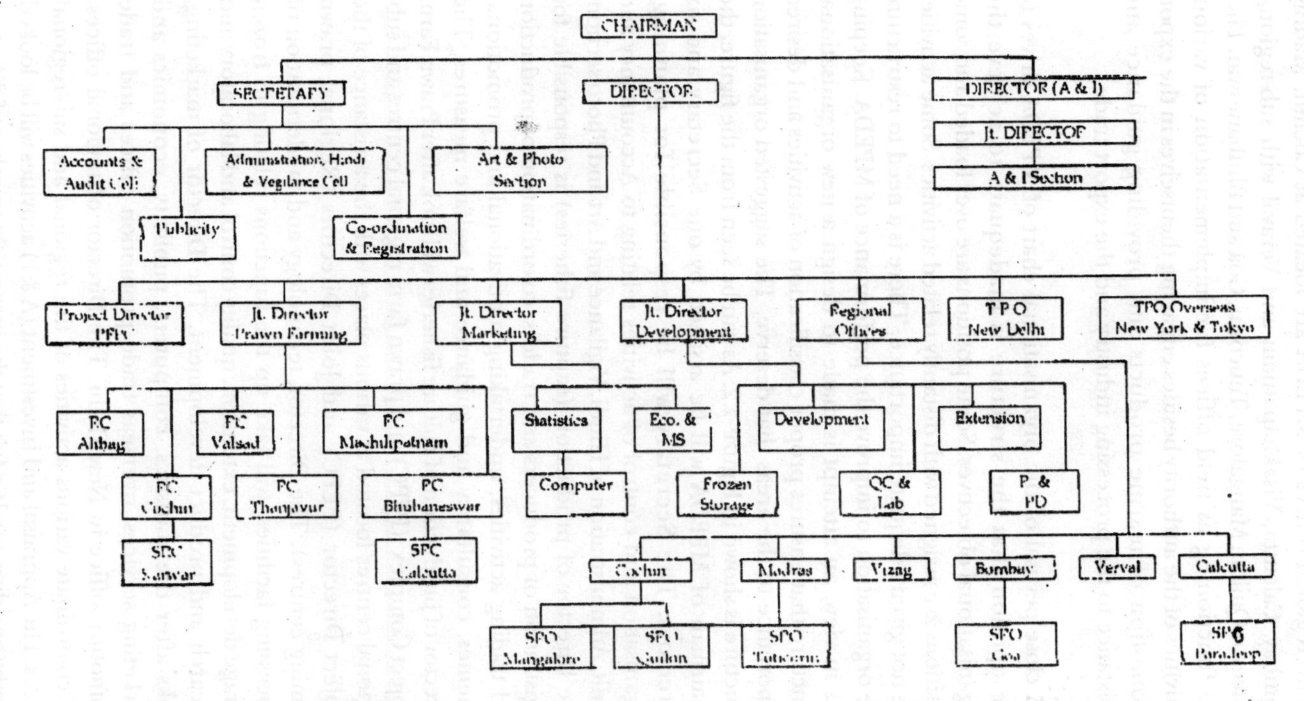

Fig. 4.1: The Marine Products Export Development Authority, Cochin Organisational Structure

The regional offices of MPEDA are located at Cochin, Madras, Bombay, Calcutta, Visakhapatnam and Veraval with sub-regional offices at Quilon, Mangalore, Tuticorin, Goa and Bhubaneswar. They are functioning as field offices for implementation of various activities of the authority besides engaging themselves in the export promotion of marine products and providing guidance and assistance to the processing industry and the export trade.

A close perusal of the organisational chart of MPEDA drives to the opinion that the structure is inadequate to achieve the organisational objectives. Some positions are over loaded and some positions are assigned with distantly related activities. Some activities are not given adequate importance. There is a need to restructure the organisation to improve the performance of MPEDA. Keeping this in view, an attempt is made to design a new organisational structure that ensures proper classification of activities and desired importance to the areas that deserve. The suggested organisation structure is shown in Figure 4.2. As can be seen from the figure, the Chairman of MPEDA will be assisted by one Secretary and six Directors. The Secretary will be responsible for planning, organisation and control of activities relating to Accountancy and Audit, Administration of Hindi, Vigilance and Art and Photo section. The Director of production (capture fisheries) is responsible for registration of producers and traders, co-ordination of production and trading activities, undertaking motivational and promotional schemes, consultancy and guidance and welfare measures. The Director of production of culture fisheries will look after Prawn Farm Project Complex (PFPC) and prawn farm regional centres and sub-regional centres located at various places with the assistance of the Project Director (PEPC) and Joint Directors (Regional prawn farming centres). The Director, technology and modernisation of processing facilities, will take up the functions relating to frozen storage development, extension, quality control and laboratory and research and product development. The Director of marketing, looks after the statistics, computers, publicity, economics and marketing services, overseas trade promotion offices and trade promotion office in New Delhi. The Director of regional offices, will co-ordinate various activities of the regional and sub-regional offices. The Appraisal and Investment (A &1) activities will be looked after by one director. It is felt that the increase in number of directors is immenent to give importance to the activities like culture fisheries and marketing and also to reduce the burden of a single director who is supposed to hold responsibility of a host of activities in the present organisation structure. The proposed change will encourage fishermen and traders of capture fisheries and also strengthens marketing activities apart from activating regional offices and regional centres for culture fisheries. The new organisational structure also recognises the importance of technological development in fisheries and provides special place to it.

INFRASTRUCTURE DEVELOPMENT

As per the provisions under MPEDA Act, no person shall export any marine products unless he has been registered as an exporter with the Authority*. The applicant will be allowed to export for a period of one month pending issues of the certificate of registration. The authority fixes the maximum limit in terms of value from time to time depending on the nature of the product, quantum to be exported and volume of samples to exhibited/distributed. The application for registration as exporter of marine products shall be made to the secretary or the other officer authorised by him. The authority will conduct an enquiry if it deems necessary for either grant or refuse such registration.

The data presented in Table 4.1. shows the number of exporters registered during 1986-87 to 1995-96. the table reveals, the number of fishing exporters which was 749 in 1986-87 increased to 1,190 in 1995-96 recording an increase of 58.88 per cent. The table further reveals the number of new exporters who were granted registration. The annual additions during the period varied between 76 and 207. The MPEDA has cancelled the registration of number of exporters

* This rule shall not apply to the export of marine products if : Central Government or MPEDA: authorise any person to export marine products, by means of gift parcel or sending of samples: as personal efforts of passengers: for any non-commercial Purposes: and for any exhibition abroad.

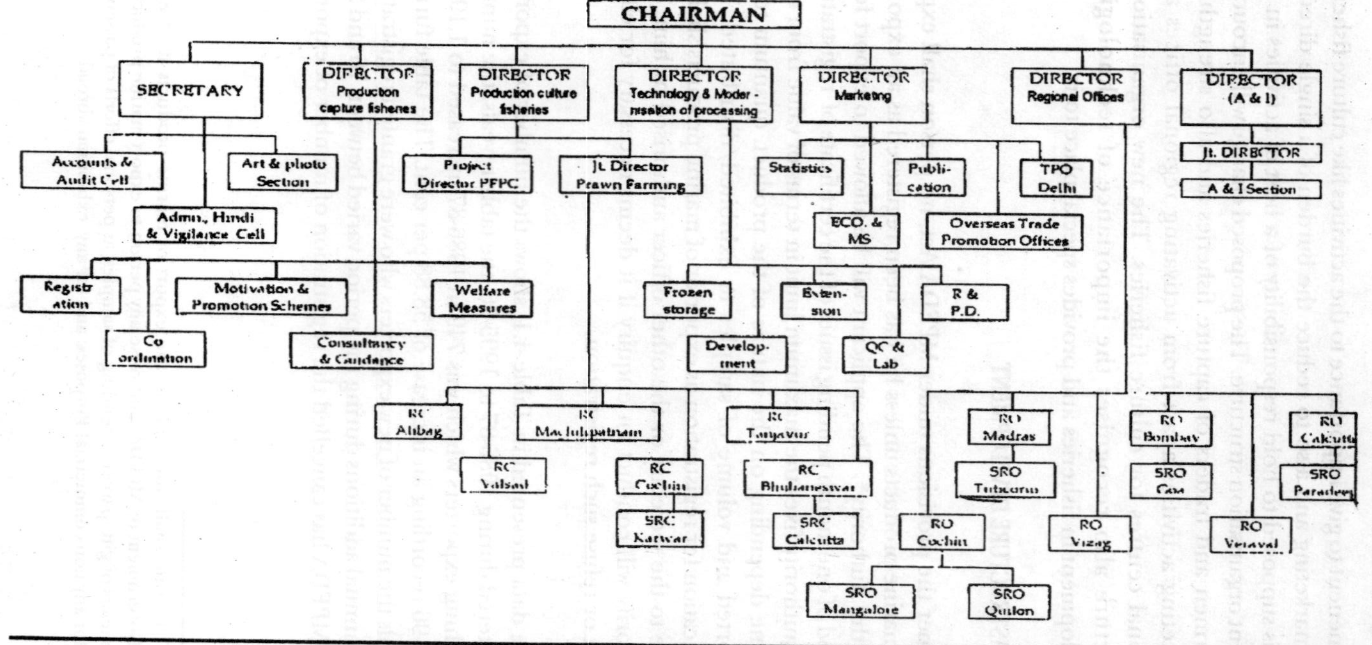

Fig 4.2: The Marine Products Export Development Authority, Cochin Re-Organisational Structure

Table 4.1: Number of Fishing Exporters Registered During 1986-87 to 1995-96

Year	Number Registered	Number Added	Number Deleted	Net Additions/ deletions	Percentage change over previous year
1986-87	749	118	150	(-) 32	(-) 4.10
1987-88	751	76	74	2	0.27
1988-89	788	119	82	37	4.93
1989-90	854	153	77	66	8.38
1990-91	888	134	110	34	3.98
1991-92	951	173	110	63	7.09
1992-93	1,030	148	81	79	8.31
1993-94	1.062	165	133	32	3.11
1994-95	1.107	207	166	45	4.24
1995-96	1,190	191	108	83	7.50

Source: Compiled from the Annual Reports of The Marine Products Export Development Authority, Cochin.

during the period*". The number of exporters deleted from the list varied between 74 and 166 in a year during the period. Due to the large number of deletions the net additions to the main list got marginalised. In the year 1986-87 the list of exporters was reduced by 32 inspite of the addition of 118 new exporters. In the subsequent year the net addition was only two when 76 new exporters were granted registrations. In the year 1995-96, the highest number of net additions (83) were made when 191 joined and 108 deleted. It can be inferred from the above, though the list of exporters is getting expanded every year, the percentage growth over previous year varied between 0.27 and 8.83 per cent during the period with the exception to 1986-87 (-4.10 per cent growth). The number of registrations. Though implementation of the rules for cancellation is a mark of efficiency of MPEDA, the size and recurrence of such cases every

* The MPEDA has a power to cancel the registration if it is satisfied that any person has obtained a certificate of registration by furnishing incorrect information or that he has contravened any of the provisions of this rule or of the conditions mentioned in the certificate or registration, or any person who has been registered as an exporter fails during the period of twelve consecutive months to export any of the marine products in respect of which he is registered, or if the Secretary of other officer is satisfied that such person has become disqualified to continue as an exporter, the Secretary or such officer may, after giving the person who holds a certificate a reasonable opportunity of making his objections, by order, cancel the registration and communicate to him a copy of such order.

year is a problem to be identified and well defined. It is necessary to know the reasons from the exporters point of view for not being able to make the business to the requirements of MPEDA. Appropriate measures need to be initiated to solve the problems and to encourage the exporters to continue in the business. Such measures would not only strengthen the small and marginal exporters but also contribute for the development of the fisheries sector as a whole.

Table 4.2: Number of Freezing Plants Registered During 1986-87 to 1995-96

Year	No. Registered	No. Added	No. Deleted	Net Additions/ deletions	Percentage change over previous year	Capacity in tonnes
1986-87	273	12	19	(-) 7	(-) 2.5	NA
1987-88	236	10	47	(-) 37	(-) 13.55	2,108.65
1988-89	222	37	51	(-) 14	(-) 5.93	2,157.66
1989-90	231	16	7	9	4.05	2,295.88
1990-91	246	18	3	15	6.49	2,678.80
1991-92	258	18	6	12	4.88	3,150.80
1992-93	289	34	4	31	12.02	3,563.45
1993-94	320	35	4	31	10.73	4,140.05
1994-95	338	30	4	18	5.63	4,735.68
1995-96	367	40	12	29	8.58	6,496.29

NA: Not Available

Source: Compiled from the Annual Reports of The Marine Products Export Development Authority, Cochin.

Table 4.2 depicts the data relating to number of freezing plants registered with MPEDA during 1986-87 to 1995-96. The number of freezing plants registered which was 273 in 1986-87 registered a declining trend to reach 222 in 1988-89. Since 1989-90, the number has been on the increase year by year to reach 367 in 1995-96. The number of freezing plants* added per annum varied between 10 and 40, while the number of freezing plants deleted varied between three and 51 per year during the period. Due to the effect of additions and deletions, the net effect to the number was negative during the first three years of the decade and afterwards it was

* The freezing plants will be generally established in fish processing plants and also established by private persons for the purpose of lending space to the exporters of marine products. Freezing is helpful to preserve the fish as fresh as possible with minimum loss in flavour, taste, odur, forum, nutritive value and digestibility of flesh. Freezing is achieved either by using a mixture of ice and salt or refrigeration.

positive. The growth over previous year was more than 10 per cent only in two years i.e., 1992-93 and 1993-94. The number of deletions was very high upto 1988-89 (51) and later the number of deletions varied between three and seven per annum during 1989-90 and 1994-95. However, in 1995-96 the number of deletions was increased to 12. The capacity of the freezing plants which was 2,108.65 tonnes in 1987-88 increased to 6,496.29 tonnes recording an increase of 208.08 per cent during the period.

Table 4.3: Number of Canning Plants Registered During 1986-87 to 1995-96

Year	No. Registered	No. Added	No. Deleted	Net Additions/ deletions	Percentage change over previous year	Capacity in tonnes
1986-87	27	1	3	(-) 2	(-) 6.90	NA
1987-88	25	-	2	(-) 2	(-) 7.41	1,816.14
1988-89	25	-	-	-	-	84.50
1989-90	24	-	1	(-) 1	(-) 4.00	83.50
1990-91	23	1	2	(-) 1	(-) 4.17	81.50
1991-92	23	-	-	-	-	81.50
1992-93	24	1	-	1	4.35	81.50
1993-94	22	-	2	(-) 2	(-) 8.33	76.50
1994-95	21	-	1	(-) 1	(-) 4.55	65.50
1995-96	14	-	7	(-) 7	(-) 33.33	52.50

NA : Not Available

Source : Compiled from the Annual Reports of The Marine Products Export Development Authority, Cochin.

The data relating to the number of canning plants* registered during 1986-87 to 1995-96 are presented in Table 4.3. The table reveals the number of canning plants which was 27 in 1986-87 was reduced to 14 in 1995-96. During the period three new canning plants were added to the total number whereas 18 canning plants were deleted from the list. The total capacity of the canning plants was also declined from 1,816.14 tonnes in 1987-88 to 52.50 tonnes in 1995-96.

* Cans are considered very effective for the package of cooked pieces of fish. Canning is used for effective preservation of the fish pieces which are used particularly for export trade. Canning plants are specialised in undertaking this process.

The number of ice plants registered was increased marginally from 137 in 1986-87 to 148 in 1995-96 recording an increase of 8.03 per cent during the period under study (Table 4.4). The number of additions per year varied between zero and 14 while the number of elections varied between zero and 22 during the period. In total, there were 39 ice plants added and 50 ice plants were deleted. The capacity of the ice plants was increased from 1,816.14 tonnes in 1987-88 to 2,064 tonnes in 1994-95. However, in 1995-96 the capacity was declined to 1,788.50 tonnes.

Table 4.5 shows the number of fish meal plants* registered during 1986-87 to 1995-96. The table reveals that there was a substantial decrease in the number of registered fish meal plants during 1986-87 to 1995-96. There were 29 registered fish meal plants in the year 1986-87 which came down to 15 fish meal plants during 1995-96 showing a decrease of 48.28 per cent. The year-wise number of additions varied between zero and five. Similarly, the number of deletions also varied in the same manner during the period. However, the total number of plants deleted (20) were more than double to the number of plants added (9). The capacity of the registered fish meal plants decreased from 422 tonnes in 1987 -88 to 329 tonnes during 1995-96, except during the year 1989-90 in which there was in increasing trend. The capacity of the total fish meal plants was 463 tonnes in 1989-90 while, it was decreased to 372.50 tonnes in 1990-91 and in the next year it was marginally increased too 375.50 tonnes.

The data relating to the number of registered peeling sheds during the period 1986-96, is shown in Table 4.6. As shown in the table, there was a marginal decrease in the number of peeling sheds during the period. There were 953 peeling sheds during 1986-87 which came down to 898 peeling sheds in the year 1995-96 recording a decrease of 5.77 per cent. The number of additions during the same

* Fish meal is the by-product of the processing of marine products. In the export processing of marine products some parts of the fish are removed. The export processing units established fish meal plants to make use of the waste material along with the landed fish of poor food value. The minsed mass is steam heated and then hydraulically operated. The process extracts oil and water from the mass and leaves dry cakes which are used for sac filling and food for chickens in the poulties.

period varied between 12 to 66. The minimum number of additions was recorded during 1988-89 and 1989-90 while the maximum number was recorded during the year 1993-94. In the case of number of deletions, the minimum number (7) was recorded during the year 1995-96 while the maximum number of deletions (88) was observed during 1992-93. The table also reveals that the capacity of the peeling sheds was more than 2,000 tonnes during all these years.

Table 4.4: Number of Ice Plants Registered During 1986-87 to 1995-96

Year	Number Registered	Number Added	Number Deleted	Net Additions/ deletions	Percentage change over previous year	Capacity in tonnes
1986-87	137	1	22	(-) 21	(-) 13.29	NA
1987-88	129	4	12	(-) 8	(-) 5.84	1,816.14
1988-89	129	-	-	-	-	1,820.64
1989-90	132	7	4	3	2.33	1,854.00
1990-91	129	1	4	(-) 3	(-) 2.27	1,894.00
1991-92	131	4	2	2	1.55	2,012.50
1992-93	133	3	1	2	1.53	2,039.00
1993-94	134	3	2	1	0.75	2,042.00
1994-95	137	2	-	3	2.24	2,064.00
1995-96	148	14	3	11	8.03	1,788.50

NA : Not Available

Source: Compiled from the Annual Reports of The Marine Products Export Development Authority, Cochin.

Table 4.7 reveals the particulars of conveyance** registered during 1986-87 to 1995-96. The number of registered conveyance increased from 443 (1986-87) to 506 (1995-96) showing an increase of about 14 per cent during the period under study. The variation in the number of additions in the conveyance ranged from five to 46 during 1986-87 to 1995-96. While the number of deletions in the conveyance varied between zero to 23 during the same period. The data relating to the number of cold storages registered during 1986-87 to 1995-96 is presented in Table 4.8. The table reveals, the number of

* The peeling sheds are build-up in the process plants wherein the unwanted parts of the fish will be removed. The larger number of casual labour mostly women will take-up this removal process.

** The finished product which is transported either in refrigerator container or insulated vehicle.

registered cold storages has shown a substantial increase during the period 1986-87 to 1995-96. There were 292 cold storages registered during 1986-87 which increased to 445 during 1995-96 recording an increase of 34.38 per cent. The total number of additions were 245 which is almost three times more than the total number of deletions were 245 which is almost three times more than the total number of deletions which is 96 only. The capacity of the cold storages also has shown an increasing trend. During 1987-88, the capacity of the registered cold storages was slightly above 39,000 tonnes which increased to a little more than 79,000 tonnes recording more than hundred per cent increase

Table 4.5 Number of Fish Meal Plants Registered During 1986-87 to 1995-96

Year	Number Registered	Number Added	Number Deleted	Net Additions/ deletions	Percentage change over previous year	Capacity in tonnes
1986-87	29	5	2	3	11.54	NA
1987-88	27	-	2	(-) 2	(-) 6.90	422.00
1988-89	24	-	3	(-) 3	(-) 11.11	419.00
1989-90	26	2	-	2	8.33	463.00
1990-91	22	1	5	(-) 4	(-) 15.38	372.50
1991-92	21	1	2	(-) 1	(-) 4.55	375.50
1992-93	18	-	-	-	-	333.50
1994-95	18	-	-	-	-	333.50
1995-96	15	-	3	(-) 3	(-) 16.67	329.00

NA : Not Available

Source: compiled from the Annual Reports of The Marine Products Export Development Authority, Cochin.

Table 4.9 shows the number of other storages* registered during the period 1986-87 to 1995-96. There were 399 other storages in 1986-87, which came down to 242 in 1994-95 showing a decrease of about 65 per cent. The number of additions varied between zero to 32, where as the number of deletions varied between four to 76. The maximum number of additions were recorded during the year 1988-89 where as the maximum number of deletions were recorded

* Storage for dried marine products like dried fish and other marine products.

during 1990-91. The number of Agar Agar Plants* registered in 1986-87 to 1995-96 in shown in Table 4.10. The table reveals that during 1986-87 to 1989-90, there were no registered agar agar plants. During 1990-91, two plants were registered with a capacity of 11 tonnes and in the next year one more plant was added with one tonne capacity. From 1992-93, there were only four registered Agar Agar plants.

Table 4.6 Number of Peeling Sheds Registered During 1986-87 to 1995-96

Year	Number Registered	Number Added	Number Deleted	Net Additions/ deletions	Percentage change over previous year	Capacity in tonnes
1986-87	953	25	21	4	1.69	NA
1987-88	942	23	34	(-) 11	(-) 1.54	NA
1988-89	923	112	31	(-) 19	(-) 2.02	NA
1989-90	924	12	11	1	0.11	NA
1990-91	928	25	21	4	0.43	2,182.16
1991-92	925	16	19	(-)3	(-) 0.32	2,184.36
1992-93	873	36	88	(-) 52	(-) 5.62	2,178.74
1993-94	862	66	77	(-) 11	(-) 1.26	2,293.79
1994-95	861	45	39	(-) 1	(-) 0.12	2,259.07
1995-96	898	44	7	37	4.30	2,665.96

NA : Not Available

Source : Compiled from the annual Reports of The Marine Products Export development Authority, Cochin.

Table 4.11 shows the information regarding the number of fishing vessels registered, as well as the additions and deletions during 1986-87 to 1995-96. An insight into the table reveals an increasing trend in the number of registered fishing vessels (except during 1994-95). There were 11,696 registered fishing vessels in 1986-87, which increased to 13,560 in 1995-96, recording an increase of 15.94 per cent. The number of additions to the registered fishing vessels varied between 127 to 754. On the other hand, the deletions during the same period varied between one to 975. The highest number of additions were recorded during 1991-92 where as the highest number of deletions were recorded during 1994-95.

---

* Agar Agar is mucilgenous product of seaweeds (seaweeds are leaf like algae which are red, brown or green which live in the sea). It is polysaccharide (a type of carbohydrate) i.e. extracted from the naturally available of cultured seaweeds. Agar Agar is used as a medium for culturing bacteria in the microbiology laboratories. Agar Agar is also used as a gel in scientific experiments.

Table 4.7: Number of Conveyances Registered During 1986-87 to 1995-96

Year	Number Registered	Number Added	Number Deleted	Net Additions/ deletions	Percentage change over previous year
1986-87	443	21	18	3	0.68
1987-88	456	46	23	13	2.93
1988-89	471	22	7	15	3.29
1989-90	481	14	4	10	2.12
1990-91	483	15	13	2	0.42
1991-92	480	18	21	(-) 3	(-) 0.62
1992-93	487	5	-	7	1.46
1993-94	487	8	8	-	-
1994-95	501	31	14	14	2.87
1995-96	506	5	-	5	1.00

Source : Compiled from the Annual Reports of The Marine Products Export Development Authority, Cochin.

Table 4.8 Number of Cold Storages Registered During 1986-87 to 1995-96

Year	Number Registered	Number Added	Number Deleted	Net Additions/ deletions	Percentage change over previous year	Capacity in tonnes
1986-87	292	14	27	(-) 13	(-) 4.26	NA
1987-88	301	17	8	9	3.08	39,041.00
1988-89	296	11	16	(-) 5	(-) 1.66	39,913.00
1989-90	304	16	8	8	2.70	42,458.00
1990-91	320	20	4	16	5.26	48,705.00
1991-92	333	19	6	13	4.06	52,425.00
1992-93	363	33	4	30	9.01	56,965.00
1993-94	394	36	5	31	8.54	69,795.00
1994-95	416	35	3	22	5.58	75,774.00
1995-96	445	44	15	29	6.97	79,400.50

NA : Not Available

Source: Compiled from the Annual Reports of The Marine Products Export Development Authority, Cochin.

Table 4.9 : Number of Other Storages Registered During 1986-87 to 1995-96

Year	Number Registered	Number Added	Number Deleted	Net Additions/ deletions	Percentage change over previous year
1986-87	399	12	6	6	1.53
1987-88	403	10	6	4	1.00
1988-89	423	32	12	20	4.96
1989-90	430	12	5	7	1.65
1990-91	371	17	76	41	9.53
1991-92	368	12	15	(-)3	(-)0.80
1992-93	371	9	6	3	0.81
1993-94	366	-	5	(-)5	(-)1.35
1994-95	242	5	4	(-)24	(-)6.56
1995-96	NA	NA	NA	NA	NA

NA : Not Available

Source: Compiled from the Annual Reports of The Marine Products Export Development Authority, Cochin.

Table 4.10 : Number of Agar Agar Plants Registered During 1986-87 to 1995-96

Year	Number Registered	Number Added	Number Deleted	Net Additions/ deletions	Percentage change over previous year	Capacity in tonnes
1986-87	-	-	-	-	-	-
1987-88	-	-	-	-	-	-
1988-89	-	-	-	-	-	-
1989-90	-	-	-	-	-	-
1990-91	2	2	-	2	-	11.00
1991-92	3	1	-	1	50.00	12.00
1992-93	4	1	-	1	33.33	-
1993-94	4	-	-	-	-	-
1994-95	4	-	-	-	-	-
1995-96	4	-	-	-	-	-

Source : Compiled from the Annual Reports of The Marine Products Export Development Authority, Cochin.

Table 4.11 Number of Fishing Vessels Registered During 1986-87 to 1995-96

Year	Number Registered	Number Added	Number Deleted	Net Additions/ deletions	Percentage change over previous year
1986-87	11,696	352	66	286	2.51
1987-88	11,815	127	8	119	1.02
1988-89	11,937	136	14	122	1.03
1989-90	12,083	164	18	146	1.22
1990-91	12,499	485	69	416	3.44
1991-92	13,245	764	8	746	5.97
1992-93	13,546	306	6	301	2.27
1993-94	13,809	264	1	263	1.94
1994-95	13,219	349	975	(-) 590	(0) 4.27
1995-96	13,560	342	1	341	2.58

Source: Compiled from the Annual Reports of The Marine Products Export Development Authority, Cochin.

REFERENCE

1. The Marine Products Export Development Authority, Act, Rules and Regulations, The MPEDA, Cochin, 1992, p. 1.

2. Central Marine Fisheries Research Institute, '40 Years of Research and Development in Marine Fisheries in India', The Author, Cochin, p. 41.

3. Ibid p. 4.

4. The Marine Products Export Development Authority, 'MPEDA - An Overview', The Author, Cochin 1994, p. 3.

5. Grans, J.M., and *et al.*, ' The Frontiers of Public Administration Code in Administration and Management of Electricity in India', Deep and Deep Publications, New Delhi, 1987, p. 53.

6. Organisation and Managerial Problems of Apex Co-operative Organisation with Special Reference to MARKFED', CO-operative Perspective, Vol. II, No.1, 1977.

7. John Child, 'Organisation: A Guide to Problems and Practices', Harper and Row Publishers, London, 1977, p. 8.

8. William B. Cornell, 'Organisation and Management in Industry and Business', The Ronald Press Company, U.S.A, 1947, p. 17.

5

Export Marketing Services-I Product Planning and Quality Control Mechanisms

The product is the heart of the marketing endeavour; the product brings buyer and seller, the firm and its market, together. It is the area of product that the interests of the firm and the interests of the customer overlap the most[1]. Product is the basis for marketing activity. A product by means is a set of tangible and intangible attributes, including packaging, colour, price, manufacturer's prestige, retailer's prestige and manufacturer's and retailer's services, which the buyer may accept as offering satisfaction of wants or needs[2]. In the words of Phlip Kotler[3], a product is anything that can be offered to a market for attention, acquisition, use or consumption that might satisfy a want or a need.

Manufactures when they consider entering into the international markets usually concerned about their profit making prospects in the product port-folio. The product being offered to the foreign customers must have something special either in terms of attraction or advantage which will motivate them to opt for this one in preference to others.[4] The manufacturer realises that the primary reason his company is accepted abroad is the product or service it offers to the host country. As result, international product policy is the cornerstone around which all other international marketing activities must be designed.[5]

Each product which is to be offered must above all, meet the needs of the potential user; therefore, each must be subjected to extreme scrutiny from the user's viewpoint before committing the company's resources to the development of products. The product decision calls for others involving the provision of production facilities and the development of effective marketing programmes. The physical product, itself, needs review to determine its appropriateness in the overseas environment.[6] Certainly, the foreign customer's definition of the firm's product is different from that of its domestic customers, either in terms of the role it performs or in terms of the bundle of utilities it offers. On a more prosaic and practical level, the packaging, labeling, branding, and warranty aspects of the product are likely to be different.[7]

Product adaptation is to be given vital importance in product planning and development for international markets. A product that is perfectly good for one market may have to be adapted for another. There can be many reasons for this. Physical conditions may be different. Functional requirements may vary from market to market. People in different places may use products differently or for different purposes.[8] The varied use conditions, income levels, consumer tastes, habits, traditions and other behavioural patterns, governmental regulations, etc., generally force the manufacturers to differentiate the offer so as to make it adaptable to the market conditions.

PRODUCT MIX

The Marine Products Export development Authority offers export marketing services to the widely spread producers and middlemen of fish and fish products to reach international markets with their products. The MPEDA acts as liaison between the importers in the foreign countries and the exporters of our country. It offers a product mix to the international market and work for mobilising orders from the importers and intum takes the responsibility of arranging the products with assured quantity and quality standards apart from the supply within the stipulated time. The product mix offered by MPEDA is presented in Exhibit 5.1. There are five product lines in the product mix of MPEDA. They are frozen shrimp, frozen fish, frozen cuttle fish, frozen squid and others. The length of the product line of frozen shrimp is very wide including 17 number of products. They are white shrimp, tiger shrimp, brown shrimp, flower shrimp, sea tiger shrimp, deepsea shrimp, brown shrimp, flower shrimp, sea tiger shrimp, scampy shrimp, karikkedi shrimp, PUD shrimp, tailon shrimp, CP shrimp, PD shrimp, PD tailon shrimp, PC shrimp, PDC shrimp, AFD shrimp and cooked shrimp. Product variants were also offered for each product in the line The product line relating to frozen fish has 17 products including pomfret (white), Pomfret (black), chinese pomfret, sea bream, snapper, ribbon fish, reef cod, yellow fin tuna, skip jack tuna, big eye tune, mackerel, sardine, king (seer) fish, fish fillets, shark meat, fresh water fish and other marine fish. The product line relating to frozen cuttle fish has nine products including fillets, whole, whole cleaned, tentacles, stripes, roe, IQF, ink and cuttle bone. The product line relating to frozen squid has 10 products including whole, whole cleaned, tubes, rings, tentacles, fillets, peeled, stuffed, roe and IQF. The product line relating to others has 14 products including pickles, canned crab meat, sea shell, mussel meat, snail meat, fish/prawn cutlets, surimi, agar-agar, squid salad, fish oil, crab shell, frozen skewers, frozen baigai and jelly fish salted.

PRODUCT DEVELOPMENT PROGRAMMES

The Marine Products Export Development Authority has taken two major lines of activity to strengthen product planning and development programme for export marketing of fish and fish products. They are encouraging and promoting the exporters for the production of export oriented fish and fish products and to ensure quality standards to promote the image of the Indian products in the international markets. A number of tasks have been designed to achieve the two important objectives.

The MPEDA has established Prawn Farm Project Complex at vallarpadom in 1986 with the administrative office located at Cochin. The main objective of setting up this complex is to conduct regular training programmes in shrimp culture, hatchery operation, design and construction of hatchery to government officials, personnel of financial institutions, researchers and entrepreneurs who are interested in taking up shrimp aquaculture as profession and also

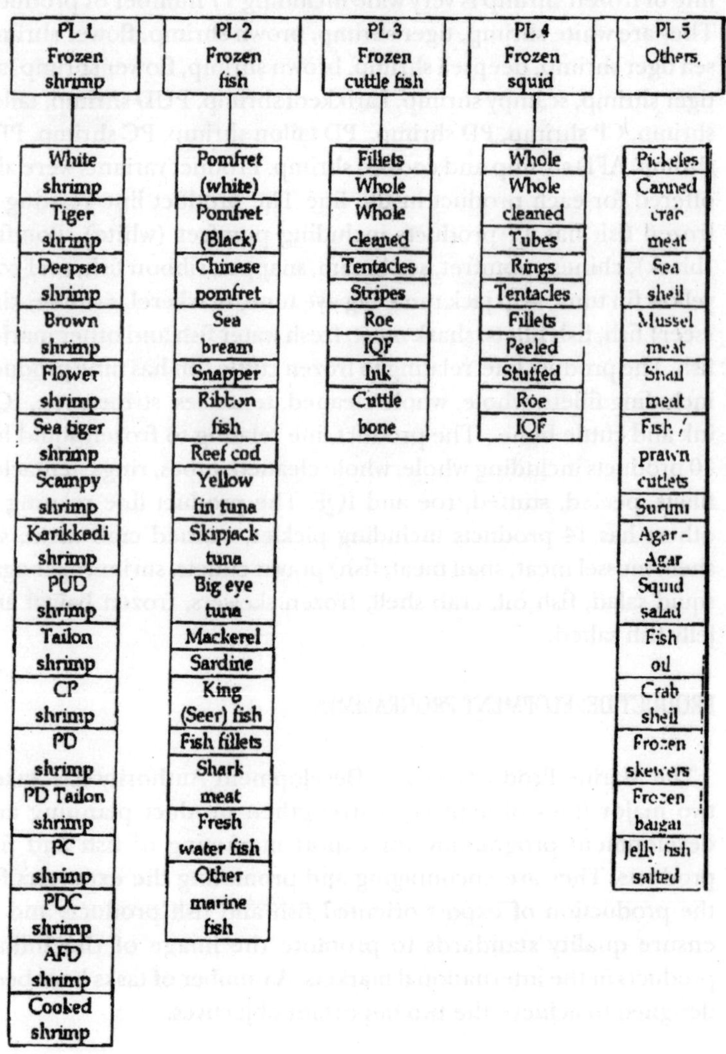

Exhibit 5.1
Product Mix

to operate the hatchery as a demonstration component for trainees. The training programmes taken up by this complex includes training on shrimp culture and hatchery management, training on shrimp hatchery operation, training in shrimp culture, training for ARDB officials, workshop in shrimp farming, development and construction work, miscellaneous and literature collection. It has also promoted prawn farming at regional centres and prawn farming at sub-regional centres to assist the farmers by providing technical assistance and consultancy during various stages of prawn farming.

The prawn farm regional and sub-regional centres carred out surveys to identify suitable areas for prawn farming in different coastal districts. Under this programme topographic survey, hydro biological survey, soil survey and meteorological survey were carred out to collect data on different parameters. Table 5.1 shows particulars of area survey carried out during 1986-87 to 1995-96. The table reveals during the decade the total area surveyed was 1.23 lakh ha. Out of the total, macro level survey was conducted. The longest area surveyed at micro level was registered in 1993-94 while in macro level survey the longest area was registered in 1992-93.

Table 5.1 : Area Survey Carried Out During 1986-87 to 1995-96

Year	Micro Level Survey in Hectares	Macro Level Survey in Hectares	Total Area Surveyed in Hectares
1986-87	1,866.14	-	1,866.14
1987-88	2,000.49	6,396.00	8,396.49
1988-89	2,012.44	12,193.60	14,206.04
1989-90	2,834.32	13,258.63	16,092.95
1990-91	3,820.52	7,494.70	11,315.22
1991-92	3,410.40	12,046.67	15,457.07
1992-93	3,668.19	18,267.66	21,935.85
1993-94	8,130.68	-	8,130.68
1994-95	5,053.67	13,134.61	18,188.28
1995-96	2,212.91	5,109.41	7,322.32
Total	35,009.76	87,901.28	1,22,911.04

Source : Compiled from the Annual Reports of The Marine Products Export Development Authority, Cochin.

Necessary inputs for prawn farming such as prawn seed, prawn feed, mohuna oil cake, etc., in limited quantities were arranged for needy farmers on cast basis. Table 5.2 depicts the particulars of inputs supplied to prawn farmers during 1986-87 to 1995-96. The supply of essential inputs to the prawn farmers was taken up by MPEDA during 1988-89 During the year 10.26 tonnes of mohua oil cake, which is useful for eradication of predators from the fish pond, and prawn feed to the tune of 4.9 tonnes and prawn seed valued at Rs. 56.32 lakhs were supplied at cost price to the identified needy farmers of prawn production. In the following year there was substantial cut in the quantity supplied in relation to mohuva oil cake (3.15 tonnes) and prawn feed (0.68 tonnes). On the other hand the prawn seed valued at Rs. 115.75 lakhs was supplied to the farmers. The supply of mohuva oil cake was terminated after 1991 and 1992 and concentrated on the supply of the other two inputs. By 1993-94 the MPEDA realised that the most important inputs for which the farmers are struggling a lot is quality prawn seed. Therefore, it stopped supplying prawn feed and substantially increased the supply of prawn seed. During the period 1993-94 to 1995-96 the value of the prawn seed supplied varied between Rs. 10.71 crores and Rs. 12.13 crores. The reason for dropping the supply of other two inputs is not that the farmers doesn't require them but the MPEDA doesn't have enough financial support to supply liberally all the three inputs. However, arrangements were made to procure seed and feed by the farmers themselves directly from the suppliers by providing the information relating to the source of availability and the details of the suppliers.

Table 5.2 : Particulars of Inputs Supplied at Cost Price During 1988-89 to 1995-96

Year	Prawn Seed Value Rs. in Lakhs	Mohua Oil Cake Quantity in Tonnes	Prawn Feed Quantity in Tonnes
1988-89	56.32	10.26	4.90
1989-90	115.75	3.15	0.68
1990-91	293.08	0.74	13.60
1991-92	628.31	0.30	124.16
1992-93	702.19	-	43.19
1993-94	1,070.68	-	2.00
1994-95	1,139.85	-	-
1995-96	1,213.23	-	-

Source: Compiled from the Annual Reports of The Maine Products Export Development Authority, Cochin.

For the promotion of squid fishing in the country, the MPEDA introduced a programme of jigging and dipnet fishing for squids in coastal waters with the technical assistance from a Japanese expert in 1985. The MPEDA also co-ordinated the research institutions relating to fishing industry in conducting experiments in respect of trawling and dipnet fishing for squids. For conducting such experimental fishing, Visakhapatnam and Cochin were selected and a special scheme was sanctioned for fabrication of improved gears and equipment in 1986-87. The MPEDA plans to conduct a resource survey of white meat fishes available in Indian waters with an intention to prepare commodity notes to attract foreign entrepreneurs for the establishment of joint ventures for processing and marketing of while fish fillets and other products from white meat fishes.

In order to promote export oriented production of fish and fish products, the MPEDA is extending support to 100% export oriented units established in the area to make use of special benefits offered by the Government of India for such units in general.

The major investment area for the fishing producers is the fishing vessel. The fishing vessels are available indigenously as well as from other countries. If the producers want to purchase a fishing vessel from a foreign country, they have to obtain permission from the Ministry of Commerce and Ministry of Agriculture with their applications processed through MPEDA. Basing on the comments made by MPEDA, the Government of India takes a decision to allow or not to allow a particular producer to buy a fishing vessel. The comments of the MPEDA also influence the financial support that will be extended by financial institutions and the governmental organisations. The producers also apply to MPEDA for purchasing indigenous fishing vessels for comments on the purchase proposal so as to get the benefit of financial assistance from various organisations. MPEDA helps 100% EOUs in obtaining required finance from various organisations for purchasing of fishing vessels by presenting the fish farmers cases to the financial institutions.

Table 5.3 shows the particulars relating to the proposals received for fishing vessels for 100% EOU by MPEDA during 1986-87 to

1995-96. The table reveals during the five years period MPEDA received 132 proposals as against the requirement of 213 fishing vessels from various export oriented units. The large number of proposals (77) was received in 1986-87 requiring 158 fishing vessels but the permission was granted by the Government of India for acquiring only five fishing vessels. In the following year 31 proposals were scrutinised and permission was accorded to acquire 10 fishing vessels. IN 1988-89, out of the 13 proposals for 13 fishing vessels the government accorded permissions for the import of 10 fishing vessels. In 1989-90, only two fishing vessels were allowed to acquire against 10 applications while in 1990-91 only one proposal was approved for acquiring a fishing vessel. During 1991-92 not even a single proposal was received for the purchase of fishing vessel. In 1992-93, eight proposals for eight fishing vessels were received and all of the were accorded permission for acquiring fishing vessels. In 1993-94 and 1995-96, 15 and 13 proposals were received and permission, were accorded to all of them respectively. After a careful scrutiny of the applications, the MPEDA forwarded the applications with comments to the Ministry of Commerce and Ministry of Agriculture. The 100% EOUs have acquired 32 fishing vessels by the end of 1990-91. Out of them, five vessels are from indigenous yards and 27 from abroad.

Table 5.3 : Proposals for Fishing Vessels from 100% Export Oriented Units Submitted to the MPEDA During 1986-87 to 1995-96

Year	Number of Proposals Received	Number of Fishing Vessels Required	Number of Vessels Acquired
1986-87	77	158	5
1987-88	31	31	10
1988-89	13	13	10
1989-90	10	10	2
1990-91	1	1	1
1991-92	-	-	-
1992-93	8	8	8
1993-94	15	15	15
1994-95	-	-	-
1995-96	13	13	13

Source: Compiled from the Annual Reports of The Marine Products Export Development Authority, Cochin.

Table 5.4 depicts the data relating the fishing vessels acquired by Indian companies (including 100% EOUs'). The table reveals that a total number of 312 fishing vessels having been acquired by Indian fishing companies by the end of 1995-96. Out of the total, 150 fishing vessels, representing 46.80 per cent are imported from abroad. The 162 fishing vessels are indigenous products. By the end of 1986-87 there were 109 fishing vessels purchased by the Indian companies, out of Table 5.4 Fishing Vessels Acquired by Indian Companies which 73.39 per cent were imported ones. During the next four years, 70 fishing vessels were acquired and out of them 45.71 per cent were imported ones. During the next four years, 70 fishing vessels were acquired and out of them 45.71 per cent were imported ones. During 1991-92 to 1995-96 as many as 133 fishing vessels were purchased and out of which only 38 vessels are imported ones. It can be inferred from the above that the Indian Government is encouraging the companies to purchase fishing vessels from Indian companies. The table further reveals that a large number of vessels were purchased during 1987-88 and later there was a sharp decline in the number of fishing vessels acquired. However, during the last five years there was an increase in the number of vessels purchased. The table reveals the number of vessels purchased per year during of the last five years varied from 11 and 45.

Tables 5.4: Fishing Vessels Acquired by India Companies

Year	Indigenous	Imported	Total
As on 31-3-'87	29	80	109
1987-88	10	20	30
1988-89	13	9	22
1989-90	8	2	10
1990-91	7	1	8
1991-92	10	4	14
1992-93	16	8	24
1993-94	31	14	45
1994-95	9	2	11
1995-96	29	10	39
Total	162	150	312

Source: Compiled from the Annual Reports of The Marine Products Export Development Authority, Cochin.

The MPEDA processed 48 proposals for the conversion of existing seafood processing units into 100% EOUs and forwarded to the Ministry of Commerce in 1992-93. In the year 1993-94, 37 proposals, 20 proposals in the subsequent year and five proposals of the same order in 1995-96 were examined and forwarded to the Ministry of Commerce for approval. It can be inferred from the above that many seafood processing units are planning to join the team of 100% export oriented units.

Table 5.5: Source-wise Export of Fishing Vessels

Country	Number of Vessels
Mexico	49
Holland	33
Australia	31
U.S.A.	18
South Korea	8
Japan	7
Singapore	2
Hong Kong	1
Taiwan (through FSI)	1
Total	150

Source: Compiled from the Annual Reports of The Marine Products Export Development Authority, Cochin

The data relating to source-wise import of fishing vessels are presented in Table 5.5. The Indian companies have imported fishing vessels from nine different countries viz., Mexico, Holland, Australia, U.S.A, S. Koera, Japan, Singapore, Hong Kong and Taiwan. Out of the total 150 fishing vessels imported, 49 fishing vessels representing 32.67 percent were imported from Mexico-the largest supplier to the Indian companies, 33 fishing vessels were imported from Holland while 31 vessels were imported from Australia. The number of fishing vessels imported from USA and South Korea was 18 and eight respectively. While seven fishing vessels were imported from Japan, two fishing vessels were imported from Singapore and one each from Hong Kong and Taiwan.

The Government of India has announced new deepsea fishing policy in 1986. As per the policy the Ministry of Commerce and the Ministry of Agriculture, would be nodal agencies for the joint ventures in deep sea fishing. The Ministry of commerce inturn entrusted MPEDA with the responsibility of receiving and examining proposals for joint ventures in deepsea fishing. The salient features of the new joint venture policy are:

a) Joint venture has to be for a minimum period of five years.
b) Foreign equity upto 40 per cent will be normally allowed.
a) Second hand vessels of age not exceeding eight years are permitted.
b) Long lease (8-10 years) of fishing vessels is allowed.
c) Foreign crew upto 50 per cent will be normally allowed.
d) Pari-passu clause is liberalised to 1: 2 (i.e., one Indian vessel for every two imported) and no such clause for 100% export oriented units (EOUs) or second hand imported vessels.

The MPEDA has introduced financial schemes for developmental projects for the creation of infrastructure facilities and to build up support to the producers to acquire new machinery and technology. Table 5.6 depicts the details of the schemes of financial assistance for the overall development of fish and fish products in the country. As seen from the table, there are 10 schemes of financial assistance offered by MPEDA as on 31-3-1996. The subsidy scheme for automatic flake/chip/tube ice making machines is intended to assist seafood processors for production of quality ice required for inplant use. The subsidy scheme for generator set was introduced with an objective of assisting processing units to have captive power as standby arrangement. In order to upgrade the efficiency of freezing machinery in the processing plants a scheme called subsidy for installation of improved plate freezers* was introduced. With an objective to assist seafood processor to efficiently transport frozen seafood products, the subsidy scheme for refrigerated truck/container/trailor with prime mover and generator set was initiated. The scheme of upgrading deficient cold storages was introduced with an objective of assisting seafood processors in increasing the efficiency in their cold storages. The objective of the subsidy scheme for acquisition of IQF machinery and equipments is to promote the

* This is one of the advanced method of preservation. In this the fish are freezed in plates.

Table 5.6: Schemes of Financial Assistance for Overall Development of fish and Fish Products

Name of the Scheme	Objective in brief
1. Subsidy for Automatic Flake /Chip/Tube Ice Making Machines	To assist seafood processor for production of quality ice required for inplant use.
2. Subsidy for Generator Set	To assist seafood processing units to have captive power as stand by arrangement.
3. Subsidy for Installation of improved Plate Freezers	To upgrade efficiency of freezing machinery in the processing plants.
4. Subsidy for Refrigerated Truck/container/Trailor with Prime mover and Generator Set.	To assist seafood processors to efficiently transport frozen seafood products.
5. Subsidy for Upgrading Deficient Cold Storages	To assist seafood processors to increase efficiency of their cold storages.
6. Subsidy for Aquisition of IQF Machinery and Equipments.	To assist seafood processors to promote production of IQF products.
7. Distribution of Insulated Fish Boxes at subsidised rate.	To ensure proper preservation of raw material to produce quality seafood products.
8. Reimbursement of part of the cost of HSD consumed by the deep sea fishing vessel.	To enable deepsea fishing vessel operators to effectively compete with their counterparts in developing countries.

(Cont.)...

9. Financial Assistance for Modification of Fishing Vessels Below 20 M OAL for Multiday Fishing Operations (2 to 3 vessels in Each State).	To encourage diversified and multiday fishing in the 50-100 M depth range.
10. Financial Assistance for Diversified Fishing (fund offered by MOFPI)	
a) Assistance for conversion of deepsea fishing vessels for diversified fishing.	
b) To subsidise cost of installation of blast freezers for onboard freezing.	To encourage commercial exploitation of under exploited non-shrimp resources.

Source: Policies and Opprotunities for Investments in Fisheries in India, The Marine Products Export Development Authority, 1995, Cochin, pp. 12 and 13.

production of IQF products while the objective of distribution of insulated fish boxes at subsidised rate scheme is to ensure proper preservation of raw-material to produce quality seafood products. To enable the deepsea fishing vessel operators to efficiently compete with their counter parts in developing countries, a financial assistance scheme called remibursement of part of the cost of HSD consumed by the deepsea fishing vessel has been offered. To encourage diversified multi-day fishing in the 50 to 100 metres depth range, a financial assistance scheme for modification of fishing vessels below 20 M OAL for multi-day fishing operators was introduced. To encourage commercial exploitation of under exploited and un-exploited non-shrimp resources a financial assistance scheme for diversified fishing was introduced.

The details of schemes of financial assistance intended for prawn farming are shown in table 5.7. The table shows, there are four schemes under operation exclusively for the development of prawn farming. The subsidy for new farm development is intended to bring new areas under scientific shrimp farming. To encourage shrimp seed production a subsidy scheme for establishment of shrimp hatchery was offered. The objective of the subsidy scheme for shrimp feed and seed is to encourage shrimp production through traditional farms. To encourage the establishment of spawner banks, a subsidy scheme for the establishment of broodstock bank introduced.

An attempt is made to know the number of beneficiaries and the amount sanctioned under various schemes intended for the overall development of fish products. Table 5.8 presents the details of the beneficiaries under subsidies for automatic flake/chip/tube ice making machine during 1986-87 to 1995-96. Under this scheme 25 per cent of the cost of the machine subject to a maximum of rupees one lakh is offered as an assistance. Though the financial assistance scheme is under operation since 1986-87 it could not attract the industry for availing itself the subsidy during the period. Since 1991-92, there were 19 beneficiaries who obtained financial assistance scheme is under operation since 1986-87 it could not attract the industry until 1991-92. There was absolutely no response from the industry for availing itself the subsidy during the period. Since 1991-92, there were 19 beneficiaries who obtained financial assistance from MPEDA to the tune of Rs. 19.00 lakhs. In other

Table 5,7: Schemes of Prawn Farming for Overall Development of Fish and Fish Products

Name of the Scheme	Objective in brief
1. Subsidy for New Farm Development	To bring new areas under sciencitific shrimp farming.
2. Subsidy for Establishment of Shrimp Hatchery.	To encourage shrimp seed production.
3. Subsidy for Shrimp Feed and Seed	To encourage shrimp production through traditional farms.
4. Subsidy for Establishment of Broodstock Bank.	To encourage establishment of spawner banks.

Source: Policies and Opportunities for Investments in Fisheries in India, The Marine Products Export Development Authority, 1995, Cochin, p. 12.

words, each beneficiary got one lakh rupees subsidy in purchasing the machines. Under the subsidy for generator set scheme, as many as 86 beneficiaries were granted an amount of Rs. 31.55 lakhs during 1986-87 to 1995-96 (table 5.9). The rate of assistance offered was 15 per cent of the cost of the generator set or Rs. 40,000 whichever was less. In other words, each beneficiary availed on an average Rs. 0.37 lakhs as subsidy for purchasing a generator set. The beneficiaries were more in number in 1993-94 (15) and 1987-88 (13).

Table 5.8 Subsidy for automatic Flake/Chip/Tube Ice Making Machines During 1986-87 to 1995-96

Year	Number of Beneficiaries	Amount Sanctioned (Rs. in Lakhs)
1986-87	Nil	Nil
1987-88	Nil	Nil
1988-89	Nil	Nil
1989-90	Nil	Nil
1990-91	Nil	Nil
1991-92	3	3.00
1992-93	1	1.00
1993-94	8	8.00
1994-95	5	5.00
1995-96	2	2.00

Source: Compiled from the Annual Reports of The Marine Products Export Development Authority, Cochin.

Table 5.9: Subsidy for Generator Sets During 1986-87 to 1995-96

Year	Number of Beneficiaries	Amount Sanctioned (Rs. in Lakhs)
1986-87	6	1.75
1987-88	13	4.37
1988-89	7	2.45
1989-90	11	3.83
1990-91	9	3.43
1991-92	7	2.77
1992-93	5	2.00
1993-94	15	5.74
1994-95	6	2.40
1995-96	7	2.81

Source: Compiled from the Annual Reports of The Marine Products Export Development Authority, Cochin.

The particulars relating to beneficiaries under subsidy for installation of improved plate freezers scheme are shown in Table 5.10. The rate of assistance under the scheme is (-) 20 per cent of cost of bonded or bored type freezing units along with compressors, condensers etc. subject to a maximum of rupees one lakh. During the period under study 117 exporters were sanctioned an amount of Rs. 100.89 lakhs. In other words, on an average, each beneficiary obtained a subsidy of Rs. 0.86 lakhs. During 1986-87 and 1987-88 a large number of respondents (37) availed the benefit under the scheme. The subsidy scheme for refrigerated truck/container/trailor with prime mover and generator set is offered on 25 per cent of purchase price on any of these items subject to a maximum of Rs. 2.00 lakhs (Table 5.11). The scheme could not attract even a single exporter until 1992-93. By the end of 1995-96 eleven beneficiaries availed subsidy to the tune of Rs. 19.42 lakhs. On an average each beneficiary was given a subsidy of Rs. 1.77 lakhs. All the 11 beneficiaries have purchased refrigerated trucks.

Table 5.10 : Subsidy for Installation of Improved Plate Freezers During 1986-87 to 1995-96

Year	Number of Beneficiaries	Amount Sanctioned (Rs. in Lakhs)
1986-87	20	15.42
1987-88	17	13.13
1988-89	8	7.17
1989-90	11	9.79
1990-91	11	9.93
1991-92	10	8.87
1992-93	13	11.94
1993-94	12	10.81
1994-95	7	6.41
1995-96	8	7.42

Source: Compiled from the Annual Reports of The Marine Products Export Development Authority, Cochin.

The data relating to the beneficiaries under subsidy for upgrading deficient cold storages scheme are shown in Table 5.12. The scheme offers subsidy of 25 per cent of the cost for improving insulation and for upgrading existing deffusers subject to a maximum of Rs. 75,000. This scheme could attract only 21 production units during 1986-87 to 1995-96. The total amount sanctioned during the period was Rs. 9.07 lakhs. On an average, each beneficiary was sanctioned a subsidy of rupees 0.43 lakhs. Under the subsidy scheme for acquisition of IQF machinery and equipment the amount, subject to a maximum of Rs. 15 lakhs, was offered as an assistance (Table 5.13). The scheme was availed by 80 beneficiaries during 1986-87 to 1995-96 and an amount of Rs. 627.17 lakhs was sanctioned for this purpose. Each beneficiary on an average got a subsidy of Rs. 7.84 lakhs. The large number of beneficiaries (21) was registered during 1990-91, while the biggest amount sanctioned (Rs. 132.42 lakhs) was registered in the year 1992-93. The scheme of distribution of insulated fish boxes at subsidised rate of 50 per cent could attract beneficiaries only during 1994-95 and in the subsequent year (Table 5.14). There were 467 beneficiaries availed a subsidy of Rs. 1.61 lakhs in 1994-95 where as 565 beneficiaries availed a subsidy of Rs. 1.74 lakhs in 1995-96.

Table 5.11: Subsidy for Refrigerated Truck/Container/Trailor with Prim Mover and Generator Set During 1986-87 to 1995-96

Year	Number of Beneficiaries	Amount Sanctioned (Rs. in Lakhs)
1986-87	Nil	Nil
1987-88	Nil	Nil
1988-89	Nil	Nil
1989-90	Nil	Nil
1990-91	Nil	Nil
1991-92	Nil	Nil
1992-93	1	2.00
1993-94	1	2.00
1994-95	4	5.69
1995-96	5	9.73

Source: Compiled from the Annual Reports of The Marine Products Export Development Authority, Cochin.

The MPEDA introduced the financial assistance scheme to reimburse a part of the cost of high speed diesel consumed by deepsea fishing vessel on an export linked formula in 1991. The details of the scheme are shown in Table 5.15. Since the introduction of the scheme an amount of Rs. 761.39 laks was sanctioned to the beneficiaries. During 1991-92, 12 companies have taken the reimbursement against 36 fishing vessels. The number of companies increased to 22 in the year 1995-96 and the number of fishing vessels increased to 50. Against the scheme of financial assistance for modification of fishing vessels below 20 m overall length for multiday fishing operations, 30 per cent of cost of modification/acquisition of equipment subject to a maximum of Rs. 1.5 lakhs per vessel was offered. So far an amount of Rs. 7.20 lakhs was granted against six vessels only.

Table 5.12: Subsidy for Upgrading Deficient Cold Storages During 1986-87 to 1995-96

Year	Number of Beneficiaries	Amount Sanctioned (Rs. in Lakhs)
1986-87	Nil	Nil
1987-88	2	0.60
1988-89	3	0.97
1989-90	4	1.50
1990-91	3	1.48
1991-92	Nil	Nil
1993-94	6	3.33
1994-95	Nil	Nil
1995-96	Nil	Nil

Source: Compiled from the Annual Reports of The Marine Products Export Development Authority, Cochin.

Table 5.13: Subsidy for Acquisition of IQF Machinery and Equipments During 1986-87 to 1995-96

Year	Number of Beneficiaries	Amount Sanctioned (Rs. in Lakhs)
1986-87	3	17.50
1987-88	4	28.62
1988-89	3	11.09
1989-90	5	24.46
1990-91	21	116.39
1991-92	12	78.44
1992-93	11	132.42
1993-94	10	100.41
1994-95	5	47.43
1995-96	6	70.41

Source: Compiled from the Annual Reports of The Marine Products Export Development Authority, Cochin.

Table 5.14: Distribution of Insulated Fish Boxes at Subsidised Rate During 1986-87 to 1995-96

Year	Number of Beneficiaries	Amount Sanctioned (Rs. in Lakhs)
1986-87	Nil	Nil
1987-88	Nil	Nil
1988-89	Nil	Nil
1989-90	Nil	Nil
1990-91	Nil	Nil
1991-92	Nil	Nil
1992-93	Nil	Nil
1993-94	Nil	Nil
1994-95	467	1.61
1995-96	565	1.74

Source: Compiled from the Annual Reports of The Marine Products Export Development Authority, Cochin.

The data relating to the number of beneficiaries, the subsidy assistance and the area developed under subsidy for new farm development scheme during 1986-87 to 1995-96 are shown in Table 5.16. Under the scheme, the subsidy offered was 25 per cent of capital investment or Rs. 30,000 per ha, which ever is less. The maximum limit for an individual/unit under the scheme is Rs. 1.5 lakhs to develop 10 ha of new area. During the decade, 1,325 farmers have taken subsidy benefit of Rs. 655.80 lakhs for the development of 4,861.27 ha of land for prawn farming. The largest number of beneficiaries (272) were registered in the year 1994-95. There is an erratic trend during the period in the case of number of beneficiaries, the area developed and also the subsidy assistance granted.

Table 5.15: High Speed Diesel Price Reimbursement Scheme During 1991-92 to 1995-96

Year	Number of Fishing Vessels	Number of Companies	amount (Rs. in Lakhs)
1991-92	36	12	91.26
1992-93	55	21	113.38
1993-94	51	20	149.75
1994-95	59	23	207.00
1995-96	50	22	200.00

Source: Compiled from the Annual Reports of The Marine Products Export Development Authority, Cochin.

Table 5.16 : Subsidy for New Farm Development for Prawn Farming During 1986-87 to 199-96

Year	Number of Beneficiaries	Subsidy Assistance (Rs. in Lakhs)	Developing Area in Ha.
1986-87	81	16.36	214.60
1987-88	47	7.28	139.38
1988-89	144	19.44	332.80
1989-90	81	20.98	349.91
1990-91	125	55.78	418.07
1991-92	116	70.00	490.00
1992-93	116	70.00	490.00
1993-94	193	113.75	805.58
1994-95	272	165.15	952.96
1995-96	150	110.06	667.97

Source: Compiled from the Annual Reports of The Marine Products Export Development Authority, Cochin.

Table 5.17 depicts the data relating to subsidy for establishment of shrimp hatchery during 1986-87 to 1995-96. The subsidy is offered to both governmental organisations as well as private organisations. The assistance offered under the subsidy scheme is 25 per cent of capital investment subject to a maximum of Rs. 5 lakhs. During 1986-87 to 1990-91, five organisations were granted subsidy of Rs. 24.50 lakhs for the establishment of five hatcheries. All the beneficiaries were governmental organisations. During 1991-92 to 1995-96, 29 organisations were given subsidy of Rs. 94.88 lakhs to establish 29 prawn hatcheries. Except one, all the beneficiaries were private organisations. In the year 1992-93, the MPEDA modified the subsidised scheme and the subsidy was extended on capital at the rate of 50 per cent subject to a maximum of Rs. 5 lakhs to government sector, 25 per cent subject to a maximum of Rs. 2.5 lakhs to corporate sector and 15 per cent subject to a maximum of Rs. 1.5 lakhs to private sector. The MPEDA encouraged private sector so as to benefit large number with lesser financial commitment.

Table 5.17: Subsidy for Establishment of Shrimp Hatchery During 1986-87 to 1995-96

Year	Number of Beneficiers Government	Private	Number of Hatcheries	Amount (Rs. in Lakhs)
1986-87	2	-	2	10.00
1987-88	1	-	1	5.00
1988-89	1	-	1	5.00
1989-90	-	-	-	-
1990-91	1	-	1	4.50
1991-92		3	3	3.89
1992-93	1	1	1	6.50
1993-94	-	2	2	3.00
1994-95	-	5	5	7.50
1995-96	-	17	17	73.99

Source: Compiled from the Annual Reports of The Marine Products Export Development Authority, Cochin.

To encourage farmers to adopt scientific farming techniques, the subsidy assistance is extended at the rate of 25 per cent of shrimp feed and seed subject to a maximum of Rs. 3,000 and Rs. 450 respectively per ha. Maximum area is limited to 50 ha per unit/ beneficier. Table 5.18 depicts the particulars relating to the number of beneficiaries, subsidy amount granted and the area covered during 1986-87 to 1995-96. The table reveals, as many as 303 farmers got benefited under the scheme with the subsidy grant of Rs. 43.82 lakhs for the development of 2,579.40 ha of shrimp farming area. The number of beneficiaries during the period shows an erratic trend vis-a-vis the area covered and the amount sanctioned. To encourage the establishment of broodstock banks by the prawn farming organisations a subsidy scheme was introduced in the year 1992-93 and a subsidy of 25 per cent of capital cost subject to maximum of Rs. 1.5 lakhs per unit. By the end of 1995-96, none beneficiaries were sanctioned an amount of Rs. 12.25 lakhs under the scheme.[9]

QUALITY MANAGEMENT

In order to ensure quality in seafood exports, the MPEDA has made it mandatory to every seafood processing plant to have a quality control laboratory for effective implementation of in-plant process quality control. It has introduced a subsidy scheme in 1980 to offer financial subsidy to the processing units to the extent of 50 per cent of the cost subject to a maximum of Rs. 50,000 per unit for setting up a mini laboratory. During the last 10 years as many as 142 processing units were benefited to the tune of Rs. 58.52 lakhs in the form of subsidy (Table 5.19).

Table 5.18 Subsidy for Shrimp Feed and Seed During 1986-87 to 1995-96

Year	Number of Beneficiaries	Covering Area in Ha.	Amount (Rs. in Lakhs)
1986-87	5	42.50	0.66
1987-88	6	48.00	0.75
1988-89	81	196.74	10.30
1989-90	3	40.00	0.60
1990-91	1	12.86	0.20
1991-92	42	448.20	6.97
1992-93	57	448.20	6.97
1993-94	24	55.77	0.87
1994-95	61	848.13	12.84
1995-96	23	439.00	3.66

Source: Compiled from the Annual Reports of The Marine Products Export Development Authority, Cochin.

The MPEDA identified the need for training the Indian quality control technologists to make them equipped with the skills and methods of testing the quality to ensure it to the international standards. It has sponsored ten technologists from the trade and two officers each from EIA and MPEDA to attend the workshop organised by regional laboratory of US FDA, New York. In 1988-89 and in the following year five day course organised by US FDA laboratories on quality control mechanisms. The MPEDA has been working since then in close co-operation with US FDA in upgrading its quality control mechanisms relation to the export of marine products.

Table 5.19: Subsidy for Setting up of Mini Laboratory During 1986-87 to 1995-96

Year	Number of Beneficiaries	Amount Sanctioned (Rs. in Lakhs)
1986-87	18	7.80
1987-88	22	8.54
1988-89	20	7.22
1989-90	29	11.22
1990-91	7	3.06
1991-92	14	6.14
1992-93	8	3.58
1993-94	7	2.52
1994-95	8	3.94
1995-96	9	4.50

Source : Compiled from the Annual Reports of The Marine Products Export Development Authority, Cochin.

Quality is the key word for any product or service in the international markets. It is particulalry more sensitive in relation to food products. No consumer will be ready to take a minimum risk quality aspects of food items since there is a possibility of getting into health problems. Food safety and wholesmeness is a factor which cannnot be left to the arbitration. This has to be viewed in the light of the fact that there is an ever increasing emphasis on the quality assurance now and generally, this is advocated either through ISO 9000 or similar quality systems. Most of the countries in the international market are very much particular with the quality standards of importing products particularly food products. They are not allowing the inferior products to their countries. Most of the countries are demanding for evidence of quality standards or an assurance through certificates from quality standards organisation of international repute and governments of the respective countries.

In the case of marine products any lapse in handling, processing, storage and distribution can lead to rejection of the product. It has been estimated that about 20 per cent of the landings are being discarded as inferior in quality due to improper handling on-board fishing trawlers and at the landing centres[10]. The exporters of the country should be careful about the quality aspects relating to fish and fish products and initiate designing of programmes for quality maintenance and improvement. In the case of fishery product it is not sufficient that the finished product meet the specification or requirements at the end of production stage. It should also have been handled, processed, packed, stored and transported under sanitary and hygienic conditions. The responsibility for the quality assurance functions remain with the various individual functions/ departments whose activities directly or indirectly influence the quality of the finished product. There is a need for integration of the quality activities of the various departments. The formal organisational structure provides only the framework and the effectiveness of the quality organisation really depends on the commitment and zeal of the top management and also in providing adequate resources as necessary to implement the quality policy[11].

Quality management is that aspect of the overall management function which determines and implements the quality policy. Quality policy is a broad guide to act and statement of the desired result or goal to be achieved within a specified action plan. The ISO 9002* specified the requirements of the quality system. In the case of marine products the chief executive of a company should at the outset clearly define and state the quality policy. Most companies are adopting Hazard Analysis Critical Control Points (HACCP) as a means of ensuring control of spoilage, safety and health requirements and ensuring integrity of the product. HACCP has been made mandatory by countries like US FDA, EC for both domestic production as well as for imported fish and fishery products.

HACCP involves identification of hazards, identification of critical control points, establishment of monitoring procedure, establishment of corrective action procedure and establishment of documentation procedure[12]. A section of the marine products industry has focused on ISO 9000 to provide suitable frame work

* The management shall–state and implement the quality policy: ensure that the quality policy communicated to and understood by all levels of the personnel; define and responsibilities and authorities for ensuring quality, provide resources for implementation and verification; appoint a management representative to implement and maintain quality system and to report to the management regarding such activities and also keep liaison with outside bodies on matters regarding quality.; periodical review of the quality system, to ensure its suitability and effectiveness– for further details refer clause 4.1 of ISO 9002.

for quality management system, while regulatory agencies have focussed on HACCP systems as a tool for ensuring safety and wholesomeness of the marine products. The emphasis on both ISO 9000 and HACCP is on prevention on non-conformance of the product through effective planned process control. The element regarding process control in ISO 9000 can very well be linked with the principle regarding monitoring of HACCP. Integration of HACCP for processing of marine products adopting HACCP principles is advocated as the base way to meet the international requirements.

In India Marine Products Industry is the first sector in which HACCP system (for export) is being introduced. But, lack of experience in undertaking hazard analysis, lack of epidemiological data and the dearth of information in technical literature of the food processing sector are some of the constraints on the adoption of HACCP. The result is that the HACCP system which was developed for food processing industries could pose a problem of ineffectiveness in addressing their needs and satisfy their objectives. There are differing limits for the same food product set by different importing countries for factors like additives and pesticide residues. The question arises as to which limit should a food processor from a developing country adjust to be able to export their product to a range of countries.

Major markets such as EU and United States of America and Canada have commenced implementing HACCP for marine products industry with the principles being extended to imported products. Other developed countries and developing countries have also commenced action on the implementation of HACCP. This development will apply pressure on the Indian marine product industry for concentrating on the export to adopt HACCP. But mutual agreement on the standards of each country and the equivalence of food safety system based on the codex guide lines and standards and other recommendations is the emerging trend in the international regulatory situations.[13]

The market trends in international scenario for fish and fish products indicating that there is a growing demand for value added fish products. Present market trends reflect a rapidly growing demand for ready to serve and ready to cook convenience products. The importance of conventional frozen and canned products is getting diminished day by day. The sophisticated consumer abroad as well the urban consumer at home demand new types of value added, hygienically prepared nutritious and attractively packed products[14].

The production of value added products has been recognised as thrust area for stepping up the country's exports. A large number of value added marine products both for export and internal markets based on shrimp, lobster, squid,, cuttle fish, bivalves, certain species of fish and minced meet from low prices fish have been identified. They include : Battered and breaded products; prawn products; squid products; clam products; fish fillets' fish fingers; fish cutlets; fish patties (burgers); individual quick frozen products; butter sandwiched prawn; minced meet; mince based products; surimi; kneaded produce and kamaboko products. The technology for their production is readily available.

There was a time when we had a lot of scope for diversification into processing and exporting different varieties of fish products packed in cartons ready for cooking. But unfortunately, this process is also not picking up due to several reasons though one cannot say the demand for fish products in India as well as in foreign markets is not encouraging. The sea food exporters are not taking up the projects in a big way for processing of value added fish products for two reasons (a) for the price that it fetches at present and (b) lack of infrastructural facilities available in India especially in several maritime states. Even converting cuttle fish and squids to steaks which are being exported at present in the raw form could be considered for export as value added products provided there is financial incentives for doing it.[15] There is a need to encourage the exporters by offering liberal financial support. A lot of research and development work is required within the country to develop new products for export. The programmes like developing consumer packs for IQF shrimp and other products, perfecting the processing methodology and diversified products identified for export, preparation of diversified seafood items for test marketing in overseas markets etc., are also to be carried out. The MPEDA should take the responsibility of the development of value added and new products for export by providing required facilities and support to the research organisations and exporters and also by creating markets for such products.

REFERENCE

1. Vern Terpstra, The University of Michigan, 'International Marketing', Dryden Press, Hinsdale, Illinois, 1972, p.207.

2. Stanton W.J., 'Fundamentals of Marketing', Mc Graw Hills, New York, 1980, p. 179.

3. Philip Kotler, Marketing Management: Analysis Planning, Implementation and Control: Printice Hall of India, New Delhi, 1988, p.445.

4. Varshney, R.L., and Bhattacharya, B., 'International Marketing Management: An Indian Perspective', Sultan Chand and Sons, New Delhi, 1996, p.199.

5. Vern Terpstra, The University of Michigan, 'International Marketing'. Dryden Press, Hinsdale, Illinois, 1972, Op. cit p.206.

6. Rathor, B.S., and Rathor, J.S., 'Export Marketing', Himalaya Publishing House, New Delhi, 1993, p.347.

7. Vern Terpstra, The University of Michigan, 'International Marketing', Dryden Press, Hinsdale, Illinois, 1972, Opcit p. 210.

8. Varshney, R.L. and Bhattacharya, B., 'International Marketing Management:: An Indian Perspective', Sultan Chand and Sons, New Delhi, 1996, Opcit p.200.

9. MPEDA Annual Report 1995-96, p.53.

10. The Marine Products Development Authority, MPEDA An Overview, the author, Cochin 1995, p. 6.

11. Bhaskaran Nair, P., 'ISO 9000 For Marine Products Industry Requirements of ISO 9002: Quality system', Seafood Export Journal, Cochin, Vol.XXV No.22, December 1994, P.19.

12. Bhaskaran Nair.P., 'ISO 9000 For Marine Products Industry Requirements of ISO 9002: Quality system', Seafood Export Journal, Cochin, Vol.XXV No.22, December 1994, Op.citp.25.

13. Bhaskaran Nair, P., 'ISO 9000 For Marine Products Requirements of ISO 9002: Process Control', Seafood Export Journal, Cochin, Vol.XXVI No.9, September 1995, p. 23.

14. Gopakumar, K., 'Marketing of value Added Products', Seafood Export Journal. Cochin. Vol.XXV, No.7, July 1993, p.25.

15. The Editor, 'Value Addition to Seafood Exports', Seafood Export Journal, Cochin, Vol. XXVII, No.6, June 1996, p.3.

6

Export Marketing Services -II Distribution and Pricing Policies

DISTRIBUTION SYSTEM

Distribution is the function that brings the firm and its customers nearer physically. It is concerned with transferring the services from the producer to the consumers[1]. A distribution channel is a live organ of marketing. It is an organised net work or a system of agencies and institutions which, in combination, perform all the activities required to link producers with users and users with producers to accomplish the marketing task[2]. The American Marketing Association defines a channel of distribution as "the structure of intracompany organisation units and extra ordinary company agents and dealers, wholesale and retail, through which a commodity, product, or service is marketed"[3]. It is necessary that any distribution plan, if it is to be effective, has to reflect the concept of total commitment to the customer[4].

The Marine Products Export Development Authority is a service organisation, offering export marketing services to the exporting or organisations of fish and fish products located throughout the coastline of India. The distribution objectives of the originations are bi-focal. On the one hand, it has to nuture the producers through the distribution of services in different packages so as to make them equipped with all resources to develop fish and fish products that are needed by the markets abroad. On the other hand, it has to distribute the services to the importers spread in various contries to facilitate trade on fish and fish products from India.

A service organisation generally uses a direct channel, serving through its branch offices, regional offices and service centres. The design of the distribution system shall be on the basis of service complexity and distribution value. The former indicates the extent of customisation and the later the personalisation added to service. Based on these two charactestics the firm should find out the combination that would suit the best to the customers as well as the firm itself[5]. The MPEDA distributes its services directly through regional offices and sub-regional offices regional centres and sub-regional centres to the target market in India and through trade promotion offices located at New Delhi, Tokyo and New York to the target market outside the country. The particulars relating to number of regional offices of MPEDA and their location are presented in Table 6.1. The number of regional offices which was four in 1986-87 increased to six in 1995-96. During 1986-87 to 1993-94 there are only four regional offices located at Cochin, Madras Bombay and Calcutta. During 1994-95 the status of the Vizag sub-regional office was elevated to regional office and in 1995-96 the status of Veraval sub-regional office was elevated to regional office.

Table 6.1 Regional Offices of The MPEDA During 1986-87 to 1995-96

Year	Number of	Location
1986-87	4	Cochin, Madras, Bombay and Calcutta
1987-88	4	Cochin, Madras, Bombay and Calcutta
1988-89	4	Cochin, Madras, Bombay and Calcutta
1989-90	4	Cochin, Madras, Bombay and Calcutta
1990-91	4	Cochin, Madras, Bombay and Calcutta
1991-92	4	Cochin, Madras, Bombay and Calcutta
1992-93	4	Cochin, Madras, Bombay and Calcutta
1993-94	4	Cochin, Madras, Bombay and Calcutta
1994-95	5	Cochin, Madras, Bombay, Calcutta, and Vizag
1995-96	6	Cochin, Madras, Bombay, Calcutta, Vizag and Veraval

Source: Compiled from the Annual Reports of The Marine Products Export Development Authority, Cochin.

The number of sub-regional offices was seven during 1986-87 to 1993-94. As a result of the status elevation of the Vizag sub-regional office to regional office in 1994-95 and Veraval sub-regional office to regional office in 1995-96, the number of sub-regional offices, came down to five (Table 6.2). The sub regional offices are located at Mangalore, Goa, Quilon, Tuticorin and Paradeep. The location of the regional offices and sub-regional offices are shown in Figure 6.1. It can be inferred from the above, bearing the changes in the status of two sub-regional offices to regional offices, there is absolutely zero expansion of distribution net work of MPEDA during the decade under study.

The regional centres and sub-regional centres are intended to offer inputs and services relating to export production. The MPEDA has increased the number of regional centres from three in 1986-87 to six in 1987-88 (Table 6.3). Since then, there has been no expansion in that respect. The regional centres are located at Cochin, Bhubaneswar, Machilipatnam, Pattukottai, Valsad and Alibag. There were two subregional centres located at Karwar and Barsat during 1986-87 to 1994-95. Two more sub-regional centres were added-one at Bhimavaram and the other at Kannur-during the year 1995-96 (Table 6.4). The location of regional and sub-regional centres are shown in Figure 6.2.

Table 6.2 Sub-regional Offices of The MPEDA During 1986-87 to 1995-96

Year	Number of Sub-Regional Offices	Location
1986-87	7	Mangalore, Goa, Veraval, Vizag, Quilon, Tuticorin and Paradeep
1987-88	7	Mangalore, Goa, Veraval, Vizag, Quilon, Tuticorin and Paradeep
1988-89	7	Mangalore, Goa, Veraval, Vizag, Quilon, Tuticorin and Paradeep
1989-90	7	Mangalore, Goa, Veraval, Vizag, Quilon, Tuticorin and Paradeep
1990-91	7	Mangalore, Goa, Veraval, Vizag, Quilon, Tuticorin and Paradeep
1991-92	7	Mangalore, Goa, Veraval, Vizag, Quilon, Tuticorin and Paradeep
1992-93	7	Mangalore, Goa, Veraval, Vizag, Quilon, Tuticorin and Paradeep
1993-94	7	Mangalore, Goa, Veraval, Vizag, Quilon, Tuticorin and Paradeep
1994-95	6	Mangalore, Goa, Veraval, Quilon, Bhubaneswar and Tuticorin
1995-96	5	Mangalore, Goa, Quilon, Bhubaneswar and Tuticorin

Source : Compiled from the Annual Reports of The Marine Products Export Development Authority, Cochin.

Fig. 6.1 Regional and Sub-Regional Offices of MPEDA.

Fig. 6.2 Regional and Sub-Regional Centres of MPEDA.

Table 6.3 Centres of The MPEDA During 1986-87 to 1995-96

Year	Number of Sub-Regional Offices	Location
1986-87	3	Cochin, Bhubaneswar and Machilipatnam
1987-88	6	Cochin, Bhubaneswar, Machilipatnam, Pattukottai, Valsad and Alibagh
1988-89	6	Cochin, Bhubaneswar, Machilipatnam, pattukottai, Valsad and and Alibagh
1989-90	6	Cochin, Bhubaneswar, Machilipatnam, Pattukottai, Valsad and Alibagh
1990-91	6	Cochin, Bhubaneswar, Machilipatnam, Pattukottai, Valsad and Alibagh
1991-92	6	Cochin, Bhubaneswar, Machilipatnam, Pattukottai, Valsad and Alibagh
1992-93	6	Cochin, Bhubaneswar, Machilipatnam, Pattukottai, Valsad and Alibagh
1993-94	6	Cochin, Bhubaneswar, Machilipatnam, Pattukottai, Valsad and Alibagh
1994-95	6	Cochin, Bhubaneswar, Machilipatnam, Pattukottai, Valsad and Alibagh
1995 -96	6	Cochin, Bhubaneswar, Machilipatnam, Pattukottai, Valsad and Alibagh

Source: Compiled from the Annual Reports of The Marine Products Export Development Authority, Cochin.

The regional offices and sub-regional offices of MPEDA shall discharge their functions relating to the implementation of various schemes of the MPEDA besides engaging themselves in the task of facilitating the export of fish and fish products. The offices provide guidance and assistance to the processing industry and the export trade relating to fish and fish products. They function in close liaison with the department of fisheries, the state government concerned, the export inspection authority and other relevant central and state government agencies.

The regional centres and sub-regional centres of MPEDA extend promotional activities of prawn farming. The centres provide technical guidance to the farmers and also supply required quality inputs at subsidized prices. The centres provide advanced training in prawn hatchery management, prawn culture management, etc.

Table 6.4 Sub-Regional Centres of The MPEDA During 1986-87 to 1995-96

Year	Number of Sub-Regional Offices	Location
1986-87	2	Karwar and Barasat
1987-88	2	Karwar and Barasat
1988-89	2	Karwar and Barasat
1989-90	2	Karwar and Barasat
1990-91	2	Karwar and Barasat
1991-92	2	Karwar and Barasat
1992-93	2	Karwar and Barasat
1993-94	2	Karwar and Barasat
1994-95	2	Karwar and Barasat
1995-96	4	Karwr, Barasat, Bhimavaram and Kannur

Source: Compiled from the Annual Reports of The Marine products Export Development Authority, Cochin.

In order to develop liaison with the Central government, the MPEDA established the trade promotion office in New Delhi in 1976. The trade promotion office maintains close liaison with the ministries concerned particularly the ministries of commerce, agriculture, finance, foreign trade, industry and shipping and transport. It facilitates useful relationship between MPEDA and the ministries concerned to ensure efficient discharge of various responsibilities. Apart from that, the trade promotion office also extends helping hand to the seafood processors and exporters in solving various problems faced by them.

The MPEDA established two overseas trade promotion offices one at Tokyo in 1978 and the other at New York in 1983. The trade promotion offices shall deliver three major functions. They are :

1. Market Intelligence :

The trade promotion offices shall gather information on prices of marine products in respective markets. Along with them they have to collect information relating to significant changes in prices of fish and fish products with reasons for such changes and anticipated changes. Important developments in seafood industry such as additional supply of products, government notification/action on quality front, tariff and non-tariff barriers, detentions, serious quality problems of the products supplied, etc., shall be reported every week by telex/fax. The offices shall carefully study the performance of the competitors and suggest suitable measures to face the competition. They have to submit monthly reports on issues such as (i) demand situation (ii) prices (iii) inventories (iv) currency situation (v) imports from other countries (vi) landings in USA and Japan (vii) quality problems (viii) trade disputes and (ix) sources of suitable technology for adoption by Indian processors and farmers.

2. Market Information and Other Works:

The trade promotion offices undertake investigation of quality problems and trade disputes arising from time to time to take necessary follow up action. They maintain close liaison with the government offices dealing with import and quality control outside India and explore the scope for arranging marketing tie-upss and joint ventures between foreign buyers and the Indian companies.

3. Promotion and Publicity:

The trade promotion officers take up promotion and publicity activities by arranging meetings for Indian exporters with buyers in the respective countries and regular meetings with importes to know the demand for the products, market situation, etc. The offices regularly conduct buyer-seller meets and maintain close liaison with important organisations and their members. The offices also advise MPEDA regarding participation in the international fairs, display of products on the stands, arrangement of meetings with buyers during fair period, releasing of advertisements in the trade journals and other publicity measures to be undertaken to promote exports. They also advise suitable measures for boosting the image of Indian seafood in the respective international markets. The offices maintain close liaison with the officials of Indian Embassy and maintain public relations in the respective countries to improve the image of the Indian seafood industry.

PRICING POLICY

The pricing policies of MPEDA are on line with the organisational objectives. In order to encourage the farmers and seafood processors to export fish and fish products exemplary services are offered to the target market at zero price. In other words, all services from MPEDA are offered at free of cost to every seafood processor and farmer in fishing sector. However, MPEDA charges reduced price for certain inputs like mohua oil cake, prawn seed and p.:awn feed.

One important pricing area where MPEDA could not develop the mechanism, is the price agreement between the importers and exporters. The Indian exporters require assistance in developing a strategical approach while getting into agreement with the importers. The absence of such approach would result only transactions but not relationships. If MPEDA develops an organisational mechanism that keeps up-to-date the pricing information relating to seafood products, demand supply positions, profiles of importers and farmers, such mechanism can develop long-term agreements and relationships between importers and exporters and ensure win-win proposition to both the parties. The trade promotion officesshall have such mechanism to facilitate price decisions between the parties to go meaningfully.

REFERENCE

1. Sinha, P.K., and Sahoo, S.C., 'Services Marketing', Himalaya Publishing House, Bombay, 1994,p.48.

2 Sontakkai, C.N., 'Marketing Management', Kalyani Publishers, New Delhi, 1992. p. 448.

3 American Management Association, Marketing Definition 'A Glossary of Marketing Terms', New York, 1960, p.10.

4 Ravi Shankar, 'Managing the Distribution', Manas Publications, New Delhi, 1992, p.7.

5 Sinha, P.K., and Sahoo, S.C., 'Services Marketing', Op.cit., p.50.

7

Export Marketing Services - III Promotional Strategies

Promotion refers to activities and processes designed to change or reinforce behaviour and/or ideas of the consumers, through communication, so that they are persuaded to buy what they might not otherwise buy, what they don't really want to buy[1]. Promotion is the link between the company and the outside public[2]. In the age of information, marketing is incomplete without effective communication with the prospective buyers about the right product at the right time that is available at the right place. Marketers must communicate the product, its features, etc., to the right target customers by formulating right message in the language that is understood by them. Proper communication requires advertising, sales promotion, personal selling, direct marketing, and public relations. Thus, marketer has to use complex marketing communication to convey the message to the target group of customers[3]. The need for designing an effective promotional programme has been gaining significance over the years. The changes that are taking place in economic, cultural and social, political, technological, competition and other fields in the marketing environment promoted the necessity to promote an organisation's goods and services.

TRAINING PROGRAMMES

The promotional programme of the MPEDA is directed towards two distinctive groups of customers. They are producers and exporters of fish and fish products in India and importers of Indian marine products. Since it is an apex organisation with an objective to provide facilitating services for the promotion of export trade of fish and fish products, the MPEDA designed a number of training programmes to the fishermen, processors and export organisations on various issues of importance. Advertising, publicity and sales promotion campaigns are also being organised.

The MPEDA has taken up extension and training programmes to traditional fishermen and artisanal fishermen on-board. The data presented in Table 7.1 depicts the year-wise number of training programmes organised by MPEDA and the number of fishermen benefited. The MPEDA identified the need for imparting training on hygienic handling of marine products, after having observed the international market environment and the special focus of importing countries on hygiene factors. The training programmes were initiated in the year 1987-88. During the initial year, seven programmes were organised and the number of beneficiaries was 337. In the subsequent year due to some preliminary problems, only five programmes were undertaken for 280 fishermen. Since 1989-90, there was a substantial increase in the number of programmes. The number of programmes increased from 24 in 1989-90 to 80 in 1991-92 and the beneficiaries also increased from 1,717 to 6,780 during the period. During 1992-93, though the number of programmes declined to 63, the number of beneficiaries has gone up substantially to 16,976. Since then though there was a substantial increase in the number of programmes, there was a decline in the number of beneficiaries. During 1995-96, 135 programmes were organised by MPEDA benefiting 7, 983 fishermen.

The MPEDA also has undertaken the training programme to the employees in peeling sheds and pre-processing centres of the exporters on hygienic handling of marine products. The data presented in Table 7.2, reveals, the number of training programmes organised by MPEDA increased from six in 1986-87 to 127 in 1995-96 recording an increase of over 21 times. The number of participants has also gone up substantially from 300 in 1986-87 to 5,465 in 1995-96 recording an increase of more than 18 times.

The process of growing baby shrimps upto a marketable size in an enclosed water body or specially created aquatic environment can be termed as shrimp farming*. Shrimps (Prawns) are aquatic organisms inhabiting the seas, estuaries** and backwaters***. There are more than 50 varieties of shrimps and six of them are identified for coastal aquaculture. Majority of them, breed* and spawn** in the sea and the young ones migrate towards coastal waters/estuaries/backwaters for growth and return to the sea for reproduction. There are a few varieties of freshwater prawns and some of them breed in the estuary and young ones grow in freshwater.

High demand for shrimp in the world markets and inability of natural fisheries to meet the demand have created a world-wide interest in their culture during the last decade. Japan was perhaps the first country to develop a system of intensive prawn farming from hatchery produced larvae and juveniles. Asian countries continue to be the global leaders in shrimp production contributing 85 per cent of the total farmed shrimps. China was the leading country in the eighties but later gave away to Thailand which now produces 1,55,000 tonnes from an area of 60,000 ha. China contributed only 50,000 tonnes from 1,40,000 ha. The leading shrimp species contributing for the world catch were *P. chinensis, P. penicilllatus, P. merguiensis and P. monodon.* There were a total of 3,012 hatcheries and 49,816 farms all over the world. The average production is estimated to be 633 kg/ha. In countries like Thailand and Indonesia, species like *P. monodon* and *P. merguiensis* are cultured on a large scale. *P. vannamei* is the dominant species in Ecuador and in other countries in the western hemisphere followed by *P. stylirostris.* Most of the area is still following extensive farming techniques, though, countries like Taiwan, Thailand, USA, etc., have been producing shrimps through semi-intensive technology[4].

---

* According to the nature of scientific management and inputs, shrimp farming systems can be broadly classified as traditional, extensive, semi-intensive and intensive. In the Traditional system of shrimp farming shrimp seeds along with fish seeds etc., are trapped during hightide when the ponds get inundated. Escape of these trapped organisms is prevented by fixing suitable screen (s) in the silence and crop is harvested at frequent intervals, owing to indiscriminate stocking of both desirable and undesirable varieties of shrimps, fishes, etc. The production under this system is normally unpredictable and often very low in quality because of predation by fishes, etc., The production under this

The technical improvements made in shrimp farming in many parts of the world through research and development has paved the way to increase our shrimp production through aquaculture by adopting extensive and semi-extenisive system of shrimp farming in areas which are congenial for taking up shrimp aquaculture. India is endowed with rich natural resources in the form of brackishwater* and estuaries for taking up shrimp culture in the coastal zone of our country. The stimulated potential brackishwater area available in our country is about 1.2 million ha. of which around 70,700 ha. are utilised mostly adopting traditional practices (50,000 ha) and partly by scientific extensive methods.

Shrimp farming has been given 'extreme focus' status in our national plans in recent years to increase export production. During the Fifth Plan period, the Government recognised brackishwater aquaculture as one of the potential secotrs besides inland and marine fisheries, which could contribute towards achievement of the development objectives and commenced promotional activity. "Pilot

---

system is normally unpredictable and often very low in quality because of predation by fishes, low stocking density and frequent harvest. The average production from traditional system is below 0.5 tonnes/ha/annum. The extensive system of shrimp farming is an improved method of traditional farming, involving construction of new ponds ranging from one to five hectares in suitable selected areas, selective stocking with fast growing shrimp seeds at a comparatively lower density ranging from a few thousands to 1,00,000 seeds per ha. with supplementary feeding. The water quality is maintained either through the natural fall and rise of tides or exchange through pumping on a low scale (upto 10 per cent). The average production under this system normally ranges from one to 1.5 tonnes/ha/crop.

The semi-intensive system of shrimp farming involves construction of ponds ranging from 0.2 to one hectare in size, selective stocking with fast growing hatchery seeds at a comparatively high density ranging from one to three lakhs per hectare maintenance of water quality by exchanging 10-12 percent daily, aerating the pond with air blowers/paddle wheels and feeding the shrimps with nutritious feed. The average production in this system ranges from four to five tonnes/ha/crop. The Intensive system of shrimp farming involves construction of concrete ponds of 0.03 to 0.1 ha. in size, selective stocking with quality shrimp seeds exclusively procured from hatcheries at a density ranging from five to 10 lakhs per ha. maintaining water quality by exchanging over 30 per cent a day, aerating the pond with mechanical aerators and feeding the shrimps with nutritionally well balanced high energy feed. The production from this system ranges from 10 to 20 tonnes/ha/crop.

Project Centres", to act as demonstration-cum-extension centres, were started during the Fifth Plan but achievements were not satisfactory. In the Sixth Plan, the "Area Development Scheme" aimed at a target of 1,500 ha in eight maritime states and three inland states with underground saline water to be brought under brackishwater fish farming in the Government sector. The scheme was concluded with the physical achievement of 1,060 ha and one shrimp hatchery with a targeted capacity of 20 million seed.

In the Seventh Plan, the Government have introduced the scheme of "integrated Brackishwater Fish Farm Development" for development of brackishwater areas both in the Government and the private sector to achieve a cumulative target of 2,160 ha of farms and six hatcheries. The scheme includes one UNDP- assisted and FAO- executed project on " Development of Coastal Aquaculture" for the establishment of five pilot farms and five pilot shrimp hatcheries. This project also includes establishment of a feed mill and training of manpower. The fish farmers development agency (FFDA) concept of fresh water aquaculture has been extended to

* Breeders refers to the mature male and female shrimps or crabs or fish. After growing to a particular size and after attaining sexual maturity breeding takes place in them usually in deepwaters of the sea fro shrimps and crabs and in the estuaries for fresh water prawns. During breeding the male deposits, the spermatophore, on to the female internal and external fertilisation takes place depending upon the species. After fertilisation the every grows inside the body and the animal with growing overy is referred to as brood or broodstock.

** The term spawn refers to the fertilised or unfertilised egg mass released into the surrounding water. Usually spawning takes place in the sea. After spawning embrionic development takes place inside the egg and the larvey are developed and comes out of the egg. The spawn is related to the size of the mother. In case of shrimps the female lays the eggs and spermatophore simultaneously.

** An estuary is a semi-enclosed coastal body of water which has a free connection with the opensea and within which sea water is measurably diluted with fresh water derived from land drainage.

*** The intrusion of sea waters into the low lying areas of land adjacent to the sea are called backwaters. At the end of the monsoon and during the post-monsoon, it is stratified and continuously supplied with fresh water at the surface and with the sea water at the bottom.

brackishwater aquaculture and accordingly Brackishwater Fish Farmers Development Agencies (BFDA) have been established in West Bengal, Orissa, Andhra Pradesh and Kerala. The Integrated Brackishwater Fish Farm Development Scheme has a total outlay of Rs. 136.5 million of which Rs. 70.0 million is the central outlay, the balance being the share of the state/union territory governments. In the Eighth Five Year Plan, the expansion of area under brackishwater aquaculture through extensive, semintensive and intensive prawn farming and increasing the productivity levels of aquaculture systems were given appropriate place. Towards the achievements of these tasks, the programmes were designed for the up-gradition of technology, increased involvement and encouragement of private sector for aquaculture related activities such as production of quality seed, feed and other inputs, creation of regularised infrastructure facilities for producing the basic inputs and requisite climate for easy availability of credit. An amount of Rs. 30 crores was granted for the Integrated Brackishwater Fish Farm Development. The targets are set to develop 20,000 ha. of brackishwater area, and to survey 5,000 ha. of brackishwater area.

Table 7.1: Training on Hygienic Handling of Marine Products to Fishermen On-board Fishing Vessel and at Fish Landing Centres During 1986-87 to 1995-96

Year	Number of Programmes	Number of Fishermen Undergone Training
1986-87	-	
1987-88	7	337
1988-89	5	280
1989-90	24	1,717
1990-91	59	3,211
1991-92	80	6,780
1992-93	63	16,796
1993-94	123	14,508
1994-95	113	11,374
1995-96	135	7,983

Source: Compiled from the Annual Reports of The Marine Products Export Development Authority, Cochin.

The MPEDA has taken up the responsibility of developing brackishwater shrimp farming in the country. It has been encouraging the private entrepreneurs to take up brackishwater shrimp farming by providing all sorts of assistance that is required.

Table 7.2 :Hygienic handling of Marine Products in Peeling Sheds/Pre Processing Centres During 1986-87 to 1995-96

Year	Number of Programmes	Number of Participants
1986-87	6	300
1987-88	11	750
1988-89	33	1,175
1989-90	42	3,074
1990-91	75	4,295
1991-92	105	4,393
1992-93	93	4,404
1993-94	103	5,224
1994-95	116	5,708
1995-96	127	5,465

Source: Compiled from the Annual Reports of The Marine Products Export Development Authority, Cochin.

Recognising the need for imparting training to the farmers who are cultivating brackishwater prawn farming, the MPEDA designed training programmes and has been executing since 1986-87. The data presented in /Table 7.3 depicts the particulars relating to the number of training programmes organised and the number of farmers/entrepreneurs trained during 1986-87 to 1995-96. The table reveals, the number of training programmes organised varied between seven and 35 during the period. The number of farmers and entrepreneurs trained per annum varied between 172 and 2,344 during the period.

TECHNICAL ASSISTANCE

Shrimp farming activity involves a lot of technical processes. The shrimp farming process can be divided into six stages. They are : i) site selection and micro level survey; ii) design and construction of farm; iii) pond preparation; iv) selective stocking with fast growing shrimp seeds; v) supplementary feeding and water quality management; and vi) harvesting and marketing. Each and every stage is crucial and any lapse or low level efficiency will influence the final result. In order to protect the farmers and also to make them successful in the activity, MPEDA is providing technical assistance right from the micro-level survey and site selection to the last process. Apart from offering consultancy services, it is directing the technical personnel of MPEDA to visit the farmers and ensure that the things are going in the right direction. The required meachanical devises to measure the quality factors at various levels are supplied to the farmers.

Table 7.3 :Training on Brackishwater Prawn Farming During 1986-87 to 1995-96

Year	Number of Training Programmes	Number of Farmers/Entrepreneurs Trained
1986-87	13	347
1987-88	23	522
1988-89	24	656
1989-90	17	459
1990-91	18	618
1991-92	7	172
1992-93	23	719
1993-94	35	919
1994-95	33	2,344
1995-96	25	695

Source: Compiled from the Annual Reports of The Marine Products Export Development Authority, Cochin.

Every year the MPEDA is providing specialised technical assistance on prawn farming to a selected number of farmers. The data presented in Table 7.4 reveals the year-wise number of farmers received technical assistance from MPEDA during 1986-87 to 1995-96. The number of farmers who received technical assistance from MPEDA on prawn farming varied between 1,029 and 3,128 per annum during the period. In all, 19,289 farmers were given technical assistance.

The MPEDA organises field surveys to prepare feasibility reports for prawn fárming and supplies to the existing as well as prospective farmers and entrepreneurs. The regional and sub-regional centres of MPEDA are taking up the job of preparing feasibility reports in respect of the areas for prawn farming and these reports will be issued to entrepreneurs to avail credit facilities from banks and for developing their areas for prawn farming. Table 7.5 presents the data relating to the year-wise number of feasibility reports issued to farmers and the area covered in the survey during 1986-87 to 1995-96.The number of feasibility reports issued varied from 139 to 603 per annum during the period. The area covered varied from 596.71 ha. to 3,424.72 ha. During the decade as many as 2,935 feasibility reports were prepared covering an area of 17,856.32 ha. On an average 1,785.63 ha. are being surveyed by MPEDA and the information is being passed on to the farmers every year.

Table 7.4 :Techanical Assistance on Prawn Farming to Existing Farmers During 1986-87 to 1995-96

Year	Number of Farmers
1986-87	1,317
1987-88	1.029
1988-89	1,505
1989-90	1,722
1990-91	1,954
1991-92	2,234
1992-93	2.136
1993-94	3,128
1994-95	2,315
1995-96	1,949

Source : Compiled from the Annual Reports of The Marine Products Export Development Authority, Cochin.

COMMUNICATION CAMPAIGN

The organisations and the individuals connected with the export of fish and fish products are spread throughout the coastal line of the country. There are big, medium and small size organisations with varied levels of expertise, skill, awareness the knowledge of issue relating to the business. MPEDA recognised the need for educating individuals and organisations relating to this activity. Since its inception, it has been publishing books and journals containing valuable information. Table 7.6 depicts the particulars relating to journals and books published by MPEDA on fishery sector. The table reveals, the MPEDA is publishing two journals namely 'MPEDA Newsletter' and 'Price Indicator for Marine Products Exports (PRIME).

Table 7.5: Particulars Relating to Ceasibility Reports of the Areas Covered for the Entrepreneurs During 1986-87 to 1995-96

Year	Number of Reports Prepared and Issued to Farmers	Area Covered in Hectares
1986-87	139	646.99
1987-88	159	596.71
1988-89	193	1,189.83
1989-90	170	1,075.96
1990-91	221	2,135.91
1991-92	280	1,653.03
1992-93	425	2,982.32
1993-94	597	3,424.72
1994-95	603	3,376.29
1995-96	148	774.56

Source: Compiled from the Annual Reports of The Marine Products Export Development Authority, Cochin.

The 'MPEDA Newsletter' is a fortnightly publication that presents the national and international news relating to imports and exports, technological developments, political developments, legal developments and the opinions of the experts in the area. The annual subscription of the newsletter was Rs. 240.00 per annum. PRIME is the weekly journal which gives day to day market information on export of marine products from India. The major focus of the journal is to publish the prices of various species in different markets. Further, it presents the market reports collected from the importing countries, day to day developments in fishery sector, technological developments, economic problems, government policies, etc. It also publishes the trade enquiries received by MPEDA through trade promotion offices, and embassies, etc. MPEDA has published 14 books on various issues relating to fisheries sector. The titles of the books on various issues relating to fisheries sector. The titles of the books are Directory of Marine Products Importers, Indian Fishery Handbook, Commercial Fishes of India-Chart, Deepsea fishing in Indian EEZ, Statistics of Marine Products (1993) Statistics of Marine Products (1994), Marine Products Export Review (1994-95), MPEDA Act, Rules and Regulations, Report of the working group on revalidation of the potential marine fisheries resources of EEZ of India, The Maritime Zones of India (Regulation of Fishing by Foreign Vessel) Act, Manual of Farming, Processing and Marketing of Giant African Snail - Achatone-Fulica, Catalogue of participants in Indian Seafood Trade Fair, Generalised System of Preference Guide (GSP) and Product Catalogue. The prices of the books vary from Rs. 20.00 to Rs. 250.00.

Table 7.6: Journals and Books Published by the MPEDA

Name of the Journal/Title of the Book	Price
Periodicals	**Annual Subscription**
MPEDA Newsletter	Rs. 240
Prime (Price Indicator for Marine Products Exports)	350
Publications	**Price/Copy**
Directory of Marine Products Importers	75
Indian Fishery Handbook	250
Commercial Fishes of India-Chart	60
Deep Sea Fishing in Indian EEZ	100
Statistics of Marine Products(1993)	150
Statistics of Marine Products (1994)	200
Marine Products Export Review (1994-95)	100
MPEDA Act, Rules and Regulations	20
Reports of the Working Group on Revalidation of the Potential Marine Fisheries Resources of EEZ of India	75
The Maritime Zones of India (Regulation of Fishing by Foreign Vessel) Act.	25
Manual of Farming, Processing and Marketing of Giant African Snail Achatona-Fulia	50
Catalogue of Participants in Indian Seafood Trade Fair	–
Generalised System of Preference Guide (GSP)	60
Product Catalogue	50

MPEDA gave special attention to aquafarming as shrimp is the major exporting item. It has brought out 20 hand-books on aquafarming, the prices of which varied between Rs. 20.00 and Rs. 200.00 (Table 7.7). The titles of the publications are Aquaculture Engineering and Water Quality Management, Aquaculture Feed, Freshwater Fishes, Fishery Potential of Andamans, Trout-Eel-Freshwater Prawn-Cray Fish, Identifying Features of cultivable species, Live Feed, Molluscs, Ornamental Fishes, Processing-Quality Control-marketing, Sea Fishes, Shrimp Hatchery, Shrimps-Lobsters-Mud Crabs, Seafood Recipes, Seaweeds, Sea Urchins, Sea cucumber,

Directory of Aquaculture, Directory of Aquaculture-Supplementary, Handbook on Shrimp Farming, A Manual on Seed production and Farming of Giant Freshwater Prawn Macrobrachium Rosenbergii.

Table 7.7 : List of Handbooks on Aqua Farming

Title of the Book	Price Rs.
Aquaculture Engineering and Water Quality Management	40
Aquaculture Feed	30
Freshwater Fishes	30
Fishery Potential of Andamans	25
Trout-El-Freshwater Prawn-Cray Fish	40
Identifying Features of Cultivable Species	30
Life Feed	25
Molluscs	40
Ornamental Fishes	30
Processing-Quality Control Marketing	50
Sea Fishes	50
Shrimp Hatchery	50
Shrimps-Lobsters-Mud Crabs	40
Seafood Recipes	20
Seaweeds,See Urchins, Sea cucumber	25
Directory of Aquaculture	200
Directory of Acquaculture-Supplementary	50
Handbook on Shrimp Farming	50
A Manual on Seed Production and Farming of Giant Freshwater Prawn Macrobrachium Rosenbergii	50

In addition to the publication of books and journals, the MPEDA is printing and distributing huge volumes of extension material in the form of folders, book-lets and stickers since 1988-89. The material is being published not only in English and Hind, but also in various regional languages of coastal India such as Telugu, Tamil, Gujarathi, Marathi, Malayalam, Kannada, Oriya, Bengali and Konkani. The details of folders, book-lets and stickers published and distributed during 1988-89 to 1993-94 are shown in Table 7.8. The MPEDA failed to continue this exercise due to financial constraints since 1994.

Films and audiovisuals have also been produced by MPEDA for the purpose of exhibiting to the farmers, processors and exporters. The data in Table 7.9 shows, there were in total seven films was produced during 1986-87 to 1995-96. Out of them, four films was

Table 7.8 : Details of Printing and Distribution of Extension Material (Folders and Booklets) During 1988-89 to 1993-94.

Year	Title	Language with number of copies	Total Copies
1988-89	Seafood Handlers Thermometer Peeling Sheds/Processing Plants	English-3000, Tamil-1000, Telugu-1000, Gujarathi-2,250, Marathi, 1000, Kannada-500	8,750
	Fishing Boats	Gujarathi-2,250, Marathi-2,000	4,250
	Folder on Squid and Cuttlefish	Tamil-2,000	2,000
	Folder on Fish and Ice	English-4,000	4,000
	Folder on Clam	Malayalam-3,000	3,000
	Folder o Hygiene and Health Chart	English-2,000	2,000
	Folder on Water Chlorination Chart	Gujarathi-2,250, Marathi-1,000	3,250
	Booklet on Squid and Cuttle Fish	English - 4,000	4,000
	Sticker on Cleanliness, Care and Cooling	English-3,000	3,000
1989-90	Hygiene and Health	Kannada-1,000, Oriya-500	1,500
	Fish and Ice	Marathi-7,000, Gujarathi-5,000, Konkani-2,000, Malayalam-2,000 Kannada-1,000, Tamil-1,250, Telugu-1,000, Oriya-500	19,750
	Shark Fin/Fish Maws	English-3,000	3,000
	Poster on Fishing Vessel	Oriya-500	500
	Poster on Peeling Shed	Oriya-500	500
	Booklet on Water Chlorination	Malayalam-500	500
	Sticker on Cleanliness, Care	Oriya-500	500
	Sticker on Bacteria and Seafoods	English-3,000	3,000
	Sticker on Indian Lobsters	English -4,000	4,000

(Cont.)...

Year	Title	Language with number of copies	Total Copies
1990-91	Folder on Hygiene and Health	Gujarathi-2,500, Marathi-3,000, Konkani-2,000, Tamil-2,500,	
		Telugu-1000, Bengali-1,000	
		Poster on fishing vessels Bengali-500	500
	Poster on peeling shed/processing plant	Bengali-500	500
	Folder on fish and ice	Bengali-1,000, Malayalam-6,000	7,000
	Folder on unhygiene and food poisioning	Malayalam-2,000	2,000
	Folder on beche-de-mer	English-3,000	3,000
	Folder on shrak fins/fish maws	Marathi-2,000, Gujarathi-2,000, Konkani, 1,500	5,500
	Folder on bacteria and seafoods	Marathi-2,000, Gujarathi-2,000, Konkani-1,500	5,500
	Booklet on Look! They destroy me, you too!	Malayalam-5,000	5,000
1991-92	Folder on processing of squid and cuttle fish	Malayalam-3,000	3,000
	Booklet on bacteria and seafoods	Gujarathi-2,000, Marathi-2,000, Konkani-1,500, Tamil-2,500,	10,000
		Telugu, 1,000, Kannada-1,000	9000
	Folder on shark fin/fish maws	Gujarathi-2,000, Marathi-2,000, Konkani-1,500, Tamil-2,500,	
		Telugu, 1,000	
	Booklet on Indian tuna fishery	English -5,000	5,000
	Booklet on MPEDA-the trend setter in seafood export promotion	English-3, Hindi-1, Malayalam-1, Tamil-1	6
	Booklet on smoke fish processing	English-1	1
	Booklet on sanitation for seafood and processing personnel	English-1	1
	Booklet on pest control is seafood processing	English-1	1

(Cont.)...

Year	Title	Language with number of copies	Total Copies
1992-93	Folder on Hygiene and Health	English-2,000, Malayalam-2,000, Tamil-10,000	14,000
	Chart on Cleaning Schedules	English-2,000	2,000
	Chart on Chlorintion Schedules	English-2,000	2,000
	Folder on Fish and Ice	Tamil-10,000	10,000
	Folder on Hygienic Handling of Fish From Landing Centre to Processing Plants	Tamil-2,000	2,000
	Folder on Bacteria and Seafoods	Tamil-10,000	10,000
	Folder on Squid and Cuttlefish	Tamil-10,000	10,000
	Folder on shark fin/fish maws/fin rays	Tamil-10,000	10,000
1993-94	Folder on shark and shark based products	English-3,000	3,000
	Folder on guidelines for traditional fisherman	Malayalam-5,000, Kannada-2,000, Telugu-1,000, Tamil-6,000, Konkani-2,000, Bengali-3,000, Gujarathi-2,000, Marathi-4,000, Oriya-5,000	30,000
	Booklet on "Look" they will destroy me, you too' for pre-processing and processing workers	Malayalam-5,000	5,000
	Folder on processing of fish maws/shark	English-3,000, Tamil-10,000	13,000
	Folder on squid and cuttle fish	Tamil-10,000	10,000
	Folder on bacteria and seafoods	Tamil-10,000	10,000

produced during the first two years (two each per year) and one film each were produced during the last three years. The production of audio-visuals started in 1988-89 and during the period 36 audio-visuals were produced. During the last two years, 28 audiovisuals were produced. The details of films and audio-visuals produced by MPEDA during 1986-87 to 1995-96 are shown in Annexure 7.1.

Table 7.9 Films and Audiovisuals Produced During 1986-87 to 1995-96

Year	Number of Films	Number of Audiovisuals
1986-87	2	-
1987-88	2	-
1988-89	-	3
1989-90	-	-
1990-91	-	4
1991-92	-	1
1992-93	-	-
1993-94	1	-
1994-95	1	14
1995-96	1	14

Source: Compiled from the Annual Reports of The Marine Products Export Development Authority, Cochin.

Seminars and workshops provide a common platform to exchange views, get clarifications and to develop plans and programmes to face the future. They play a key role in the development of inter-personal understanding and relationships. MPEDA is organising seminars and workshop in various places in the country on various issues of importance involving all sections of the society who are contributing for the growth and development of fisheries sector particularly the export of marine products. The data presented in Table 7.10 reveals, during 1986-87 to 1995-96, the MPEDA has organised 27 seminars and five workshops. The details of the seminars and workshops organised by MPEDA are presented in Annexure 7.2.

MPEDA started releasing advertisements within the country since 1989-90. The focus of these advertisements are detailed in Table 7.11. The advertisements are mostly aimed at building up public relations with persons and organisations who are directly or indirectly involved or influential in the business. During 1990-91, a special supplement was brought out in the 'Economic Times' (daily newspaper) in connection with the inauguration of MPEDA Head Quarters Building. Since 1992-93, the focus was shifted towards popularising the activities, programmes and achievements of MPEDA and also highlighting the role of MPEDA in promoting export of marine products.

MPEDA is organising promotional campaigns in the importing countries through publication of books, printing and distribution of folders, book-lets brochures, posters and catalogues and by releasing advertisements in various journals. Further, it campaigns in the selected importing countries, by participating in trade fairs and exhibitions and also by taking part in international seminars and conferences.

Table 7.10: Seminars and Workshops Organised by the MPEDA During 1986-87 to 1995-96

Year	Seminars	Workshop
1986-87	1	-
1987-88	2	1
1988-89	4	2
1989-90	3	-
1990-91	3	-
1991-92	11	-
1992-93	1	-
1993-94	1	1
1994-95	-	1
1995-96	1	-

Source: Compiled from the Annual Reports of The Marine Products Export Development Authority, Cochin.

Table 7.12 presents the particulars relating to books published by MPEDA for importers. The major publication of MPEDA is the Directory of Exporters of Marine Products from India priced at Rs. 100.00. The directory is updated every year. A classified list of exporters was published in three different areas such as frozen shrimp and lobster tail, frozen cuttlefish, squid and other fish and canned and dried marine products. These publications are valued at Rs. 30.00, Rs. 25.00 and Rs. 15.00 respectively. The data presented in Table 7.13 shows the particulars relating to the folders, book-lets brochures, posters and catalogues printed and distributed by MPEDA during 1986-87 to 1995-96. The table reveals that during the decade two types of folders, 10 book-lets, none brochures, five posters and one catalogue were printed and distributed in different languages and in required number of copies. The details of the printing and distribution of this extension material are shown in Annexure7.3.

Table 7.11 The Focus of Advertisement with in India During 1989-90 1995-96

Year	Particulars
1989-90	A limited scale internal press advertisement programme mainly as a public relation activity was undertaken
1990-91	Apart from the regular limited scale internal press advertisement programme, a special supplement of the 'Economic Times' (all issues) was brought out in connection with the inauguration of the MPEDA head quarters building on June 11, 1990. A specially designed corporate advertisement was also released in all national and regional news papers to coincide with the inauguration of head quarters building.
1991-92	A limited scale internal press advertisement programme was carried out
1192-93	A limited scale internal press advertisement programme was carried out. - Press releases were issued on important activities of MPEDA
1993-94	Attractive advertisements were released in some of the leading Indian news papers and magazines highlighting activities/ achievements of MPEDA.
1994-95	Attractive advertisements were released in some of the leading Indian news papers, magazines highlighting activities/ achievements of MPEDA.
1995-96	Attractive advertisements released in 50 selected leading Indian news papers/magazines highlighting the role of MPEDA in promoting export of marine products.

Source:Compiled from the Annual Reports The Marine Products Export Development Authority, Cochin.

Table 7.14 shows the data relating to the media used for the release of advertisements by MPEDA in abroad. The mass communicatioin ampaign through advertisements was started in 1987-88 in print media targeted to overseas importers, Indian trade missions, other trade interesta and agencies in foreign countries. The number of journals used is fluctuating during the period ranging from 13 journals to 48 journals.

Table 7.12: Books Published by MPEDA for Importers

Title of the Book	Price/Copy Rs
Directory of Exporters of Marine Products from India	100
Classified list of exporters:	
i) Frozen Shrimp and Lobster Tail	30
ii) Frozen Cuttlefish, Squid and Other Fish	25
iii) Canned and Dried Marine Products	15

Table 7.13: Folders, Booklets, Brochures, Poster and Catalogues for Importers During 1986-87 to 1995-96

Year	Folders	Booklets	Brochures	Posters	Catalogues
1986-87	1	1	-	-	-
1987-88	1	1	1	-	-
1988-89	-	-	3	-	-
1989-90	-	1	1	1	-
1990-91	-	1	2	1	1
1991-92	-	4	-	-	-
1992-93	-	-	1	2	-
1993-94	-	2	-	1	-
1994-95	-	-	1	-	-
1995-96	-	-	-	-	-
Total	2	10	9	5	1

Source: Compiled from the Annual Reports of The Marine Products Export Development Authority, Cochin.

Table 7.14 Media used for the Release of Advertisements by MPEDA in Abroad During 1986-87 to 1995-96

Year	Number of Journals
1986-87	-
1987-88	27
1988-89	25
1989-90	20
1990-91	48
1991-92	18
1992-93	17
1993-94	13
1994-95	15
1995-96	16

Source: Compiled from the Annual Reports of The Marine Products Export Development Authority, Cochin.

The MPEDA has been actively taken part in trade fairs and exhibitions relating to fisheries sector within the country and outside the country. The data presented in Table 7.15 reveals, during the period from 1986-87 to 1995-96, the MPEDA has participated in 95 trade fairs and exhibitions - (52 fairs and 43 exhibitions), among which 35 are within India and 60 are outside India. It has participated more in number of exhibitions participation was registered in 1995-96 (17). The list of fairs and exhibitions within the country and when it comes to overseas market, the participation is more in number of fairs. The highest number of participation was registered in 1995-96 (17). The list of fairs and exhibitions participated by MPEDA in India is shown in Annexure 7.4. The list of overseas trade fairs and exhibitions in which in a few international seminars and conference to rise the voice of Indian fisheries sector, and to develop marketing opportunities. Table 7.16 presents the number of seminars and conferences in which MPEDA represented during 1986-87 to 1995-96. During the decade, MPEDA participated in five seminars and six conferences. The details of the seminar and conferences are presented in Annexure 7.6.

Table 7.15 Participation in Trade Fair and Exhibitions within India and Overseas During 1986-87 to 1995-96

Year	Within India		Overseas		Total
	Fairs	Exhibitions	Fairs	Exhibitions	
1986-87	1	2	2	2	7
1987-88	-	3	3	1	7
1988-89	-	2	4	2	8
1989-90	1	4	6	1	11
1990-91	-	2	5	1	8
1991-92	-	1	5	1	7
1992-93	-	5	2	1	8
1993-94	1	2	5	1	11
1994-95	1	4	5	1	11
1995-96	1	5	10	1	17
Total	5	30	47	13	95

Source: Compiled from the Annual Reports of The Marine Products Export Development Authority, Cochin.

Table 7.16 International Seminars and Conferences Attended During 1986-87 to 1995-96

Year	Seminars	Conferences
1986-87	-	-
1987-88	1	-
1988-89	3	-
1989-90	-	2
1990-91	1	1
1991-92	-	1
1992-93	-	1
1993-94	-	1
1994-95	-	-
1995-96	-	-

Source: Compiled from the Annual Reports of The Marine Products Export Development Authority, Cochin.

As a part of establishing relationships with various persons and institutions of importing countries, the MPEDA is extending invitation to the persons of eminence and importance to India. The data presented in Table 7.17 shows the number of persons visited India from abroad during 1986-87 to 1995-96. During the decade as many as 55 persons visited the country. The details of the persons visited are presented in Annexure 7.7.

Table 7.18 shows the trade enquiries received by MPEDA from within the country and outside the country during 1986-87 to 1995-96. The number of trade enquiries received shows the fluctuative trend during the period. The number has varied between 271 and 699. It is significant to note, during the last two years, the number of trade enquiries received was declined significantly. The table further reveals that the majority of trade enquires are from abroad in all the years.

The exporters of our country are facing problems relating to shipment of fish products. Finding space in a cargo-ship, and frequent hikes in freight rates, are the major problems. Non-availability of space for cargoes during seasons, in-frequent shipping facility, labour problems for loading, losses due to natural calamities and procedural complexities are some more problems being faced by the exporters, Unless these problems are solved amicably the exporters may not find it convenient to export fish and fish products.

They may get discouraged and demotivated due to the problems. The MPEDA is extending its helping hand to the exporters to find some solutions to the problems. It is acting as a liaison organisation between exporters and the concerned union governmental authorities to find proper solutions to ensure smooth shipment of the fish and fish products. The activities taken up by the MPEDA against different shipping problems during 1986-87 to 1995-96 are detailed in Annexure 7.8.

Table 7.17. Number of Persons Visited from Abroad During 1986-87 to 1995-96.

Year	Number of Persons
1986-87	6
1987-88	2
1988-89	6
1989-90	10
1990-91	-
1991-92	5
1992-93	-
1993-94	4
1994-95	7
1995-96	15

Source: Compiled from the Annual Reports of The Marine Products Export Development Authority, Cochin.

Table 7.18 Trade Enquiries Received from India and Abroad During 1986-87 to 1995-96

Year	India	Abroad	Total
1986-87	-	276	276
1987-88	-	271	271
1988-89	236	259	495
1989-90	172	275	447
1990-91	246	297	543
1991-92	230	408	638
1992-93	191	354	545
1993-94	281	418	699
1994-95	187	352	539
1995-96	132	363	495

Source: Compiled from the Annual Reports of The Marine Products Export Development Authority, Cochin.

The MPEDA has been striving for exploring the new markets for the Indian Products. It has been encouraging the exporters who are on the look out of introducing new products to the international markets and introducing the existing products to the new markets. For the purpose, it has introduced financial assistance scheme for air freighting samples to the markets outside the country. However, due to financial constraints, it could offer only the maximum of Rs. 5,000 to each exporter and that too for a limited number.

Annexure 7.1

Films and Audiovisual Brought up by MPEDA During 1986-87 to 1995-96

1986-87

a) "Deep Sea Trawler", a film showing fishing and processing on-board has been acquired for screening at the demonstration-cum-audio visual programmes.

b) 'Modernisation of Indian Seafood Industry" A film showing various aspects of fishing and processing of seafood in India was under production.

1987-88

a) Five Copies of 6mm print of the extension film title "Indian Seafood the New Era".

b) A new film on "Mariculture" have been procured for audio-visual programme.

1988-89

a) Three video tapes on hygienic handling of seafoods have been procured

1989-90

1990-91

The following video cassettes have been copied and a copy of each was forwarded to regional offices for arranging audiovisual programmes:

a) Evaluating fresh seafood quality.

b) Handling and evaluating seafood.

c) Shell fish sanitation.

Two video copies of the film "Indian Seafod-the New Era" were taken and a copy and forwarded to TPO Tokyo.

1991-92

MPEDA have produced a video cassettes "MPEDA-The Trend Setter in Seafood Export Promotion". For arranging audio-visual programmes.

Some cassettes on hygiene is seafood processing have also purchased.

All field officers have been equipped with audio-visual and public address systems.

Field officers have also been engaged in vocational guidance and dissemination of information to the industry as a whole.

1992-93

A number of cassettes procured during the year on hygiene in seafood processing and other aspects of seafood industry for arranging audio-visual programmes.

1993-94

A number of cassettes procured during the year on hygiene in seafood processing and other aspects of seafood industry for arranging audio-visual programmes.

M/s. MAA Communication Pvt. Ltd., Cochin has been engaged for production of a 16 mm colour documentary film on the entire gamut of activities of the seafood industry.

1995-95

Documentary film on various aspects of hygiene and sanitation, quality control measures and food manufacturing practices are either produced by MPEDA or procured from outside agencies and screened to the participants at the extension education programmes.

During the year, production of a 16 mm colour documentary on good manufacturing practices was almost completed.

14 Video cassettes on all subjects released to marine products were procured from outside agencies.

1995-96

Documentary film on various aspects of hygiene and sanitation, quality control measures and food manufacturing practices are either produced by MPEDA or procured from outside agencies and screened to the participants at the extension education programmes.

During the year, production of a 16mm colour documentary on good manufacturing practices was almost completed.

14 Video cassettes on all subjects released to marine products were procured from outside agencies.

Annexure 7.2

Seminars/Workshops/Training Programmes Organised by MPEDA during 1986-87 to 1995-96

1986-87

"FAO Technical Consultation of fish inspection and assurance quality for Asia and Pacific" at Cochin sponsored by FAO/ INFOFISH was hosted by the Authority, in which 50 delegates including Indian and overseas participants attended.

1987-88

Financial assistance was given for organising the following:

a) Seminar on Tropical Marine Living Resources at Cochin.
b) First Indian Fisheries Forum at Managalore.
c) National Seminar on Esturaries Management at Trivandrum.

1988-89

MPEDA extended the support to the organisation of the following:

1. Fisheries seminar at Cochin by All Kerala Deevara Sabha.
2. World Environmental Programme Organised by Greater Cochin Development Authority
3. Resources estimation using acoustics organised by the IFP Cochin.
4. Management seminar organised by Rajagiri College of Social Sciences Ernakulam.
5. National workshop on technology for small scale fish workers at Trivendram.
6. Seminar on advances in fisheries technology by the maharaja College, Ernakulam.

1989-90 Support was extended for organising the following:

a. Seminar on Advances in Fisheries Technology at Maharaja College, Cochin.
b. Fisheries Seminar by Dheevara Sabha, Cochin.
c. National Seminar on "Aquatic Pollution Strategies for Prevention and Management" at Trivandrum.

1990-91

"The New Exaim Poliy for 1990-93", one day seminar organised by MPEDA at Ernakulam, in association with Species Board for the benefit of trade and officials of MPEDA. MPEDA's officials were participated/attended in the following Seminars.

1. Seminar cum workshop on Export Finance, foreign Exchange and Project Finance organised by FIEO at Madras.
2. Seminar on export possibilities of food and industries organised by the Institute of Marketing and Management at Delhi.
3. International Seminar on food and agro based products.

1991-92

Financial support was extended for organising 11 seminars on subjects relating to aquaculture by various organisations.

1992-93

MPEDA contributed financially to the seminars conducted to review the status of various aspects of aquaculture and to popularise the concept of scientific aquaculture/seminars have been organised by the developmental agencies under Central and State Governments.

1993-94

MPEDA contributed financially to the seminars conducted to review the status of various aspects of aquacultre and to popularise the concept of scientific aquaculture/seminars have been organised by the developmental agencies under Central and State Governments.

1994-95

MPEDA contributed financially to the seminars conducted to review the status of various aspects of aquacultre and to popularise the concept of scientific aquaculture/seminars have been organised by the developmental agencies under Central and State Governments.

MPEDA organised a 3 day workshop on shrimp disease in association with INFOFISH about 70 farmers and Indian experts attended the workshop.

The Joint Director (Prawn Farming) was deputed to attend "Aquatech-95", International Conference on Aquaculture organised by INFOFISH Kuala Limpur, in Colombo (Srilanka).

1995-96

MPEDA contributed financially to the seminars conducted to review the status of various aspects of aquacultrue and to popularise the concept of scientific aquacultre/seminars have been organised by the developmental agencies under Central and State Governments.

MPEDA organised a "National Seminar on Environmental and Social Impact of Coastal Aquaculture and Related Problems in India" at Madras.

Annexure 7.3
Printing and Distribution of Extension Material by MPEDA During 1986-87 to 1995-96

Year	Material
1986-87	1. Multi colour and multi lingual publicity folders for international fairs and exhibitions.
	2. Corporate Booklet on the occasion of 7th Indian Seafood Trade Fair.
1987-88	3. Multi colour and multi lingual publicity folders for international fairs and exhibitions.
	4. A brochure on Indian Seafood Industry.
	5. A Booklet on 'Surimi' products for distribution in Foodex Fair Tokyo.
1988-89	6. A publicity brochure in Japanese language for distribution in the Hoters and Foodex Jaupon-1989 at Tokyo.
	7. A multi coloured brochure on Indian Marine Products for distribution in international fairs.
	8. Another brochure on the role and functions of MPEDA.
1989-90	9. Multicolour illustrated poster on commercial fishes in India.
	10. Product-wise classified booklets of registered exporters.
	11. Multi-colour and multi lingual promotional brochure on Indian Marine Products.
1990-91	12. Multi colour and multi lingual promotional brochure (English, French and Spanish)
	13. Poster on Commercial Fishes in India.
	14. Product catalogue on Indian Seafoods.
	15. Promotional brochure in Japanese language.
	16. A corporate booklet on major functions and contributions of MPEDA
1991-92	17. Corporate booklet om MPEDA
	18. Three classified booklets on Exporters of Indian Marine Products.
	19. 3,000 copies of publicity posters.
1992-93	20. Posters on Commercial fishes of India sent to more than 60 Indian Missiions abroad.
	21. A brochure on MPEDA activities.
	22. 3,000 copies of poster on commercial fishes of India.
1993-94	23. Two sets of corporate booklet on MPEDA activities
	24. 5, 0000 copies of poster on commercial fishes in India.
1994-95	25. Multi-lingual brochure on Indian seafoods.
1995-96	

Annexure 7.4
Fairs and Exhibitions Participated by MPEDA During 1986-87 to 1995-96

Year	Fair/Exhibition	Number
1986-87	Exhibition on fisheries development - Trivandrum September, 1986.	1
	World Food Day Exhibition, Malipuram, October, 1986.	1
		2
1987-88	Exhibition on the 'Role of Marine Products in the Developing Economy of the Country', Bhubaneswar, June, 1987.	1
	Silver Jubilee celebrations Exhibition, Pondicherry, August, 1987.	1
	Decennial Celebration Exhibition, Bhavan's Vidya Mandir, Cochin, August, 1987	1
		3
1988-89	The 8th Indian Seafood Trade Fair, Madras (February 10-12, 1989).	1
	National Agriculture Fair, New Delhi (march-April 1989)	1
		2
1989-90	National Maritime Day Celebration Exhibition, Visakhapatnam, April 1-5, 1989. Spice Fair, Cochin April, 9-11, 1989.	1
	The Exhibition on Fisheries and Veterinary Sciences, Madras (September, 20-22, 1989).	1
	The Exhibition on Nehru's Vision on Public Sector Undertakings in India, Bangalore, November 7.24, 1989.	1
	Exhibition in connection with the 77th Indian Science Congress, Cochin, January, 26-February 17th, 1990.	1
		5

(Cont.)...

Year	Event	No.
1990-91	First World Spice Congress, Bangalore, November 1-3, 1990.	1
	International Seafood Festival, Goa, November 27-December, 2, 1990	1
		2
1991-92	MPEDA participated in the International Seafood Festival, Goa during November, 20-24, 1991.	1
1992-93	MPEDA participated in the "INDFEST '92", at Cochin during May 5-24, 1992.	1
	Participated in the "Second World Spice Congress" organised by the Spices Board, Cochin at Leela Beach, Goa during Nobrmbrt 5-7, 1992 as an exhibitor.	1
	Participated as an exhibitor in the Food and Cultural Festival of Goa held at Goa during 25-29 November, 1992 organised by the Goa Tourism Department.	1
	Participated in the Malabar Mahotsavam and Seafood Exhibition held at Calicut during 5-11 February, 1993 by taking a stall and our stall was given the "Best Stall" award of the show.	1
	Participated in the Aquafest 93-Aquaculture Show and Exhibition, held at Cochin during 24-28 February, 1993 by the Industrial fisheries Association, Cochin by taking a stall.	1
		5
1993-94	Trissur Pooram Exhibition, 28th April to 12th May, 1993.	1
	INFOFEST-93, National Book Fair, November 20-28,	1
	1993 at Town Hall, Cochin.	1
	Maha Mela-93-24th December, 1993 to 2nd January, 1994 at Vali, Fort cochin.	1
		3

(Cont.)...		
1994-95	INFOFEST Book Exhibition, 26-11-94 to 4.12-1994 Ernakulam.	1
	State level agriculture fair, December 14-18, 1994, Trivandrum.	1
	Matsya Vijanana Mela 94 24-12-94 to 1-1-1995, Mangalore.	1
	CENFEST 95- 10-2-95 to 5-3-3995, Ponnani.	1
	Agri Expo 95, New Delhi - March 8-11, 1995.	1
		5
1995-96	Agricultural and Agro Process Export Exhibition Kumbakonam-7th July, 1995	1
	National Rubber Conference-Kochi-November 3-4, 1995.	1
	National food Fair-Kochi-December 2-10, 1995.	1
	National Food Fair-Kochi-December 2-10, 1995.	1
	Agrivision 2000, Bangalore-December 23-January 12, 1996.	1
	AHARA 1996-New 8-11 March, 1996.	1
	Agri Expo, New Delhi-March 1996.	1
		6

Annexure 7.5

Overseas Trade Fairs and Exhibitions Participated by MPEDA During 1986-87 to 1995-96

Year	Particulars	Number
1986-87	Annual Harare Agriculture Show, Harare (August 25 to September 7, 1986)	1
	Sial International food products Exhibition, Paris (October 20-24, 1986)	1
	The 5th International Food and Drink Exhibition, London(February 1-5, 1987)	1
	Hoteres and Foodex Japan, Tokyo (March 11-15, 1987)	1
		4
1987-88	Indian Trade Exhibition, Singapore, April 6-12, 1987.	1
	International Food Fair of Scandinavia, Copenhagen, Dernmark, April 10-14, 1987.	1
	Anuga Food Fair, Cologne, FRG, October 10-15, 1987.	1
	Hoteres and Foodex Japan 88, Tokyo March 8-12, 1988.	1
		4
1988-89	Seafood Asia '88, Singapore (September 8-11', 88).	1
	Sial International Food Products Exhibition, Paris (October 17-21, 1988).	1
	6th International Food and Drink Exhibition, London(January 29-February 2, 1989).	1
	New York Seafood Show, New York (October, 25-26, 1988)Boston Seafood Show, Boston (March 7-9, 1989).	1
	Hoteres and Foodex Japan 89, Tokyo (March 7-11, 1989).	
		6
1989-90	Anuga Food Fair, Cologne, October, 14-19, 1989.	1
	19th Kobe Import Fair, Kobe, October, 19-22, 1989.	1

(Cont.)...

	New York Seafood Show, New York, October, 24-25, 1989	1
	Alimentaria 90 International Food Fair, Barcelona, March, 3-8, 1990.	1
	Hoteres and Foodex Japan, Tokyo, March, 13-17, 1990.	1
	Boston Seafood Show, Boston, March, 20-22, 1990.	1
		6
1990-91	International Fishing Fair (1st Seafood Show) Ancona (Itlay) May, 24-27, 1990.	
	Sial International Food Products Exhibition, Pairs, October 22-26, 1990	1
	Sea Fare South East Orlando (West Coast), USA, October, 31-November 1,1990.	1
	Sea Fare International, Long Beach (West Coast), USA,February, 12-14, 1991.	1
	Boston Internal Seafood Show Boston, USA March 12-14, 1991.	1
	Boston International Seafood Show, Boston, USA, March 12-14, 1991.	1
	Hoteres and Foodex Japan 1991, Tokyo, March 12-16, 1991.	1
		6
1991-92	The 7th International Food and Drink Exhibition, London, April 28-May 2, 1991.	1
	Hoteres and Foodex, Osaka, Japan, September, 17-20, 1991.	1
	Anuga Food Fair, Cologne, Germany, October, 12-17, 1991.	1
	Alimentary International Food Fair, Barcelona, Spain, March 7-12, 1992.	1
	Hoteres and Foodex, Japan 1992, Tokyo, March, 10-14,1992.	1
	Boston Seafood Show, Boston, USA, March, 17-19, 1992.	1
		6

(Cont.)...

1992-93	15th Sial International Food Products Exhibition, Paris, 25-29 October, 1992.	1
	Hoteres and Foodex, Tokyo, Japan, 9-13 March, 1993.	1
	Boston Seafood Show, Boston, March, 16-18, 1993.	1
1993-94	European Seafood Exposition, Brussels, Belgium April 20-22, 1993.	1
	International Food and Drink Exhibition, London, April 25-28, 1993.	1
	Tokyo International Seafood Show, June 10-12, 1993, Tokyo, Japan	1
	International Seafood Process Exhibition (SEAPEX), Lorient, France, Sept. 8-12, 1993.	1
	Anuga Food Fair, Cologne, Germany, October, 25-29, 1993.	1
	Alimentaria 94, March 1-6, 1994, Barcelona.	1
	Hoteres and Foodex Fair, Japan, March 7-11, 1994.	1
	Boston Seafood Show, Boston, March 15-17, 1994.	1
		8
1994-95	Food and Hotel Asia '94, 12-15 April 1994, Singapore.	1
	European Seafood Exposition, April 19-21, 1994.	1
	Second Tokyo International Seafood Show 21-23, June, 1994.	1
	Sial Food Fair, Paris, October 23-27, 1994.	1
	Foodex Japan, 1995, March 7-11, 1995.	1
	International Boston Seafood, Show, March 14-16, 1995.	1
		6
1995-96	European Seafood Exposition May 9-22, 1995-Brussels.	1
	3rd Tokyo International Seafood Show, June, 13-15, 1995.	1
	Seafood China, 16-19, October, '95 at Beijing.	1

(Cont.)...

Fish Africa 1995, South Africa, November, 30-2nd December, 1995.	1
MEFEX '96, Behrain, 13-16 January 1996.	1
The Bangkok Seafood Show 1996, January 29-22nd Feb.1996.	
Alimentaria '96, Barcelona, March 4-9, 1996.	1
The International Boston Seafood Show, March 12-14, 1996.	1
Foodex 1996, Japan, March 12-15, 1996.	1
Fine Food, Brisbane, March 17-19, 1996.	1
Food and Hotel Asia 1996, Singapore, April 16-19, 1996.	1
	11

Annexure 7.6
International Seminars and Conferences Represented During 1986-87 to 1995-96

1986-87	
1987-88	The Japan External Trade Organisation (JETRO) sponsored an International Seminar on Shrimp Industry at Tokyo during September 1987. Chairman of the Authority represented India and made a presentation on Indian shrimp industry and trade.
1988-89	Resident Director, TPO, New York represented MPEDA at the 43rd NFI convention during April 1988 at New York. Chairman, MPEDA participated in the FAO/SEAFDEC/INFOFISH sponsored seminar on Investment on Fisheries at Bangkok during October, 1988. Director, MPEDA represented India in the 3rd session of the INFOFISH Governing Council held at Dhaka in November 1988.
1989-90	The Resident Director, TPO, New York, represented MPEDA at the 44th Annual Contribution of the National Fishery Institute (NFI) at Las Gegas on April 9-12, 1989. The Authority hosted the Shrimp Industry meeting at the 'Seafood 90 Japan International Conference at Kyoto (Japan) on March 12-14, 1990, for which an amount of US $ 4,000/- was contributed. Chairman, MPEDA, was the Moderator of the meeting and an Indian exporter of marine products participated as a lead speaker.
1990-91	The Resident Director, TPO, New York, represented MPEDA (1) in the Seminar 'Srimpology 2000, New orleans, USA, in October, 1-2, 1990 and (2) in the 45th Annual Convention of National fisheries Institute (NFI), San Francisco, November, 4-7, 1990. As the National Liaison Office of INFOFISH in India, the Authority Co-ordinated the organisational arrangements for hosting the 5th session of the INFOFISH Governing Council at Goa on October, 31-November 2, 1990.
1991-92	Chairman participated in the 46th Annual Convention of NFI held during October 30-November 2, 1991, in New Orleans, USA.
1992-93	Chairman participated in the International Conference Shrimp 1992, Hong Kong held during 14-16, September, 1992.
1993-94	MPEDA participated in the 48th Annual NFI convention at Washington, USA from 3rd to 6th November, 1993.
1994-95	-
1995-96	-

Annexure 7.7

Foreigners Invited by MPEDA to India During 1986-87 to 1995-96

Year	Particulars of the persons visited from abroad	Number
1986-87	Managing Director, JMPIA, Tokyo	1
	Acting President, JMPIA, Tokyo	1
	Director, JETRO, Tokyo	1
	President Shrimp World Inc. New Orleans	1
	Publisher, Quick frozen food International, New York	
	Editor-in-chief, AFZ, Fishch magazine, Hamburg	1
		6
1987-88	Leading seafood Importers from Finalnd	2
1988-89	Director, USFDA	1
	President shore lobster and Shrimp corporation New Jersey	1
	Director Association of Seafood Importers Inc. New York	1
	Regional Manager, Fisheries lab of borocholm-Balticsea, Denmark	1
	Editor, Seafood International, London	1
		6
1989-90	Assistant Deputy Minister of Agriculture and Fisheries and two other officials from UAE	3
	Senior Editor, Seafood leader, a leading fishery journal in the US	1
	Four member fishery delegation from USSR	4
	Representatives of influential Italian fishery magazine 'IL PESSCE'	2
1990-91		
1991-92	President, Japan Marine Products Importers Association (JMPIA) Tokyo	1
	Director, Seafood business USA	1
	Director, Fishery Agency, Japan	1
	Representatives of CONFREPECHE France	1
	Representatives of Arista Industries Inc. USA	1
		5
1992-93	–	
1993-94	Prof. of State University of Ghent, Belgium	1
	Representative of M/s. New Toyo seafoods company Ltd. Japan.	1
	President JMPIA, Japan	1
	Editor of II PESCW, Italy	1
		4
1994-95	Visit of the Italian Health Ministry Officials	2
	Visit of French Health authority Officials	3
	Visit of EC evaluation team	2

1995-96	MPEDA co-ordinated the visits of importers/officials and also Indian officials for discussion with the trade and visit to processing plants in India.	7 2
	2 Experts from Germany visited MPEdA and Indian Institute of Packing, Bombay. Meetings were arranged with fish processing and packing industries at Cochin and Bombay.	
	A 10 member Norwegian delegation visited MPEDA and had discussions with the officials	10
	3 Officials of USFDA visited seafood processing units in Bombay, Madras, Cochin and Government laboratories also to witness and assess the quality themselves, the quality of process and product of Indian seafood plants and to have an exchange of 2 ideas with the seafoof plants and to have an exchange of ideas with the seafood industry and the inspection agencies the officials expressed their satisfaction over the progress of Indian seafood industry. They also appreciated the close relationship of Trade and India Government.	15

Annexure 7.8
Shipping Problems Handled by MPEDA During 1986-87 to 1995-96

1986-87 Quarterly reefer cargo projections were communicated to concerned authorities facilitating the shipping lines to provide adequate shiping space for the export of frozen marine products of different destinations. The MPEDA comments on proposed legislation for 40 per cent cargo support to Indian lines forwarded to the Ministry and the all India Shippers Council with a request that the marine products may be exempted from the purview of the legislation for the time being.

1987-88 Since the reefer vessels were not calling at Vizag port regularly, the MPEDA made the arrangements for the shipment of frozen cargo from Vizag by taking up the matter with the Shipping Corporation of India, Bombay. The MPEDA suggestions on various issues like port charges at Cochin port, break bulk vessels/direct sailing, freight rates/terminal handling charges etc. were furnished to the Ministry and taken up at the'SCOPE SHIPPING' meetings. The requirements of space in air crafts for export of chilled/ fresh fish for Kuwait, Singapore etc. has been collected from the exporters and communicated to the Ministry.

1988-89 The exporters in Vizag, Paradeep, Calcutta, Veraval and Probundar were assisted to solve their problems in shipping their frozen cargo by persuading the shipping lines viz. SCI, APL, TAIYO fisheries etc. to place their reefer vessels/containers.

Hike in Freight rates

The details of freight hike on export of marine products from Bombay, Cochin, Calcutta, Madras to main markets have been furnished to the Ministry of Commerce in order to take up the matter with the Ministry of Surface Transport.

Scope Shipping Meetings

MPEDA suggestions on various aspects of shipping problems viz. freight rate, wharfage at Calcutta port, non-availability of reefer sailings/containers facilities from minor ports to different destinations at UK/continent, USA etc. and non-availability of container facilities at Gujarat port is furnished to the Ministry of Commerce to be taken up in the Scope Shipping Meetings

Shipping -reefer Cargo Projections

In order to facilitate the shipping lines concerned to provide adequate refer cargo coverage the estimated projection of frozen marine products for exports to major foreign markets was communicated to the Ministry of Commerce, Shipping Agents Association, Shippers Association, Directional General of Shipping etc.

1989-90

Shipping problems

Exporters in Gujarat, West Bengal, Andhra Pradesh and Orissa have been assisted to solve their problems to ship their frozen cargo by persuading the concerned shipping lines to place their reefer vessels/containers at the ports specify.

Hiking freight rates

The details of freight hikes on major items of marine products were furnished to the ministry for taking up the matter suitably with the Ministry of Surface Transport.

Shipping reefer cargo projections

The cargo projections for marine products for exporters on quarterly basis from various Indian ports to major foreign markets were made regularly and communicated to concerned authorities to facilitate the shipping lines to berth timely reefer vessel at various Indian Ports.

1990-91

Shipping problems

The shipping problems faced by exporters of Madras and Calcutta regions have been taken up with the high commissioner of India, Singapore and Ministry of Commerce and solved their problems of shipment of marine products to Japan and European Countries during May-June 1990.

The shippers of Orissa region brought to the notice of MPEDA to solve their problem of not placing reefer vessels at paradeep port by the shipping lines. The MPEDA requested the Shipping Corporation of India of Calcutta to place a small refer vessel at paradeep port regularly so as to help the exporters to ship out their frozen cargo to the destinations.

Shipping reefer cargo projections

Estimated reefer cargo projections of frozen marine products on quarterly basis from various Indian ports to major foreign markets were compiled and communicated to the concerned authorities to facilitate shipping lines to schedule reefer sailings at various Indian ports in time.

As deserved by Ministry of Commerce a detailed note relating to shipping problems was prepared and forwarded for considerations of the sub-committee on infrastructure constituted by a board of Trade.

1991-92

Shipping Problems

The problems faced by the exports at Cochin port due to "Goslow" call of dock labour was brought to the notice of the chairman. The matter was taken up strongly with the port trust authorities and the problems has been solved tempararily.

Matters relating to shipping/Air -freighting which were brought to the notice of MPEDA have been taken up with the concerned authorities. As desired by Western India Shippers' Association, Bombay, a brief note on the problem faced by the seafood exporters was prepared and sent to WISA, for presentation at its annual general meeting.

1992-93

Shipping Problems

MPEDA helped in establishment of integrated container freight station cum frozen at Tuticorin with Tuticorin Port trust.

The exporters of Orissa brought to the notice of MPEDA the problem of withdrawal of "Sea land" vessels from Paradeep Port. Necessary action was taken to persuade "Sea land" vessels to continue to place their vessels at this port.

Similarly, the problems faced by Mangalore seafood exporters due to the withdrawal of vessels by M/s. Cyclone Shipping Corporation was taken up with the concerned and the problems were settled amicably.

Further matters relating to shipping air freighting brought to the notice of MPEDA has taken up with the concerned authorities.

Reefer cargo projections

In order to enable the exporters to get reefer vessels and air cargoes for smooth export operations the export projections were collected and send to the concerned for providing adequate reefer and air cargo space.

One exporter has informed us about the loss of two stuffed containers in the cyclonic storm which hit Tuticorin port.

MPEDA took up the matter with the concerned shipping lines to sort out the issue amicably.

1993-94

Air cargo projections

Air cargo projections for marine products from Cochin, Bombay, Madras, Calcutta for the period of September, 1993 to August 1994 were collected and sent to all concerned for providing adequate reefer space.

1994-95

Reefer cargo projections

Quarterly estimated reefer cargo projections were sent to the Ministry of Commerce/Ministry of Transport and other concerned Authorities.

The exporters were suitably informed of the revised procedure of customs/ Central Excise for movement of empty containers from docks for factory stuffing.

Sessions of Scope Shipping

Sessions of Scope AIR/SCOPE AIR/SCOPE SHIPPING were attended and the issues raised by trade/Ros/SROs were discussed. Follow-up action was taken up so as to remove the problems of exporters.

1995-96

In-house stuffing facilities

In September, 1995, customs authorities issued notice duly withdrawing the in-house stuffing facilities to export cargo of marine products at various ports. MPEDA took up the matter with the Ministry of Commerce and customs authorities as a result the in-house stuffing facilities to all frozen and perishable items including seafoods were restored.

Sessions of Scope Air/Scope Shipping

The 32nd session of Scope air and the 24th session of Scope Shipping were held at Cochin on 16th and 17th November, 1995. The Chairman, MPEDA attended the meeting and participated in the deliberations. The problems of the industry were presented before the session and necessary follow-up action were taken up so as to solve the problems of exporters.

Estimated projection of reefer cargo

Estimated reefer cargo projections for marine products from various Indian ports were collected and forwarded to the Ministry and Shipping lines concerned to provide adequate reefer container facilities.

REFERENCE

1. Mamoria, C.B., and Mamoria, S., "Marketing Management', Kitab Mahal, Allahabad, 1997. p.415.

2. Chunawalla, S.A., 'Marketing Principles and Practice', Himalaya Publishing House, Mumbai, 1997, p.343.

3. Chhabra, T.N., and Grover, S.K., 'Marketing Management', Dhanapatrai and Co. (Pvt) Ltd., Delhi, 1997, p.5.3.

4. The Marine Products Export Development Authority, The Author, Handbook on Shrimp Farming, Cochin, 1994, p.5.

8

Exporters Profile and Views

The objective of this chapter is to study the business operations of the exporting units and the personal profile of the exporters of fish and fish products. The views of the exporters on various aspects relating to export of fish and fish products from India are collected and presented. The findings of the study will be useful to the policy makers to understand the problems and opinions of the exporters and design such programmes which will be really of benefiting to the exporters.

EXPORTERS PROFILE

The age of the exporting units surveyed are shown in Table 8.1. The table reveals, the age of 70 per cent of the units varied between five years and 15 years. Ten per cent of the units were established during the last five years while 3.3 per cent of the units had an experience of more than 25 years. The particulars relating to the age of the respondents (all of them are owners of the exporting units) are presented in Table 8.2. The table reveals, about 78 per cent of the total respondents are in the age group of 30 to 50 years. Twenty per cent of the respondents are above 50 years of age while the remaining 3.3 per cent are below 30 years age. Table 8.3 depicts the educational background of the respondents. Out of the total, 50 per cent of the respondents are graduates and 13.33 per cent are post-graduates. The table reveals, a little over 13 per cent of the respondents had technical qualification in fisheries while 23.34 per cent of the respondents had technical qualification in areas other than fisheries.

Table 8.1: Age of the Exporting Unit

Age (years)	Percentage of Establishments
Less than 5	10.00
5-10	30.00
10-15	30.00
15-20	13.34
20-25	3.33
25 and Above	3.33
Total	100.00

Table 8.2: Age of the Respondents

Age (Years)	Percentage
20-30	3.30
30-40	36.67
40-50	40.00
50-60	13.33
60 and Above	6.67
Total	100.00

Table 8.3 : Educational Background of the Respondents

Particulars	Percentage
Primary Education	–
Secondary Education	–
Graduation	50.00
Post-Graduation	13.33
Technical (Fisheries)	13.33
Technical (others)	23.34
Total	100.00

The respondents were asked to reveal the first three reasons, in the order of influence, for entering into the business. After assigning weightages* ages to various reasons, the total factor weightage against each reason was presented in Table 8.4. The table reveals, vocational advantage is the most influencing factor (96 points) followed by high profitability (92 points) and inheritence (86 points). An attempt is made to know the persons who motivated the respondents to enter into the business. The respondents were asked to give three sources that motivated them in the order of influence. After assigning the factor weightage the scores are calculated and presented in Table 8.5. The table reveals, self motivation occupy first position (108 points) followed by parents (96 points), friends (86 points) and relatives (70 points). Out of the total, 36.67 per cent of the respondents had business experience before entering into the present line of activity (Table 8.6). The nature of the earlier business include fishing trawlers leasing and hiring (10 respondents) civil contracts (4 respondents) edible oil business (2) deepsea fishing (2) electronics and electricals (2) and representatives to importers (2). Out of the total, only six respondents representing 10 pre cent, took formal training before starting the business and the others have not undergone training before starting the business (Table 8.7).

Table 8.4 : Reasons for Entering into the Business

Reasons	Score
Inherited business	86
Lack of employment elsewhere	8
Less investment required	20
Have technical know-how	58
High profitability	92
Locational advantage	96

An attempt has been made to know the particulars relating to registration of the respondents with MPEDA as exporters of fish

* The factor weightsage for the reasons were given as following:
First influencing factor -3 points
Second influencing factor - 2 points
Third influencing factor -1 point

and fish products. The data presented in Table 8.8 shows that 80 per cent of the respondents got registered with MPEDA during the last ten years. The experience of 20 per cent of the respondents as registered exporters varied between 10 and 20 years. The study reveals, the MPEDA took seven days to 30 days to register the respondents after they have applied for registration. In 60 per cent of the cases, the time taken was about two weeks for registration. When respondents are asked whether they have faced any problems in obtaining registration from MPEDA, 60 per cent revealed, they did not face any problem whereas 40 per cent revealed they have faced some problems like procedural complexities, irresponsible behaviour of MPEDA employees, etc.

Table 8.5 : Who Motivated You to Enter into the Business?

Particulars	Score
Self	108
Parents	96
Relatives	70
Friends	86

Table 8.6 : Were you in any other Business Activity Before Entering into the Present Business?

Particulars	Percentage	Details of Previous Business Activity Name of the business	Number
Yes	36.67	Civil contracts	4
		Edible oil business	2
		deepsea fishing	2
No	63.33	Fishing Trawlers leasing (hiring)	10
		Delear in electronics and electricals	2
		Foreign buyers representative	2
Total	100.00	Total	22

INCOME AND EXPENDITURE

An attempt has been made to know the break-up of various costs incurred by the respondents. The details as presented in Table 8.9.

It can be seen from the table, the percentage share of cost of goods sold in the total cost of production was 94.02 per cent on an average. While the administrative and other overheads accounted for 3.16 per cent, marketing expenses were to the tune of 2.82 per cent. In the area of marketing, the expenditure is made under broad heads of advertising, packaging, transportation, storage and sales promotion. Among them packaging charges is the major expenditure item followed by storage and transportation.

Table 8.7: Have you Taken any Training Before Starting the Business?

Particulars	Percentage
Yes	10.00
No	90.00
Total	100.00

Table 8.8 : When did you got Registered as an Exporter with the MPEDA?

Years (range)	Percentage
0-5	26.67
5-10	53.33
10-15	13.3
15-10	6.67
Total	100.00

Table 8.9: Details of Expenditure During 1996-97

Particulars	Expenditure (Rupees in lakhs) Total percentage
Cost of goods sold	94.02
Administrative and other overheads	3.16
Marketing expenses	
a) Advertising	0.04
b) Packing charges	1.04
c) Transportation	0.74
d) Storage	0.91
e) Sales promotion	0.09
Total	100.00

The details relating to the annual turnover of the respondents are shown in Table 8.10. The turnover during 1996-97 was ranging between less than one crore rupees and Rs. 30 crores and above. As many as 43.33 per cent of the respondents had a turnover ranging from Rs. 10 crores to Rs. 20 crores. The turnover of 20 per cent of the respondents varied between one crore rupees and Rs. 10 crores. The turnover of 16.67 per cent of the respondents was in the range of Rs. 20 crores to Rs. 30 crores, while the same number of respondents achieved a turnover of Rs. 30 crores and above.

Table 8.10 :Turnover of the Respondents from the Units During 1996-97

Range-wise annual turnover (Rupees in crores)	Percentage
Less than 1 crore	3.33
1-5	13.33
5-10	6.67
10-15	16.67
15-10	26.66
20-25	6.67
25-30	10.00
30 and Above	16.67
Total	100.00

Table 8.11: Business Results for the Years 1995-96 and 1996-97

(Rupees in lakhs)

Particulars	Total profit	Average
1995-96	956.02	31.87
1996-97	1,407.00	46.90
Percentage of increase or decrease over previous year	47.17	

Table 8.11 reveals range-wise business results of the same units during 1995-96 and 1996-97. The total profit earned by all the concerns was Rs. 956 crores in 1995-96 which was increased to Rs. 14.07 crores in 1996-97 recording an increase of 47.17 per cent. In other words, the average profits earned by the units which was Rs. 31.87 lakhs in 1995-96 increased to Rs. 46.90 lakhs in 1996-97. The respondents revealed the profitability varies from consignment to consignment and during a year they may loose on some

consignments and gain on some consignments. Overall, the respondents revealed that they earned the profits by the end of the financial year. The range-wise profits earned by the respondents was shown in Table 8.12. The table reveals, the profits earned by about 47 per cent of the respondents was less than Rs. 20 lakhs each in 1995-96. The percentage of the respondents under this profit category reduced to about 38 per cent in the subsequent year. There are about 27 per cent of the respondents who earned a profit ranging from Rs. 20 lakhs to Rs. 60 lakhs each in 1995-96. The percentage of this profit category increased to 30 per cent in the subsequent year. The concerns that earned a profit ranging from Rs. 60 lakhs to one crore each constitute 20 per cent to the total in 1995-96 and the same was 22.33 per cent in 1996-97. The concerns which earned one crore rupees and above were 6.67 per cent in 1995-96 and 10 per cent in 1996-97.

Table 8.12: Range-wise Business Results for the Last Two Years 1995-96 and 1996-97

Range of profits (Rupees in lakhs)	Percentage of units 1995-96	1996-97
Less than 10	30.00	16.67
10-20	16.67	21.00
20-40	16.66	13.33
40-60	10.00	16.67
60-80	10.00	10.00
80-1 crore	10.00	12.33
1 crore and Above	6.67	10.00
Total	100.00	100.00

ORGANISATION SYSTEM

The fish and fish products exporters have varied forms of organisations. They include sole-proprietary, partnership, public limited company and private limited company. The data presented in Table 8.13 reveals, the majority of the respondents representing 52.33 per cent are having public limited companies. The reasons for preference include economies of large-scale, greater scope for expansion and the possibility for professional management. Out of the total, 30 per cent are private limited companies. The reasons for preference include economies of large-scale along with greater freedom of operations. Only 10 per cent preferred partnership form of organisation to derive the benefits of having services from friends, relatives to carry out the business operations successfully. Out of the total, 6.67 per cent preferred to remain as sole, proprietors to have total freedom and control over business operations.

Table 8.13 : Form of Organisation

Particulars	Percentage	Reasons for Preference
Sole proprietor	6.67	Complete freedom, no interference by others, ownership control.
Joint family	—	—
Partnership	10.00	To have the services of friends and relatives in all aspects of the business
Private Company	30.00	To enjoy the economies of large scale, greater freedom of operations
Public Company	53.33	To enjoy the economies of large scale, greater scope for expansion, professional management
Co-operative	—	—
Total	100.00	

The employment particulars of the sample units are presented in Table 8.14. The units are engaging full-time employees and part-time employees to carry out the operations. The employees under managerial cadre are all full-time employees. Below the managerial cadre, there are two cadres such as technical staff and non-technical staff. Technical staff includes assistant processing manager, technologist, technical supervisor, technical assistant and female contract labour for processing, and non-technical staff includes accountant, clearical staff, receptionist, attenders, sweepers, tea boy, watch man, etc. The contract labour are engaged only in the category of technical staff. All non-technical staff are full-time employees. The table reveals, there are 170 employees under managerial cadre including ten female employees. On an average, each unit has three managerial personnel one each in the categories of MD/ED, office manager and plant manager. The number of technical staff used by the sample units was 3,600, out of which 2,600 are contract labour and 1,000 are full-time workers. The full-time technical staff in all the organisations are male members while contract labour in all the organisations are women. The reason being the women are most suitable for certain technical processes and in such processes the requirement is only seasonal. In the category of non-technical staff there are 730 employees comprising 604 men and 126 women. Some respondents revealed that they are experiencing shortage of skilled workers.

Table 8.14 : Details of Employment

Cadre	Number					
	Full time			Contract Labour		
	Male	Female	Total	Male	Female	Total
A. Managerial:						
1. Managing/ Executive Director	50	-	50	-	-	-
2. Office Manager	50	10	60	-	-	-
3. Plant Manager	60	-	60	-	-	-
A. Total	160	10	170	-	-	-
B. Others:						
1. Technical Staff	1,000	-	1,000	-	2,600	2,600
2. Non-technical Staff	604	126	730	-	-	-
B. Total	1,604	126	1,730	-	2,600	2,600
Grand total (A+B)	1,764	136	1,900	-	2,600	2,600

Note: Technical staff includes, assistant processing manager, technologist, technical supervisor, technical assistant and female contract labour for processing.

Non-technical staff includes, accountant, clearical staff, receptionist, attenders, sweepers, tea boy, watchman, etc.

CAPITAL STRUCTURE

An attempt has been made in the study to know the capital structure of the responding units. The data presented in Table 8.15 reveals, the component of working capital constitutes 58.23 per cent in the total capital, the remaining being the fixed capital. On an average each unit invested Rs. 298.50 lakhs on working capital and Rs. 250.02 lakhs on fixed capital. The table reveals the proportion of own funds in the fixed capital is more while the reverse is true in the case of working capital. Out of the total, 61.62 per cent of the fixed capital was mobilised from the own sources of the units. Where as 69.54 per cent of the working capital was raised from external sources. The sources of borrowed capital are banks, and friends and relatives. Out of the total borrowed funds, either for fixed or working capital, 97.50 per cent were provided by banks. The friends and relatives contributed only 2.50 per cent in the total borrowed capital (Table 8.16.).

Table 8.15 : Capital Structure

(Rupees in lakhs)

	Own		Borrowed		Total	
Particulars	Percentage share	Average	Percentage share	Average	Percentage share	Average
Fixed capital	61.62	133.92	30.46	116.10	41.77	250.02
Working capital	38.38	33.40	69.54	265.10	5.23	298.50
Total	100.00	167.32	100.00	381.20	100.00	548.52

The survey revealed, 60 per cent of the exporters are manufacturers cum exporters and the 40 per cent as merchant exporters. The manufacturer cum exporter will have his own plant and processing infrastructure facilities, but they take the facilities for lease or rent to carry out their operations. There are two types of processing plants namely pate freezers and blast freezers. The plate freezers are used for the processing of shrimp whereas the blast freezers are used for the processing of fish. The data presented in Table 8.17 reveals, the 60 exporters surveyed are having 108 plate freezers and 12 blast freezers with the maximum capacity of 324 metric tonnes and 72 metric tonnes respectively. The utilisation percentage during a year is varying between 35 per cent and 75 per cent in the case of plate freezers and 20 per cent and 70 per cent in the case of blast freezers. The average percentage of utilisation for plate freezers was 55 while for blast freezers it was 45 per cent. The respondents revealed, they are keeping plate freezers idle for 60 days and blast freezers for 90 days in a year due to lack of work. The respondents revealed during a year the period from August to December is the peak season and January to March is the moderate season. April to June is the off season and during this period they were forced to keep the plants idle.

Table 8.16 : Sources of Borrowed Capital

(Rupees in lakhs)

Sources	Fixed capital	Working capital	Total	Average
Banks	96.18	98.08	97.50	371.67
Friends and relatives	3.82	1.92	2.50	9.53
Indigenous bankers	-	-	-	-
MPEDA	-	-	-	-
Total	100.00	100.00	100.00	381.20

Problems with bank finance: Too many hurdles, too many formalities, complicated procedures, demand for security, indifferent attitude of bank staff.

Table 8.17 : Details of Processing Plants

Particulars	Number	Max. capacity	Max. % utilisation	Min.% utilisation	Average% utilisation	No.of idle days in a year
Plate Freezers	108	324 Mtns	75	35	55	60
Blast Freezers	12	72 Mtns	70	20	45	90

Mtns=Metric tonnesa

The data presented in Table 8.18 reveals the range-wise number of working days of the responding units. As can be seen from the table, 50 per cent of the units are working for 150 to 180 days with full capacity and 36.67 per cent of the units work for 180 to 240 days with full capacity. Ten per cent of the units work for 180 to 240 days with full capacity while 3.33 per cent of the units work for only 60 to 90 days with full capacity. The table further reveals, 40 per cent of the units work with partial capacity (ranging from 40 to 45 per cent capacity utilisation) for 150 to 180 days in a year, 33.34 per cent work for 60 to 90 days and 23.33 per cent work for 180 to 240 days with partial capacity utilisation. As many as 83.33 per cent of the units keep their plants idle for 30 to 60 days in a year where as the remaining have no work for 60 to 90 days in a year. The respondents revealed, during non-season period they will take up other works such as repairs and maintenance of plant and machinery, buildings and other assets and the other developmental activities of business such as new market survey, attending training programmes, installation of new plant and machinery, etc. The units sponsor the employees for special training programmes being organised by the EIA, MPEDA,CIFT, etc. Apart from the training programmes the units are taking up welfare measures for their employees. The survey reveals, all the units are offering welfare schemes such as employees state insurance scheme and provident fund scheme. Pension scheme is being offered by 70 per cent of the units.

Table 8.18 : Details of Working Days in a Year

Particulars	Number of days					Total
	30-60	60-90	150-180	180-240	240-300	
Full capacity	—	3.33	50.00	36.67	10.00	100.00
Partial capacity (40-45%)	3.33	33.34	40.00	23.33	—	100.00
No work	83.33	16.67	—	—		100.00

SUPPLIER RELATIONS

An attempt is made to know the number of suppliers of raw shrimp and fish to the units during 1992-93 to 1996-97. The data presented in Table 8.19 shows that the number of suppliers for the 60 units increased from 2,620 in 1992-93 to 7,950 in 1996-97 recording an increase of 203.44 per cent. The average number of suppliers per unit increased from 43.67 to 132.50. It can be inferred from the above that the units are building-up their supplier network over the years.

Table 8.19 : Number of Suppliers During Last Five Years 1992-93 to 1996-97

Year	Number of suppliers Total	Average	Percentage of growth rate
1992-93	2,620	43.67	—
1993-94	4,470	74.50	70.61
1994-95	6,470	107.83	44.74
1995-96	6,760	112.67	4.48
1996-97	7,950	132.50	17.60

The units are building the chain of raw-material suppliers through various means which include company personnel, friends and relatives, existing suppliers and placing an open invitation for the new suppliers and also by persuading the suppliers of the competitors. The data presented in Table 8.20 reveals, the units are building-up supplier network mostly through company personnel. Existing suppliers are the second major source while the suppliers who came on their own are the third major source.

Relationship with suppliers is an important aspect for any business unit to ensure smooth, dependable, timely and adequate quantity of raw-material supply for an uninterrupted execution of production schedule and also to face the competition. An attempt is made to know how the respondents are maintaining relationships with their suppliers and the data is presented in Table 8.21. The table reveals, the advance payment of money to the suppliers is the preferred means (166 points) for many to maintain relationships with the suppliers followed by prompt payment (116 points) and offering of competitive price (72 points). The majority of the respondents revealed (60 per cent) that they don't feel threat from competitors in breaking the suppliers chain.

Table 8.20 : Ways and Means for Building the Chain of Raw-material Suppliers

Particulars	Score
Through company personnel	154
Through friends and relatives	24
Suppliers who came on their own	82
Through existing suppliers	90
Persuading the suppliers of competitors	14

Table 8.21: Methods Adopted for Maintaining Relations with the Supplies

Particulars	Score
By offering advance payments	166
By prompt payment	116
By offering competitive prices	72
By supplying information and technical assistance	—
By training the employees to exhibit good behaviour	6

The study revealed all the respondents are producing shrimp. Fish is also produced by a few respondents in limited quantities. The data presented in Table 8.22 shows range-wise production of fish and shrimp during 1992-93 to 1996-97. The table reveals, there is a decline in the number of production units that product only shrimp during the period as the percentage of such units declined from 93.34 per cent in 1992-93 to 70 per cent in 1996-97. On the other hand, the fish producing units increased from 6.67 per cent in 1992-93 to 30 per cent in 1996-97. However, the share of fish production in the total production of the units varied from below 10 per cent to 20 percent during 192-93 to 1995-96. During 1996-97, 23.33 per cent of the units had less than 10 per cent of share of fish in their total production while 3.33 per cent had 20 to 30 per cent share of fish in their production. Only 3.33 per cent of the units had 60 to 70 per cent share of fish in their total production. It can be inferred from the above that more and more units are introducing fish as their new product line, as an expansion to their product mix.

MARKET INFORMATION

Marketing information relating to supply and demand positions in various traditional markets, changes in regulations, competitive positions, market expectations, etc., are required to the exporters to orient their organisations towards the requirements of the external environment. Marketing information is the basic input for the organisations to become adaptable for the changes in the external environment. The data shown in Table 8.23 reveals the sources of marketing information for the sample units. The table reveals, agents and brokers are the major source for marketing information to the exporters followed by the association of the exporters. Apart from the two the exporters are getting information

Table 8.22 : Range-wise Share in Percentage of Production of Fish and Shrimp

Percentage (Range)	Percentage of total units									
	Fish					Shrimp				
	1992-93	1993-94	1994-95	1995-96	1996-97	1992-93	1993-94	1994-95	1995-96	1996-97
Below 10	3.33	6.67	13.33	13.33	23.33	–	-	-	-	-
10-20	3.33	6.67	3.33	3.33	-	-	-	-	-	-
20-30	-	-	-	-	3.33	-	-	-	-	-
30-40	-	-	-	-	-	-	-	-	-	3.33
40-50	-	-	-	-	-	-	-	-	-	-
50-60	-	-	-	-	-	-	-	-	-	-
60-70	-	-	-	-	3.33	-	-	-	-	-
70-80	-	-	-	-	-	-	-	-	-	3.33
80-90	-	-	-	-	-	3.33	6.66	3.33	3.33	-
90-100	-	-	-	-	-	3.33	6.67	13.33	13.33	23.34
100 per cent	-	-	-	-	-	93.34	86.67	83.34	83.34	70.00

by observing competitors and co-exporters, through trade journals and MPEDA. The MPEDA could not become a major source for the exporters as far as marketing information is concerned. It is unfortunate that the organisation though having supply of market information as one of the important objectives, could not turn to be useful source to the exporters. The findings of the study indicate that the information being supplied by the MPEDA is not been felt useful and important by the exporters for their business purposes. Therefore, there is a need for MPEDA to review the communication programmes and check their degree of effectiveness and usefulness to the target audience. It should include in its communication all such features of information which support the exporters effectively in their decision making process relating to various activities.

Table 8.23 : Sources of Market Information

Particulars	Score
MPEDA	14
Trade journals	22
Association	110
Competitors/co-exporters	68
Agents and brokers	138

An attempt is made to know how the prices are being fixed in the business. The exporters have to arrive at pricing decisions in two different situations. First, when they buy raw-shrimp and fish from the suppliers, the exporter has to arrive at the pricing decision in the role of a buyer. Secondly, when the exporter offers it for sale to various importers, he has to arrive at the pricing decision in the capacity of a seller. The pricing methods used for the purposes by the respondents include cost plus pricing, market price, negotiated price and the price suggested by the exporters association. The data presented in Table 8.24 depicts that the majority are purchasing from suppliers the produce at market price. As many as 83.33 per cent are following this method. A few are adopting negotiation price and some are following the price suggested by exporters association in purchasing the raw-shrimp/fish. In the case of pricing to the importers, the exporters are mostly adopting negotiated pricing method. Out of the total, more than 50 per cent are following this method for finalising the price. Next to the negotiated price, mark-up pricing is followed by many. Out of the total 26.67 per cent are following mark-up pricing. Market price and suggested price by exporters association are also being followed by 13.33 per cent and 6.67 per cent respectively in deciding pricing for their produce. The respondents express that they are facing some problems with the suppliers as far as the fixation of price is concerned. They revealed, the suppliers as far as the fixation of price is concerned. They revealed, the suppliers are demanding for higher price every time and it has become very difficult for them to convince the suppliers on the changing situations in the market. The respondents also expressed that they are also facing problems with the importers too in pricing decisions. The major problem being language barrier in communication. The exporters are not eloquent with the foreign languages and as such they are unable to participate in the negotiations freely with confidence. Some exporters are of the view that the hospitality expenses are tooheavy for them to continue the negotiations with foreign importers. The respondents are looking for the helping hand from MPEDA in this respect. The apex body can build -up a team of negotiations on behalf of the exporters of the country. These specialist negotiators shall take active part in arranging importer and exporter meets and facilitate for effective communication which yield fruitful negotiations.

Table 8.24 : How do You Fix the Price of Various Products?

Particulars	Pricing methods			
	Cost based on supplier price plus margin	Market price	Bargained price/ negotiated price	Suggested price by exporters association
Methods used for supplier price	—	83.33	10.00	6.67
Methods used for sale price	26.67	13.33	53.33	6.67

Cold storage plants stand as a very useful infrastructure for the exporters of fish and fish products. The exporters require cold storage facility since the fisnished product is required to be kept under-20°C. The exporters having their own cold storage plants will be in an advantageous position in price negotiation with importers compared to the exporters without their own cold storage plants. The study revealed, 60 per cent of the respondents have their own cold storage plants while the other 40 per cent are reining the storage space. The data shown in Table 8.25 reveals the particulars of the cold storage plants owned by the respondents. The 60 per cent of the respondents have 56 cold storage plants. The total investment on all the cold storage have 56 cold storage plants. The total investment on all the cold storage plants was a little over Rs. 66 crores. In other words, the investment on each plant was about Rs. 1.84 crores. Annual maintenance expenditure was to the tune of Rs. 7.88 crores and the average maintenance expenditure per unit being Rs. 21.89 lakhs. The respondents revealed that the capacity utilisation of the storage plant varies between 70 per cent to 100 per cent and the average per cent utilisation stands at 78.06 per cent. The un-utilised space of the storage plants is offered for lease or rent to the merchant exporters. The 40 per cent of the respondents who do not have their own cold storage plants are utilising the storage space of 24 private cold storage plants. The cost incurred by them was Rs. 4.76 crores per annum in 1996-97.

The exporters are using insulated vans, refrigerated vans and refrigerated containers for the purpose of transport from production point to shipment. The data shown in Table 8.26 reveals that the respondents are using 380 insulated vans, out of which 336 owned by the exporters and 44 are taken for rent. Fifty refrigerated vans are used for the purpose and out of which 38 are owned and 12 are rented. Only 16 refrigerated containers are being used by large size exporters and all the 16 are owned by them.

Table 8.25 : Details of Cold Storage Plants Owned by Exporters

Particulars	Details	Average
Number of plants	56	1.56
Investment(Rupees in lakhs)	6,610	183.61
Annual maintenance expenditure (Rupees in lakhs)	788	21.89
Capacity utilisation (percentage)	70-100	78.06

Note: The unutilised space (idle space) of the storage plants will be leased to merchant exporters.

Table 8.26 : Details of Transport Used

Particulars of transport used	Own	Rented	Total
Insulated vans	336	44	380
Refrigerated vans	38	12	50
Refrigerated containers	16	-	16

MARKETING

An attempt is made to know to whom the respondents are selling their produce. The survey revealed, 96 per cent of the respondents are selling their produce to foreign agents while four per cent sell to customer companies directly. When enquired about the criteria adopted by the respondents in selecting the agents and the customer companies, the respondents revealed that they consider the factors such as goodwill, financial soundness, selling ability, on-line experience and personal relations for the purpose. The data presented in Table 8.27 reveals, financial soundness is the major criteria (170 points) followed by goodwill for selecting the foreign agents. In the selection of the customer companies also the financial soundness and the goodwill are the major influencing factors. The terms of payment from the importer is common to all the exporters. It is an irrevocable transferable letter of credit opened on sight basis. The majority of the respondents are operating their production activities based on advance orders plus the regular production schedule to sell the finished products after being produced (80 per cent) Table 8.28. Fifteen per cent of the respondents are taking up the responsibility of production activity based on the orders received in advance while five per cent are having their fixed schedule of production without getting influenced by the orders.

Table 8.27 : Criteria Adopted in Selecting the Agents of Importers

(Score)

Particulars	Foreign agents	Customer companies
Goodwill	110	150
Financial soundness	170	170
Selling ability	40	-
Experience on line	26	-
Personal relations	14	40

Table 8.28 : How do you Operate Your Production Activities

Particulars	Percentage
Based on the orders received in advance	15
Production on traditional lines to find customers	5
Regular production plus order base	80

An attempt was made to know how the respondents are promoting their products to the foreign agents as well as the importing companies. The data presented in Table 8.29 reveals personal selling and sales promotion are mostly used for promotion. All respondents are using personal selling and 80 per cent of the respondents are using sales promotion techniques for promotion. Advertising is not a popular devise as considered by the respondents, only 10 per cent use advertising for promotion.

Table 8.30 depicts the measures taken by the respondents in retaining the existing customers. The respondents are trying to retain the existing customers through assured quality, assured supply, timely response, maintenance of good personal relations and responding positively to the changes suggested by customer. The table reveals, assured quality is the mostly used variable to retain the existing customers as it secures a score of 128 points. Assured supply is the second major variable (94 points) followed by timely response (72 points).

Table 8.29 : How do you Promote Your Products?

Particulars	Percentage
Through advertisements	10
Personal selling	100
Sales promotion	80

Table 8.30 : Measures Taken in Retaining the Existing Customers

Particulars	Percentage
Assured quality	128
Assured supply	94
Timely response	72
Maintaining personal relations	26
Responding positively to the changes suggested by customers	40

9

Performance Appraisal

The focus of this chapter is to appraise the overall performance of The Marine products Export Development Authority with the help of the analysis of capital, liabilities and assets and income and expenditure pattern and the opinions of the exporters on the role of the MPEDA in promoting export trade of fish and fish products.

FINANCIAL PERFORMANCE

The data presented in Table 9.1 depicts the growth of capital fund of the MPEDA during 1986-87 to 1995-96. Since the MPEDA is an organisation promoted by the Government of India under a special act, the capital fund of the MPEEDA increased form Rs. 5.68 crores in 1986-87 to Rs. 12.07 crores in 1995-96 recording an increase of 112.50 per cent. The Government of India allocate some proportion of the cess collected to the capital fund. Also some proportion of the surplus income over expenditure will be diverted towards the capital fund. The proportion of allocation to the capital fund from either sources varied year by year. The capital fund will be utilised primarily for the purpose of purchasing fixed assets.

The MPEDA also develops different funds for some specific purposes. The amount allocated to the specific funds which was Rs. 23.03 lakhs in 1986-87 rose to Rs. 1,,162.73 lakhs in 1995-96 recording an increase of 4,948.76 per cent. The data shown in Table 9.2 reveals that the MPEDA has developed five different specific funds during 1986-87 to 1995-96. They are provident fund, terminal benefit of staff of MPEP Council, equity participation scheme investment fund account, bio-technology fund, and food processing fund.

Table 9.1 : Capital Fund of MPEDA During 1986-87 to 1995-96

(Rupees in lakhs)

Year	Capital Fund
1986-87	567.54
1987-88	531.07
1988-89	509.54
1989-90	628.14
1990-91	646.88
1991-92	988.12
1992-93	1,141.43
1993-94	1,245.62
1994-95	1,190.62
1995-96	1,206.85

Source: Compiled from the Annual Reports of the Marine Products Export Development Authority, Cochin.

The provident fund is the fund collected from the salary savings of the employees for their benefit. It is voluntary contribution. The MPEDA does not contribute anything to it. However, on the contribution to the provident fund, it pays 12 per cent interest. The table reveals, the amount under the head of provident fund which was Rs. 21.55 lakhs in 1986-87 increased to Rs. 119.89 lakhs in 1995-96 recording an increase of 456.33 per cent.

The table denotes the fund relating to the terminal benefits of the staff of MPEP Council which was in operation up to 1988-89. The fund is originally provided to meet the contingent expenditure relating to the termination of the employees of the erstwhile Marine Products Export Promotion Council. After the establishment of the MPEDA in 1972 the majority of the employees of the MPEP Council were transfered to the MPEDA and the remaining were terminated by offering certain financial benefits. After meeting all those termination expenditure, a fund of Rs. 1.48 lakhs remained unutilised. In 1988-89, the MPEDA took a decision to terminate this fund and transfer the amount to capital fund.

Table 9.2 : Specific Funds of MPEDA During 1986-87 to 1995-96.

(Rupees in lakhs)

Fund	Years									
	1986-87	1987-88	1988-89	1989-90	1990-91	1991-92	1992-93	1993-94	1994-95	1995-96
Provident Fund	21.55	29.59	38.84	44.62	48.54	58.85	61.61	82.60	101.56	119.89
Terminal Benefit of Staff of MPEP Council	1.48	1.48	1.48	-	-	-	-	-	-	-
Equity Participation Scheme-Investment Fund Account	-	-	100.23	165.44	254.22	301.86	417.28	579.29	624.66	952.72
Bio-Technology Fund	-	-	-	24.65	17.88	15.35	0.35	0.35	31.12	29.23
Food Processing Fund	-	-	-	-	48.00	52.16	32.12	63.39	62.31	60.89
Total	23.03	31.07	140.55	234.71	368.64	428.21	511.36	725.63	819.65	1,162.73

Source: Compiled from the Annual Reports of The Marine Products Export Development Authority, Cochin.

The table further elucidates, the equity participation scheme investment fund account which was initiated in 1988-89 to build-up confidence in the financial institutions that are granting loans to the exporters for purchasing deep sea fishing vessels and also to have a close monitoring and control over such exporters. The MPEDA under this scheme purchases the equity shares of the exporting companies. The fund under the scheme was increased from Rs. 100.23 lakhs in 1988-89 to Rs. 952.72 lakhs in 1995-96 recording an increase of 850.53 per cent.

The bio-technology fund was developed in 1989-90 with a view to promote research in aquaculture. The allocations to this fund was erratic and varied between Rs. 0.35 lakhs and Rs. 29.23 lakhs. The food processing fund is developed in 1990-91 to provide facilities for value added processes and diversified fishing. The fund which was Rs. 48.00 lakhs in 1990-91 increased to a tune of Rs. 60.89 lakhs in 1995-96 recording an increase of 26.85 per cent.

The data relating to accounts payable by the MPEDA are shown in Table 9.3. Due to liquidity problems the MPEDA often goes for credit purchases. The table reveals, the amount due under the accounts payable which was Rs. 3.00 lakhs in 1986-87 increased year by year to reach Rs. 216.10 lakhs in 1995-96. Table 9.4 depicts the value of fixed assets of MPEDA during 1986-87 to 1995-96. The table reveals, the value of fixed assets which was Rs. 123.92 lakhs in 1986-87 increased to Rs. 461.82 lakhs in 1995-96 recording an increase of 272.68 per cent.

The MPEDA has investments and deposits under various heads. The amount utilised for investments and deposits which was Rs. 80.22 lakhs in 1986-87 increased gradually over the years to reach Rs. 1,218.08 lakhs in 1995-96 (Table 9.5). In other words, the investments and deposits were increased by over 1,400 per cent during the period. The table reveals that the investments and deposits were made in the areas of general provident fund investment, equity participation scheme deposit, other deposits, bio-technology scheme investment, food processing scheme investment and other investments including investments in joint ventures. A close observation of the table reveals that the focus of investments was shifted from general provident fund investment to equity participation scheme investment. In the case of deposits also the focus was towards equity participation scheme deposit in the year 1995-96 while general deposits was the focus earlier.

Table 9.3 : Accounts Payable by MPEDA During 1986-87 to 1995-96

(Rupees in lakhs)

Year	Accounts Payable
1986-87	3.00
1987-88	3.60
1988-89	30.37
1989-90	18.25
1990-91	86.47
1991-92	13.12
1992-93	16.35
1993-94	22.58
1994-95	18.59
1995-96	216.10

Source: Compiled from the Annual Reports of The Marine Products Export Development Authority, Cochin.

Table 9.4 : Value of Fixed Assets of MPEDA During 1986-87 to 1995-96

(Rupees in lakhs)

Year	Fixed Assets
1986-87	123.92
1987-88	169.49
1988-89	165.38
1989-90	170.15
1990-91	172.35
1991-92	172.44
1992-93	164.02
1993-94	381.34
1994-95	466.57
1995-96	461.82

Source: Compiled from the Annual Reports of The Marine Products Export Development Authority, Cochin.

The data relating to current assets of MPEDA during 1986-87 to 1995-96 are presented in Table 9.6. The current assets are under five broad heads. They are work-in-progress, advances, accounts receivable, cash and bank balance and other current assets. The

Table 9.5 : Investments and Deposits of MPEDA During 1986-87 to 1995-96

(Rupees in lakhs)

Investments and Deposits	Years									
	1986-87	1987-88	1988-89	1989-90	1990-91	1991-92	1992-93	1993-94	1994-95	1995-96
General Provident Fund	14.43	23.45	32.03	37.04	41.52	51.29	53.85	79.30	98.53	116.32
Provident Fund (Council)	5.01	5.01	5.01	5.01	5.01	5.01	-	-	-	
Equity Participation Scheme Investment	—	25.00	2.05	53.67	67.27	130.99	216.16	571.11	569.41	574.41
Equity Participation Scheme Deposit	—	—	44.20	111.77	186.95	170.88	201.12	8.68	55.25	378.30
Deposits	55.30	51.91	184.14	107.55	131.40	186.43	349.80	251.86	159.50	58.93
Bio-technology Scheme Investment	—	—	—	24.65	17.15	0.35	0.35	0.35	31.12	29.23
Food Processing Scheme Investment	—	—	—	—	48.00	52.16	32.12	63.38	62.31	60.89
Other Investments (Investment in Joint Venture)	5.48	29.90	53.97	—	—	—	—	—	—	—
Total	80.22	135.27	321.40	339.69	497.30	597.11	858.41	974.68	976.12	1,218.08

Source : Compiled from the Annual Reports of the Marine Products Export Development Authority, Cochin.

total value of current assets which was about Rs. 395.00 lakhs in 1986-87 had fallen to Rs. 200.55 lakhs in 1988-89 and later increased to a maximum of Rs. 659.91 lakhs in 1991-92. There was a sudden decline in 1993-94 to about Rs. 368.00 lakhs and there was only a marginal improvement in 1995-96 during which year the current assets are valued at Rs. 408.03 lakhs. The work-in- progress in prawn farm project complex situated at Vallarpadam was mostly responsible for value fluctuations in current assets. During 1995-96, there was no work-in-progress at the complex situated at Vallarpadam was mostly responsible for value fluctuations in current assets. During 1995-96, there was no work-in-progress at the complex and in the previous year, it was only Rs. 2.34 lakhs, compared to Rs. 237.52 lakhs in 1986-87. Cash and bank balance is the major item among current assets (excluding work-in-progress during 1986-87 to 1990-91). In 1986-87, the cash and bank balance was to the tune of Rs. 70.10 lakhs which was increased to Rs. 307.93 lakhs in 1995-96 recording an increase of 339.27 per cent. On the other hand, the accounts receivable which was Rs. 55.58 lakhs in 1986-87 declined to Rs. 0.99 lakhs in 1995-96. The advances were gone up from Rs. 28.49 lakhs to Rs. 75.75 lakhs during the period recording an increase of 165.88 per cent and other current assets which were valued at Rs. 3.26 lakhs in 1986-87 increased to Rs. 23.36 lakhs in 1995-96 recording an increase of 616.56 per cent.

The MPEDA Act 1972 provides for levy of cess on all marine products which are exported at such rate not exceeding three percent *ad valorem* as the Central Government may, by notification in the official gazette fix the rate of cess[1]. By a notification issued in July, 1972, the Government of India fixed the rate of cess leviable on marine products as 0.5 per cent on FOB value of exports. The cess is collected by the customs authorities and deposited in the consolidated fund of Government of India. The Government in turn through the Ministry of Commerce allocates budgets for the plan and non-plan expenditure of the Authority every year[2]. The details of cess collected during 1985-86 to 1994-95, are shown in /table 9.7. The table reveals, the amount collected in the form of cess which was Rs. 199.00 lakhs in 1985-86 increased to Rs. 1,776.54 lakhs in 1994-95 recording an increase of 792.73 per cent.

Table 9.6 : Value of /Current /Assets of MEPDA During 1986-87 to 1995-96

(Rupees in lakhs)

Investments and Deposits	Years									
	1986-87	1987-88	1988-89	1989-90	1990-91	1991-92	1992-93	1993-94	1994-95	1995-96
+ Work-in-progress	237.52	165.87	79.04	226.97	253.72	253.95	255.97	100.28	2.34	-
Advances	28.49	31.65	37.84	47.45	64.99	83.68	82.70	85.00	77.04	75.75
Accounts Receivable	55.58	37.30	39.83	38.98	43.18	42.45	45.03	30.75	7.40	0.99
Cash and Bank Balance	70.10	29.40	37.53	51.80	64.21	269.74	254.77	412.09	252.10	307.93
* Other Current Assets	3.26	3.31	6.31	6.06	6.24	10.09	8.24	10.19	16.29	23.36
Total	394.95	267.53	200.55	371.26	432.34	659.91	646.71	368.31	355.17	408.03

+ The Work-in-progress is related to prawn Farm Project Complex works at Vallarpadam.

*Other current assets includes stock of priced publications stock of stationery, stamps in hand, stock of Mohua oil cake and prawn feed, stock of spares etc.

Source: Compiled from the Annual Reports of The Marine Products Export Development Authority, Cochin.

Table 9.7 : Cess Collected During 1985-86 to 1994-95

(Rupees in lakhs)

Year	Cess Collected
1985-86	199.00
1986-87	230.35
1987-88	265.60
1988-89	298.92
1989-90	317.50
1990-91	346.68
1991-92	687.95
1992-93	883.72
1993-94	1,251.81
1994-95	1,776.54

Source: MPEDA—An Over View 1995, p.16.

Table 9.8 depicts the source-wise income of the MPEDA during 1986-87 to 1995-96. The income sources are, funds received from the Government of India, departmental receipts in the form of registration fees and miscellaneous income and amount received from other sources such as department of oceanic development, food processing industries and department of bio-technology. The total income of the MPEDA which was Rs. 443.68 lakhs in 1986-87 increased to Rs. 1,228.64 lakhs in 1995-96 recording an increase of 176.92 per cent. There were, of course, certain fluctuations in the income during the period. Out of the total income, lions share is from the Government of India and the other two sources contribute marginally to the total income.

The item-wise expenditure of the MPEDA during 1986-87 to 1995-96 was shown in /Table 9.9. There are six heads of expenditure. They are: 1) non-plan expenditure which includes administration expenditure and contingencies; 2) plan expenditure which includes publicity and propaganda expenditure for export promotion and marketing, developmental expenditure for capture fisheries, culture fisheries, induction of new technology, modernisation of processing facilities, etc., and expenditure on product development; 3) depreciation; 4) bio-technology scheme; 5) oceanic development scheme; and 6) food processing. The total expenditure of the MPEDA which was Rs. 395.61 lakhs in 1986-87 increased to Rs. 1,403.87 lakhs in 1995-96 recording an increase of 254.86 per cent.

Table 9.8: Source-wise Income of MPEDA During 1986-87 to 1995-96

(Rupees in lakhs)

Income	Years									
	1986-87	1987-88	1988-89	1989-90	1990-91	1991-92	1992-93	1993-94	1994-95	1995-96
Funds received from Government of India*	437.53	637.00	665.42	663.36	824.00	1,053.80	1,129.61	1,258.05	842.95	1,240.58
Less: Amount transferred to Equity Participation Scheme Fund	—	—	42.50	58.00	40.00	30.00	45.00	50.00	—	50.00
	437.53	637.00	622.92	605.36	784.00	1,023.80	1,081.61	1,208.05	842.95	1,190.58
Less: Amount ulitised for acquisition of fixed assets	—	—	—	167.07	42.53	—	—	26.74	9.21	16.24
1. Balance of Fund received from Government of India	437.53	637.00	622.92	438.29	741.47	1,023.80	1,084.61	1,181.31	833.74	1,174.34
2. Departmental Receipts (Registration fees and other receipts including miscellaneous income)	6.15	4.88	5.33	9.07	8.92	11.13	17.51	24.55	53.80	47.90

(Cont.)..

Income	Years									
	1986-87	1987-88	1988-89	1989-90	1990-91	1991-92	1992-93	1993-94	1994-95	1995-96
3. Amount received from other sources:										
a) Department of Oceanic Development	—	—	—	—	20.70	66.25	92.92	68.57	—	—
b) Food processing industries	—	—	—	—	88.00	—	49.00	207.50	28.00	—
c) Department of Biotechnology	—	—	—	48.75	17.00	15.00	—	—	31.12	6.40
Total Recipts from other sources (a+b+c)	—	—	—	48.75	115.70	81.25	141.92	276.07	59.12	6.40
Total Income (1+2+3)	443.68	641.88	628.25	496.11	876.09	1,116.18	1,244.04	1,481.93	946.66	1,228.64

* Proceeds of cess made over by the Government of India under section 15 of the MPEDA act from consolidated fund of India.

Source: Compiled from the Annual Reports of The Marine Products Export Development Authority, Cochin.

Table 9.9 : Item-wise Expenditure of MPEDA During 1986-87 to 1995-96

(Rupees in lakhs)

Income	Years									
	1986-87	1987-88	1988-89	1989-90	1990-91	1991-92	1992-93	1993-94	1994-95	1995-96
1. Non-Plan Expenditure: Administration and Contingencies	79.76	102.37	107.39	117.48	154.04	156.22	175.38	201.37	217.46	248.23
2. Plan Expenditure:										
a) Publicity and Propaganda (Export promotion and marketing)	65.34	68.09	95.82	107.93	-	-	-	-	-	-
b) Development (capture fisheries, culture fisheries, induction of new technology, modernisation of processing facilities etc).	239.26	411.05	380.91	248.05	467.11	377.82	582.43	668.55	661.05	901.53
c) Product development	11.25	6.62	9.83	6.85	139.44	169.73	178.27	238.07	217.05	224.63
Total Plan Expenditure	315.85	485.76	486.56	362.83	606.55	547.55	760.70	906.62	878.10	1,126.16

(Cont.)....

3. Depreciation	-	-	-	14.51	13.58	13.79	12.72	20.41	22.98	23.08
4. Bio-technology scheme	-	-	-	48.75	17.00	15.00	-	-	31.12	6.40
5. Oceanic development scheme	-	-	-	-	20.70	66.25	92.92	68.57	-	-
6. Food processing	-	-	-	-	88.00	-	49.00	207.50	28.00	-
Total processing	-	-	-	-	88.00	-	49.00	207.50	28.00	-
Total Expenditure (1+2+3+4+5+6)	395.61	588.13	593.95	543.57	899.87	798.81	1,090.72	1,404.47	1,177.66	1,403.87

Source: Compiled from the Annual Reports of The Marine Products Export

UPto 1988-89, the expenditure was only under two heads i.e., the plan expenditure and the non-plan expenditure and since 1989-90 new heads of expenditure were appeared. Out of the total expenditure lions share goes to plan expenditure followed by non-plan expenditure.

Table 9.10 depicts the data relating to the total income and expenditure of MPEDA during 1986-87 to 1995-96. The table reveals, the MPEDA has surplus income over expenditure during 1986-87 to 1988-89. However, during 1989-90 and 1990-91 there was a deficit of Rs. 47.46 lakhs and Rs. 22.78 lakhs respectively. During 1991-92 the MPEDA had the surplus income of more than three crore rupees over expenditure and in the subsequent year also it had a surplus of more than Rs. 1.5 crores. In 1993-94, the surplus was reduced to Rs. 77.46 lakhs and during 1994-95 and 1995-96, the annual deficit raised to the tune of Rs. 231.00 lakhs and Rs. 175.23 lakhs respectively. It can be inferred from the above that during the decade the MPEDA had surplus income over expenditure for six years and committed expenditure over income for four years. The expenditure over income was substantial during the last two years and there is a need to review the expenditure pattern in order to get the financial situation under control.

Table 9.10: Income and Expenditure of MPEDA During 1986-87 to 1995-96

(Rupees in lakhs)

Year	Income	Expenditure	Surplus/Deficit
1986-87	443.68	395.61	48.07
1987-88	641.88	588.13	53.75
1988-89	628.25	593.95	34.30
1989-90	496.11	543.57	(-) 47.46
1990-91	876.09	899.87	(-) 23.78
1991-92	1,116.18	798.81	317.37
1992-93	1,244.04	1,090.72	153.32
1993-94	1,481.93	1,404.47	77.46
1994-95	946.66	1,177.66	(-) 231.00
1995-96	1,228.64	1,403.87	(-)175.23

Source: Compiled from the Annual Reports of The Marine Products Export Development Authority, Cochin.

EXPORTERS PERCEPTION OF MPEDA'S PERFORMANCE

One of the important measures for the appraisal of the performance of a service organisation is to know the opinions, and the levels of satisfaction of the target market and to study their interation with the organisation. Keeping this in view, an attempt is made in the study to know the interactions, views and opinions of the exporters on MPEDA. Table 9.11 depicts the particulars relating to frequency of respondents contacts with MPEDA officials. The data shown in the table reveals, 53.33 per cent of the respondents do not have any pre determined time schedule to contact the MPEDA officials. They are contacting the officials as and when the need arises. One third of the respondents revealed that they will contact the MPEDA officials once in a month regularly, where as 13.34 per cent of the respondents revealed that they contact the MPEDA officials once in six months.

All the respondents revealed that the MPEDA officials visit their organisations to supervise how the activities are going on. The data presented in Table 9.12 reveals the frequency of visits by the MPEDA officials to the exporting organisations. As can be seen from the table, 40 per cent of the respondents revealed that the officials visit only once in a year during seasonal times while 26.67 per cent of the respondents revealed that the MPEDA officials visit their organisations twice in a year. Out of the total 33.33 per cent of the respondents revealed that the officials visit their organisations once in a month. All the respondents opined that the visits of the MPEDA personnel are useful for the betterment of their organisations and they want greater frequency of the visits of the MPEDA personnel to their organisations. All the respondents revealed that they do not face any problems with the personnel of the MPEDA.

Table 9.11 : Frequency of Contacts with MPEDA Officials

Particulars	Percentage
Once in a month	33.33
Once in two months	-
Once in three months	-
Once in six months	13.34
Once in a year	-
During peak seasons only	-
As and when required	53.33
Total	100.0

Table 9.12 : Frequency of Visits by MPEDA Officials

Particulars	Percentage
Once in a month	33.33
Twice in a year	26.67
Once in a year	40.00
Total	100.00

Table 9.13 : Details of Assistance from MPEDA

Particulars	Percentage availed the assistance
Financial Assistance	
Diesel Subsidy,	
Subsidy for processing plants including generator set,	
Subsidy for cold storage and laboratory,	
Financial assistance for modification of fishing vessel,	
Financial assistance for modification of fishing vessel,	
Financial assistance for diversified fishing, and	
Financial assistance for air freighting the samples.	60.00
Technical Assistance	
Subsidy for setting up of mini laboratory for effective in plant quality control, and	
Training of quality control officers in FDA laboratory to acquaint seafood quality control.	48.33
Managerial Assistance	8.33
Marketing Assistance	
Market information,	
Market research, and	
Participation in fairs and exhibitions.	56.67

The study revealed that out of the total 60 per cent of the respondents received special assistance from the MPEDA. The data presented in Table 9.13 shows the details of assistance provided by the MPEDA to the respondent organisations. The respondents have received assistance in four different areas i.e., financial assistance, technical assistance, managerial assistance and marketing assistance. The financial assistance received by the 60 per cent of the respondents from the MPEDA extended in the form of diesel subsidy, subsidy for processing plants including generator set, subsidy for cold storage and laboratory, financial assistance for modification of fishing vessels, for diversified fishing and for air freighting the samples. The respondents revealed that the financial assistance from the MPEDA reduced their investment burden and also was helpful in reducing cost of production.Out of the total, 56.67 per cent of the respondents availed marketing assistance from the MPEDA in the form of marketing information, marketing research and participation in fairs and exhibitions. The respondents revealed that the marketing assistance from the MPEDA helped them to get new markets and new customers and also to be adaptable to the changing marketing environment. They revealed however, that the information supplied by MPEDA is of little value for them as they could not obtain latest information about foreign markets. The technical assistance was availed by 48.33 per cent of the respondents in the form of subsidy for setting up of mini laboratory for effective in-plant quality control and training of quality control officers in FDA laboratory to make them acquainted with the latest techniques in seafood quality control. The respondents revealed that they were extremely benefited with the assistance and they could substantially reduce wastages and rejections. Managerial assistance is provided to 8.33 per cent of the responding organisations. The respondents revealed that the managerial assistance helped them to strengthen the organisation system and to run the business on professional lines.

An attempt is made in the study to know the opinions of the respondents on the performance of the MPEDA in offering marketing services. The data presented in Table 9.14 reveals, 90 per cent of the respondents rated the performance of MPEDA as satisfactory. While 6.67 per cent of the respondents rated the performance as very good, 3.33 per cent of the respondents rated the performance as excellent. None of the respondents rated the performance as poor or very poor. It can be inferred from the above, the MPEDA could establish a positive image through the efficient production and delivery of the services. However it has still to work hard with innovative schemes and greater involvement in the operations of the exporters to get an improved rating.

Table 9.14 : Opinions of Exporters on the Performance of MPEDA

Particulars	Percentage
Excellent	3.33
Very Good	6.67
Satisfactory	90.00
Poor	-
Very Poor	-
Total	100.00

The respondents were further asked to give their opinion on the role of the MPEDA in promoting the export of marine products. The data shown in Table 9.15 reveals, 60 per cent of the respondents opined that the existence of the MPEDA is certainly resulting in promotion of export of fish and fish products from the country. While 13.33 per cent of the respondents are of the opinion that the existence of MPEDA hasn't promoted the export of marine products, the remaining 26.67 per cent said that they don't have any specific opinion on it.

Table 9.15 : Do you Feel the Existence of MPEDA is Really Promoting the Export of Marine Products?

Particulars	Percentage of Respondents
Yes	60.00
No	13.33
Can't say	26.67
Total	100.00

Table 9.16: Expectations of the Respondents from MPEDA.

Suggested Changes	Percentage of Respondents
MPEDA should publish the up to date list of importers and their addresses	28.33
MPEDA should take up publicity campaign in favour of Indian exporters in markets abroad	40.00
MPEDA should supply regularly the accurate market information	76.67
MPEDA should conduct regular training for exporters technical personnel for improving and maintaining quality of the products.	56.67
MPEDA should work for obtaining licences and subsidies for exporters liberally.	46.67

An attempt is made in the study to know the expectations of the respondents from the MPEDA. The data presented in Table 9.16 depicts the expectations of the respondents. As many as 76.67 per cent of the respondents opined that the MPEDA should supply accurate market information regularly and with greater frequency. Though the MPEDA is supplying market information it is not comprehensive and not representing the latest market position. The respondents are of the view that the information relating to what has happened is of little use for their business and they need such information that helps them in designing their future course of action. Out of the total, 56.67 per cent of the respondents are of the view that the number of training programmes being organised by the MPEDA is inadequate and as such the technical personnel of the exporters are following traditional methods in quality management. The respondents felt that there is a need to take up more number of training programmes for the technical personnel so as to improve and maintain quality of the exportable fish and fish products. As many as 46.67 of the respondents opined that the MPEDA should use its good offices to obtain grants of subsidies and licences from the concerned authorities of the Union Government and save delay in the execution of various programmes. As many as 40.00 per cent of the respondents opined that the MPEDA should take up publicity campaign in favour of Indian exporters in the markets abroad. They feel that publicity is having a very pivotal role to play in influencing the importers to buy marine products. Since the market is very sensitive, the word of mouth communication through opinion leaders and campaign through credible third parties build-up strong positive image and thereby establishes lead over competitors. The independent exporting organisations with their limited financial and organisational resources are unable to promote their products. Therefore, the MPEDA should take up such initiative and design publicity campaign in the foreign markets. Out of the total, 28.33 per cent of the respondents want that the MPEDA should publish the up-to-date list of importers and their current addresses.

An attempt is made in the study to know the opinion of the respondents on the future prospects of marine products. The data presented in Table 9.17 reveals, the majority of the respondents representing 73.33 per cent are hopeful of a bright future to this business activity. The remaining 26.67 per cent have not denied a bright future to this activity but preferred not to reveal their opinion. The respondents, however, revealed that there are many challenges the business is facing at present in the international scene. The particulars shown in Table 9.18 indicates that growing competition from other countries, difficulty in knowing the quality requirements of the consumers of the importing countries, increasing cost of production, political bans on import of Indian marine products in certain countries, frequent fluctuations in exchange rates, uncertainty and fluctuation in the supply of marine catch and excessive dependence on Japan for exporting marine products are the major challenges. Out of the total, 73.33 per cent of the respondents are of the view that the excessive dependence on Japan market for exporting Indian marine products is not good for the future of the industry as any changes in the market would collapse the business prospects. About 62 per cent of the respondents expressed that the frequent fluctuations in exchange rates are causing lot of problems to them and they are quite unsure of the returns due to the fluctuations. As much as 46.67 per cent of the respondents opined that the cost of production is going-up day by day. Since the market prices are not in their control, the increase in cost of production is eating away the margins. They fear that if the same trend continues the activity becomes unprofitable and discourages the new entrepreneurs to enter into the business. Some countries are creating problems for importing Indian marine products due to some political reasons or due to communication gaps. About 40.00 per cent of the respondents opined that such bans in any part of the world will demoralise the Indian exporters and also damage the image of the Indian products in the other parts of the world.

Table 9.17 : Do you Feel that there is a bright future for the exports of marine products in the country

Particulars	Percentage of respondents
Yes	73.33
No	—
Can't say	26.67
Total	100.00

Table 9.18 : What are the Challenges the Business is Facing at Present?

Particulars	Percentage of Respondents
Growing competition from other countries	38.33
Difficulty in knowing the quality requirements of the importing countries customers	30.00
Increasing cost of production	46.67
Political banning of Indian Material in Certain Countries	40.00
Frequent fluctuations in exchange rates	61.67
Uncertainty and fluctuations in the supply of marine catch	26.67
Excessive dependence on Japan for exporting the marine products	73.33

The respondents suggested certain measures to be taken up by the Government of India for the development of export trade for fish and fish-products. Table 9.19 depicts the suggested measures of the respondents. Out of the total, 86.67 per cent of the respondents strongly feel that the Government must take an active initiative and avoid political bans on Indian products in some countries. The Government of India should develop bi-lateral relations with the countries and enter into agreements that promote export and import trade in both the countries for mutual benefit. As many as 83.33 per cent of the respondents opined that the Government of India should take up market research programmes through the MPEDA and other market research organisations, to explore new markets for Indian marine products to avoid excessive dependency on Japan. The results of the research studies will be helpful in identifying the potential markets around the globe and as such to design a promotional programme to create demand for our products in the markets. Out of the total, 75 per cent of the respondents wanted the Government to take-up special programmes to avoid uncertainty and fluctuations in the supply of marine catch.

Table 9.19 : What Measures do You Suggest to Improve the Business?

Particulars	Percentage of Respondents
Government must be active in avoiding in political banning of the Indian Marine products in some countries	86.67
Efforts must be taken to avoid uncertainty and fluctuations in the supply of marine catch	75.00
The Government of India must take steps to explore new markets for Indian products in various marine products importing countries to avoid excessive dependency of Japan markets.	83.33

10

Conclusions and Strategies for Development

EXPORT OF INDIAN MARINE PRODUCTS

Fish and fish products are the important food items for the larger population spread throughout the world. Several fish producing countries, apart from meeting the demand in the demestic market, are exporting fish and fish products to many countries to meet the demand in the international market and also to earn foreign exchange.

The study revealed the total exports of marine products to various markets in world was 85,843 tonnes in 1986-87 increased to as high as 3.07 lakh tonnes in 1994-95. However, in the subsequent year the exports declined to 2.96 lakh tonnes. The growth of exports of marine products shows an erratic trend during the period. On the other hand the value of exports which was Rs. 460.76 crores in 1986-87 tremendously increased to Rs. 3,501.11 crores in 1995-96 recording an enviable increase of 760 per cent.

There are four major markets identified for the export of marine products in the world. They are Japan, USA, Western Europe countries and other countries. The study revealed, the major share of export was to the Japan market during 1986-87 to 1989-90.

Afterwards the South East Asia emerged as a major market in terms of quantity export. The share of Japan market in the total export which was 43.44 per cent in 1986-87 came down to 17.48 per cent in 1995-96. The share of South East Asian market on the other hand increased from 15.54 per cent in 1986-87 to 37.97 per cent in 1995-96. The quantity export of marine products to all the markets has shown a positive trend.

In terms of value of exports from India, Japan is the undisputed leader in exports in all the years during 1986-87 to 1995-96. However, the share of Japan has been on the decline during the period. In the year 1986-87, as much as 67.42 per cent of the total exports were made to Japan, while in the year 1995-96 the share of the market fell to 45.03 per cent. Western Europe and South East Asia improved their share significantly during the period. While the share of Western Europe increased from 12.70 per cent in 1986-87 to 26.05 per cent in 1995-96, the South East Asia increased its share from 5.26 per cent in 1986-87 to 14.31 per cent in 1995-96. The share of USA which was 12.22 per cent in 1986-87 declined marginally to 10.46 per cent in 1995-96.

The export of the Indian marine products is routed through sea-ways to reach the markets in various countries. In India there are 11 major ports and a large number of minor ports. The major ports are Cochin, Bombay, Madras, Vizag, Calcutta, Paradeep, Tuticorin, Goa, Kandla, Manglore and Jawaharlal Nehru Port (Bombay).

There are four major marine products exported from India. They are frozen shrimp, frozen fish, frozen squid and frozen cuttle fish. As regards quantity-wise export of marine products, the study revealed, frozen shrimp and frozen fish put together account for 66 per cent to 73 per cent out of the total export during the period under study.

In terms of value of marine products export, the share of frozen shrimp varied between 82.04 per cent and 66.78 per cent during the period 1986-87 to 1995-96. The foreign exchange earnings by the export of frozen shrimp which was Rs. 377/.93 crores in 1986-87 increased to Rs. 2,356.43 crores in 1995-96 recording an increase of 524 per cent. Frozen fish occupies second position in contribution to the foreign exchange resource with a contribution ranging from Rs. 22.20 crores in 1986-87 to Rs. 446-57 crores in 1994-95 and Rs. 372.26 crores in 1995-96.

The Indian frozen shrimp has been exported to Japan, European Union, USA, South East Asian countries and other countries for several years. The study revealed that Japan is the major importing country of the Indian frozen shrimp in terms of quantity. The export to this country which was 30,961 tonnes in 1986-87 increased to 41,955 tonnes in 1995-96 recording an increase of 35.51 per cent during the decade. USA was the second major importing country of frozen shrimp during 1986-87 to 1989-90.

During the period the share of export to this country varied between 21.60 per cent and 23.71 per cent, while export increased quantitatively by 53.62 per cent. The export to European Union registered a significant growth from 6,466 tonnes in 1986-87 to 29,397 tonnes in 1995-96 recording an increase of about 355 per cent. The share of the European Union in the total export increased from 13.14 per cent to 30.71 per cent. The export to South East Asian countries started in 1992-93 and since then there was a marginal increase in the export to these countries.

In terms of value also Japan occupies first position in importing Indian frozen shrimp. Through frozen shrimp export to this country, the foreign exchange earnings, which was Rs. 282.53 crores in 1986-87, increased to Rs, 1,426.04 crores in 1995-96 recording an increase of over 400 per cent. The share of European Union increased from 9.83 per cent to 21.01 per cent, while the share of USA declined from 13.90 per cent to 12.31 per cent. Out of the total frozen shrimp imports to Japan, India occupies third position, the first and second positions being occupied by Indonesia and Thailand respectively.

Regarding quantity-wise export of frozen fish during 1986-87 to 1995-96, the study revealed that South East Asia is the major importer of Indian frozen fish. The export to this group of countries increased from 9,664 tonnes to 83,429 tonnes during the period. The share in the total export of frozen fish to South East Asia also increased from 73.56 per cent in 1986-87 to 83.35 per cent in 1995-96. Though

Japan was the second the major importer upto 1989-90, the share of this market was declined to reach 1.88 per cent in 1995-96.

In value terms the foreign exchange earnings of India from South East Asia through frozen fish export increased from Rs. 13.76 crores in 1986-87 to Rs. 252.62 crores in 1995-96 recording an increase of over 1,700 per cent. The earnings from USA increased from Rs. 0.35 crores in 1986-87 to Rs. 41.05 crores in 1995-96. The earnings of this product increased from Rs. 6.91 crores in 1986-87 to Rs. 25.51 crores in 1995-96 from Japan market.

The study revealed that the European Union is the major market for Indian frozen squid outside the country. Export to this Union which was 9,211 tonnes in 1986-87 increased to 29,288 tonnes in 1995-96 recording an increase of 218 per cent. The share of this market in the total frozen squid export varied between 65.05 per cent and 94.58 per cent during the period.

Among the markets for frozen cuttle fish outside India, European Union emerged as the major market since 1987-88. There was a sudden increase in quantity exports from 1,825 tonnes in 1986-87 to 6,618 tonnes in 1987-88 and since then, the exports were increased to European Union to reach 17,899 tonnes in 1995-96. The share of European Union in the total, which was 38.88 per cent in 1986-87 increased to about 72 per cent in the subsequent year and since then there was a fluctuative trend. The Japan market which was the leader in 1986-87 with 45.53 per cent share in the total export of frozen cuttle fish from India, fell to second position with a substantial decline in share to 16.22 per cent in the subsequent year.

Regarding foreign exchange earnings through he export of frozen cuttle fish during 1986-87 to 1995-96, the study revealed that, the foreign exchange earnings from European Union increased from Rs. 3.16 crores in 1986-87 to Rs. 135.56 crores in 1995-96. The earnings from Japan market which was Rs. 9.23 crores in 1986-87 suffered major fluctuations during 1987-88 to 1993-94. The earnings were more than doubled in 1994-95 over previous year to reach Rs. 35.53 crores and it further increased to Rs. 37.67 crores in 1995-96. The earnings from South East Asia were marginal upto 1992-93. In

1993-94, the earnings were about Rs. 33 crores and in the subsequent year the earnings increased to Rs. 70.79 crores from South East Asia.

The world seafood trade is expanding very fast due to increase in per capita consumption of seafood in many industrialised nations. The gap between supply and demand is widening and it is projected by FAO that the gap will be to the tune of 20 million tonnes by the turn of the century. India's marine fish production has touched 2.0 million tonnes as against the estimated potential of 3.9 million tonnes. Since the fish production from capture fisheries is stagnating due to over exploitation and spiralling fuel cost, culture fisheries is picking up very fast to augment fish production. When countries like China, Taiwan, Thailand, Indonesia, Philippines and Vietnam have made rapid strides in coastal aquaculture during eighties and the first half of nineties, India's progress is very slow, despite rich potentials in terms of cultivable fishery resources, material wealth and large human capital of the country.

The seafood industry in many countries is undergoing a rapid change to process more and more 'ready to cook' and 'ready to eat' in convenient packs. Indian seafood industry, by and large, remains still as a supplier of raw-material to the re-processors in foreign countries and 90 per cent of export goes in bulk packs. Because of the effort taken by the Marine Products Export Development Authority, only 10 per cent of our seafood export has started moving in as value-added individually quick frozen packs. To export more quantity in value added form, the industry has to be modernised with induction of new technology.

India depends heavily on one product (shrimp) and one market (Japan) for its marine products exports. Therefore, there is a need for diversification in products and markets. The trend in the marine products export during the last five years is quite encouraging. The market for Indian frozen shrimp expanded significantly to European Union and USA, South East Asia became major market for Indian frozen squid and the frozen cuttle fish. New markets were opened for Indian marine products throughout the year. There is a need to accelerate the efforts to promote the export of marine products.

THE ORGANISATION OF THE MARINE PRODUCTS EXPORT DEVELOPMENT AUTHORITY

The Marine Products Export Development Authority (MPEDA) was constituted in the year 1972 under the Marine Products Export Development Authority Act, 1972. The MPEDA replaced the erstwhile Marine Products Export Promotion Council which was till then looking after the promotion of export of marine products from India. The role envisaged for the MPEDA under the statute was comprehensive covering fisheries of all kinds, export standards, processing, marketing extension and training in various aspects of the fisheries sector.

The objectives of Marine Products Export Development Authority are : a) regulating marine products export; b) laying down standards and specifications; c) rendering financial assistance to processors and exporters; d) helping the industry in relation to market intelligence, export promotion, trade enquiries and the import of essential items; e) providing training in different aspects of the marine products industry, with special reference to quality control, processing and marketing and f) promotion of prawn farming for export production.

The MPEDA's managing body comprises of a Chairman, the director of marine products export development, three members of Parliament, five members to represent one each from Ministry of Agriculture, Ministry of Finance, Ministry of Foreign trade, Ministry of industry and Ministry of Shipping and Transport, Government of India. The Central Government can also nominate other members not exceeding 20 who are in its opinion capable of representing.

The chairman of the MPEDA will be appointed by the Central Government. The Director of Marine Products Export Development Authority is an ex-officio and shall be nominated by the Central Government. All the positions of the managing body are on term basis. The term of the managing body is five years. The chairman is the Convenor of the body and is responsible for all the activities of MPEDA. The Chairman is assisted by two directors and one secretary.

The Secretary takes the responsibility of the functions relaing to Accounts and Audit Cell, Publicity, Administration of Hindi and Vigilence Cell, Co-ordination and Registration, Art and Photographic Section. The Director, Appraisal and Investment, is supported by the Joint Director and he will be responsible for appraisal of various project proposals and offer suggestions on investment projects. The other Director takes the major responsibility of organising the activities of MPEDA. He will be assisted by three Joint Directors, one Project Director at the Central Office and Joint Director/Deputy Director incharge of regional centres and the Resident Directors at overseas trade promotion offices and the Trade Promotion Office established in New Delhi. The Project Director under him was assigned the function of organising the prawn farm project complex.

The joint Director, prawn farming, is responsible for undertaking farming activities at various regional centres. The joint Director of marketing is responsible for collection, analysis and interpretation of statistics relating to fisheries sector, and also delivers the functions relating to economics and marketing services. The Joint Director, Development, takes care of developmental activities, extension activities, frozen storage, quality control and laboratory and research and product development.

The MPEDA has two overseas trade promotion offices one at Tokyo (Japan) and the other at New York (USA) and each office is headed by a resident director. The Trade Promotion Office at New Delhi acts as liaison office with central ministries connected with fisheries sector. The regional offices and sub-regional offices are functioning as field offices for implementation of various activities of the authority besides engaging themselves in the export promotion of marine products and providing guidance and assistance to the processing industry and the export trade.

A close perusal of the organisational chart of MPEDA drives to the opinion that the structure is inadequate to achieve the organisational objectives. Some positions are over loaded and some positions are assigned with distantly related activities. Some activities are not given adequate importance. There is a need to restructure the organisation to improve the performance of MPEDA. Keeping this in view, a new organisational structure that ensures, proper classification of activities and desired importance to the areas that deserve was suggested. As per the new structure, the Chairman of MPEDA will be assisted by one Secretary and six Directors. The Secretary will be responsible for planning, organisation and control of activities relating to Accountancy and Audit, Administration of Hindi, Vigilance and Art and Photo section. The Director of production (capture fisheries) is responsible for registration of producers and traders, co-ordination of production and trading activities, undertaking motivational and promotional schemes, consultancy and guidance and welfare measures. The Director of production of culture fisheries will look after Prawn Farm Project Complex (PEPC) and prawn farming regional centres and sub-regional centres located at various places with the assistance of the Project Director (PEPC) and Joint Directors (Regional prawn farming centres). The Director, technology and modernisation of processing facilities, will take up the functions relating to frozen storage, development, extension, quality control and laboratory and research and product development. The Director of marketing, looks after the statistics, computers, publicity, economics and marketing services, overseas trade promotion offices and trade promotion office in New Delhi. The Director of regional offices, will co-ordinate various activities of the regional and sub-regional offices. The Appraisal and Investment (A&I) activities will be looked after by one director. It is felt that the increase in number of directors is immenent to give importance to the activities like culture fisheries and marketing and also to reduce the burden of a single director who is supposed to hold responsibility of a host of activities in the present organisation structure. The proposed change will encourage fishermen and traders of capture fisheries and also strengthens marketing activities apart from activating regional offices and regional centres for culture fisheries. The new organisational structure also recognises the importance of technological development in fisheries and provides special place to it.

As per the provisions under MPED A Act, no person shall export any marine products unless he has been registered as an exporter with the Authority. The application for registration as exporter of marine products shall be made to the secretary or the other officer authorised by him. The authority will conduct an enquiry if it deems necessary for either grant or refuse such registration.

The study revaled that the number of registered exporters which was 749 in 1986-87 increased to 1,190 in 1995-96 recording an increase of 58.88 per cent. The annual additions during the period varied between 76 and 207. The MPEDA has cancelled the registration of number of exporters during the period. The number of exporters deleted from the list varied between 74 and 166 in a year during the period. The number of registrations deleted every year is off-setting the growth of the number of registrations. Though implementation of the rules for cancellation is a mark of efficiency of MPEDA, the size and recurrence of such cases every year is a problem to be identified and well defined. It is necessary to know the reasons from the exporters point of view for not being able to make the business to the requirements of MPEDA . Appropriate measures need to be initiated to solve the problems and to encourage the exporters to continue in the business. Such measures would not only strengthen the small and marginal exporters but also contribute for the development of the fisheries sector as a whole.

Regarding the number of fishing vessels registered, as well as the additions and deletions during 1986-87 to 1995-96, the study revealed an increasing trend in the number of registered fishing vessels (except during 1994-95). There were 11,696 registered fishing vessels in 1986-87, which increased to 13,560 in 1995-96, recording an increase of 15.94 per cent. The number of additions to the registered fishing vessels varied between 127 to 754.

Export Marketing Services-1

Product Planning and Quality Control Mechanisms

The Marine Products Export Development Authority offers export marketing services to the widely spread producers and middlemen of fish and fish products to reach international markets with their products. The MPEDA acts as liaison between the importers in the foreign countries and the exporters of our country. It offers a product mix to the international market and work for mobilising orders from the importers and inturn takes the responsibility of arranging the products with assured quantity and quality standards apart from the supply within the stipulated time. There are five product lines in the product mix of MPEDA. They are frozen shrimp, frozen fish, frozen cuttle fish, frozen squid and others. The length of the product line of frozen shrimp is very wide including 17 number of products, the product line relating to frozen fish has 9 products, the product line relating to frozen squid has 10 products and the products and the product line relating to others has 14 products.

The Marine Products Exports Export Development Authority has taken two major lines of activity to strengthen product planning and development programme for export marketing of fish and fish products. They are encouraging and promoting the exporters for the production of export oriented fish and fish products and to ensure quality standards to promote the image of the Indian products in the international markets. A number of tasks have been designed to achieve the two important objectives.

The MPEDA has established Prawn Farm Project Complex at Vallarpadom in 1986 with the administrative office located at Cochin, to conduct regular training programmes in shrimp culture, hatchery operation, design and construction of hatchery to government officials, personnel of financial institutions, researchers and entrepreneurs who are interested in taking up shrimp aquaculture as profession and also to operate the hatchery as a demonstration component for trainees.

The Prawn farming regional and sub-regional centres carried out surveys to identify suitable areas for prawn farming in different coastal districts. The study revealed during the decade of 1986-87 to 1995-96, the total area surveyed was 1.23 lakh ha. Out of the total, macro level survey was conducted in 87,901 ha while in over 35,000 ha. micro level survey was conducted.

The Government of India has announced new deep-sea fishing policy in 1986. As per the policy the Ministry of Commerce and the Ministry of Agriculture, Government of India would be nodal agencies for the joint ventures in deepsea fishing. The Ministry of Commerce in turn entrusted mpeda with the responsibility of receiving and examining proposals for joint ventures in deepsea fishing.

The MPEDA has introduced financial schemes for developmental projects for the creation of infrastructure facilities and to build up support to the producers to acquire new machinery and technology.

An attempt was made to know the number of beneficiaries and the amount sanctioned under various schemes intended for the overall development of fish and fish products. As regards the details of the beneficiaries under subsidies for automatic flake/chip/tube ice making machine during 1986-87 to 1995-96, the study revealed that 25 per cent of the cost of the machine subject to a maximum of one lakh rupees was offered as an assistance. There was absolutely no response from the industry for availing itself the subsidy during 1986-87 to 1990-91. Since 1991-92, there were 19 beneficiaries who obtained financial assistance from MPEDA to the tune of Rs. 19.00 lakhs. Under the subsidy for generator set scheme, the study revealed, as many as 86 beneficiaries were granted an amount of Rs. 31.55 lakhs during 1986-87 to 1995-96. The rate of assistance offered was 15 per cent of the cost of the generator set or Rs. 40,000 whichever was less. Each beneficiary availed on an average Rs. 0.37 lakhs as subsidy for purchasing generator set.

Regarding the particulars to beneficiaries under subsidy for installation of improved plate freezers scheme, the study revealed that 117 exporters were sanctioned an amount of Rs. 100.89 lakhs. On an average, each beneficiary obtained a subsidy of Rs. 0.86 lakhs. The subsidy scheme for refrigerated truck/container/trailer with prime mover and generator set is offered on 25 per cent of purchase price on any of these items subject to a maximum of Rs. 2.00 lakhs. By the end of 1995-96 eleven beneficiaries availed subsidy to the tune of Rs. 19.42 lakhs. On an average each beneficiary was given a subsidy of Rs. 1.77 lakhs.

The subsidy for upgrading deficient cold storages scheme offers subsidy of 25 per cent of the cost for improving insulation and for upgrading existing defusers subject to a maximum of Rs. 75,000. This scheme could attract only 21 production units during 1986-87 to 1995-96. The total amount sanctioned during the period was Rs. 9.07 lakhs. Under the subsidy scheme for acquisition of IQF machinery and equipment the amount, subject to a maximum of Rs. 15 lakhs, was offered as an assistance. The scheme was availed by 80 beneficiaries during 1986-87 to 1995-96 and an amount of Rs. 627.17 lakhs was sanctioned for this purpose. The scheme of distribution of insulated fish boxes at subsidised rate of 50 per cent could attract beneficiaries only during 194-95 and in the subsequent year. There were 467 beneficiaries availed a subsidy of Rs. 1.61 lakhs in 1994-95 where as 565 beneficiaries availed a subsidy of Rs. 1.74 lakhs in 1995-96.

The MPEDA introduced the financial assistance scheme to reimburse a part of the cost of high speed diesel consumed by deepsea fishing vessel on an export linked formula in 1991. The study revealed, since the introduction of the scheme an amount of Rs. 761.39 lakhs was sanctioned to the beneficiaries. Against the scheme of financial assistance for modification of fishing vessels below 20 M overall length for multiday fishing operations, 30 per cent of cost of modification/acquisition of equipment subject to a maximum of Rs. 1.5 lakhs per vessel was offered. As per the study, so far an amount of Rs. 7.20 lakhs was granted against six vessels only.

Under the scheme of subsidy for new farm development for prawn farming the subsidy offered was 25 per cent of capital investment or Rs. 30,000 per ha, which ever is less. The maximum limit for an individual/unit under the scheme is Rs. 1.5 lakhs to develop 10 ha.of new area. The study revealed during the decade of 1986-87 to 1995-96, 1,325 farmers have taken subsidy benefit of Rs. 655.80 lakhs for the development of 4,861.27 ha. of land for prawn farming.

In order to ensure quality in seafood exports, the MPEDA has made it mandatory to every seafood processing plant to have a quality control lab for effective implementation of in-plant process quality control. It has introduced a subsidy scheme in 1980 to offer financial subsidy to the processing units to the extent of 50 per cent of the cost subject to a maximum of Rs. 50,000 per unit for setting up a mini laboratory. During the last 10 years as many as 142 processing units were benefited to the tune of Rs. 58.52 lakhs in the form of subsidy.

The MPEDA identified the need for training the Indian quality control technologists to make them equipped with the skills and methods of testing the quality to ensure it to the international standards. It has sponsored ten technologists from the trade and two officers each from EIA and MPEDA to attend the workshop organised by regional laboratory of US FDA, New York.

Quality is the key word for any product or service in the international markets. It is particularly more sensitive in relation to food products. No consumer will be ready to take a minimum risk on quality aspects of food items since there is a possibility of getting into health problems. Most of the countries in the international market are very much particular with the quality standards of importing products particularly food products. The study revealed that 20 per cent of the landings are being discarded as inferior in quality due to improper handling on-board fishing trawlers and at the landing centres. The exporters of the country should be careful about the quality aspects relating to fish and fish products and initiate designing of programmes for quality maintenance and improvement.

Quality management is that aspect of the overall management function which determines and implements the quality policy. Quality policy is a broad guide to act and statement of the desired result or goal to be achieved within a specified action plan. The ISO 9002 specified the requirements of the quality system. In the case of marine products the chief executive of a company should at the outset clearly define and state the quality policy, Most companies are adopting Hazard Analysis Critical Control Points (HACCP) as a means of ensuring control of spoilage, safety and health requirements and ensuring integrity of the product. HACCP has been made mandatory by countries like US FDA, EC for both domestic production as well as for improted fish and fishery products.

The study revealed that in India Marine Products Industry is the first sector in which HACCP system (for export) is being introduced.

But, lack of experience in undertaking hazard analysis, lack of epidemiological data and the dearth of information in technical literature of the food processing sector are some of the constraints on the adoption of HACCP. The result is that the HACCP system which was developed for food processing industries could pose a problem of ineffectiveness in addressing their needs and satisfy their objectives.

Major markets such as EU and United States of America and Canada have commenced implementing HACCP for marine products industry with the principles being extended to improted products. Other developed countries and developing countries have also commenced action on the implementation of HACCP. This development will apply pressure on the Indian marine product industry for concentrating on the export to adopt HACCP. But mutual agreement on the standards of each country and the equivalence of food safety system based on the codex guide lines and standards and other recommendations is the emerging trend in the international regulatory situations.

Export Marketing Services -II

Distribution and Pricing Policies

The Marine Products Export Development Authority is a service organisation, offering export marketing services to the exporting organisations of fish and fish products located throughout the coastline of India. The distribution objectives of the organisation are bi-focal. On the one hand, it has to nurture the producers through the distribution of services in different packages so as to make them equipped with all resources to develop fish and fish-products that are needed by the markets abroad. On the other hand, it has to distribute the services to the importers spread in various countries to facilitate trade on fish and fish products from India.

A service organisation generally uses a direct channel, serving through its branch offices, regional offices and service centres. The design of the distribution system shall be on the basis of service complexity and distribution value. The MPEDA distributes its services directly through regional offices and sub-regional offices, regional centres and sub-regional centres to the target market in India and through trade promotion offices located at New Delhi, Tokyo and New York to the target market outside the country. Regarding the number of regional offices of MPEDA and their location, the study revealed, the number of regional offices, regional centres and sub-regional centres to the target market in India and through trade promotion offices located at New Delhi, Tokyo and New York to the target market outside the country. Regarding the number of regional offices of MPEDA and their location, the study revealed., the number of regional offices which was four in 1986-87 increased to six in 1995-96. During 1986-87 to 1993-94 there are only four regional offices located at Cochin, Madras, Bombay and Calcutta. During 1994-95 the status of the Vizag sub-regional office was elevated to regional office and in 1995-96 the status of Veraval sub-regional office was elevated to regional office. The number of sub-regional offices was seven during 1986-87 to 1993-94. As a result of the status elevation of the Vizag sub-regional office to regional office in 1994-95 and Veraval sub-regional office to regional office in 1995-96, the number of sub-regional office to regional offices came down to five. The sub regional offices are located at Mangalore, Goa, Quilon, Tuticorin and Paradeep. The study revealed that the bearing the changes in the status of two sub-regional offices to regional offices, there is absolutely zero expansion of distribution net work of MPEDA during the decade under study.

The regional centres and sub-regional centres are intended to offer inputs and services relating to export production. The MPEDA has increased the number of regional centres from three in 1986-87 to six in 1987-88. Since then, there has been no expansion in that respect.

The regional offices and sub-regional offices of MPEDA shall discharge their functions relation to the implementation of various schemes of MPEDA besides engaging themselves in the task of facilitating the export of fish and fish products. The offices provide guidance and assistance to the processing industry and the export trade relating to fish and fish products. They function in close liaison with the department of fisheries, the state Government concerned, the Export Inspection Authority and other relevant central and state government agencies.

The regional centres and sub-regional centres of MPEDA extend promotional activities of prawn farming. The centres provide technical guidance to the farmers and also supply required quality inputs at subsidized prices. The centres provide advanced training in prawn hatchery management, prawn culture management, etc.

In order to develop liaison with the Central Government the MPEDA established the trade promotion office in New Delhi in 1976. The trade promotion office maintains close liaison with the ministries concerned. Apart from that, the trade promotion office also extends helping hand to the seafood processors and exporters in solving various problems faced by them.

The MPEDA established two overseas trade promotion offices one at Tokyo in 1978 and the other at New York in 1983. The trade promotion offices shall deliver three major functions. They are: i) market intelligence; ii) market information and other works; and iii) promotion and publicity. The offices maintain close liaison with the officials of Indian Embassy and maintain public relations in the respective countries to improve the image of the Indian seafood industry.

The study revealed that all services from MPEDA are offered at free of cost to every seafood processor and farmer in fishing sector. However, MPEDA charges reduced price for certain inputs like mohua oil cake, prawn seed and prawn feed.

One important pricing area where MPEDA could not develop the mechanism, is the price agreement between the importers and exporters. The Indian exporters require assistance in developing a strategical approach while getting into agreement with the importers. The absence of such approach would result only transactions but not relationships. If MPEDA develops an organisational mechanism that keeps up-to-date the pricing information relating to seafood products, demand supply positions, profiles of importers and farmers, such mechanism can develop long-term agreements and relationships between importers and exporters and ensure win-win proposition to both the parties. The trade promotion offices shall have such mechanism to facilitate price decisions between the parties to go meaningfully.

Export Marketing Services -III

Promotional Strategies

As an apex organisation with an objective to provide facilitating services for the promotion of export trade of fish and fish products, the MPEDA designed a number of training programmes to the fishermen, processors and export organisations on various issues of importance. Advertising, publicity and sales promotion campaigns are also being organised.

The study revealed that the MPEDA identified the need for imparting training on hygienic handling of marine products, after having observed the international market environment and the special focus of importing countries on hygiene factors. The training programmes were initiated in the year 1987-88. During the initial year, seven programmes were organised and the number of beneficiaries was 337. In the subsequent year due to some preliminary problems, only five programmes were undertaken for 280 fishermen. Since 1989-90, there was a substantial increase in the number of programmes.

The MPEDA also has undertaken the training programme to the employees in peeling sheds and pre-processing centres of the exporters on hygienic handling of marine products. The study revealed the number of training programmes organised by MPEDA increased from six in 1986-87 to 127 in 1995-96 recording an increase of over 21 times. The number of participants has also gone up substantially from 300 in 1986-87 to 5,465 in 1995-96 recording an increase of more than 18 times.

Recognising the need for imparting training to the farmers who are cultivating brackishwater prawn farming, the MPEDA designed training programmes and has been executing since 1986-87. The study revealed, the number of training programmes organised varied between seven and 35 during the period. The number of farmers and entrepreneurs trained per annum varied between 172 and 2,334 during the period.

Every year the MPEDA is providing specialised technical assistance on prawn farming to a selected number of farmers. In all, 19,289 farmers were given technical assistance. The MPEDA organises field surveys to prepare feasibility reports for prawn farming and supplies to the existing as well as prospective farmers and entrepreneurs. The study revealed that the number of feasibility reports issued varied from 139 to 603 per annum during 1986-87 to 1995-96. The area covered varied from 596.71 ha. to 3,424.72 ha. During the decade as many as 2,935 feasibility reports were prepared covering an area of 17,856.32 ha. On an average 1,785.63 ha. are being surveyed by MPEDA and the information is being passed on to the farmers every year.

The organisations and the individuals connected with the export of fish and fish products are spread throughout the coastal line of the country. There are big, medium and small size organisations with varied levels of expertise, skill, awareness and knowledge of issues relating to the business. MPEDA recognised to need for educating individuals and organisations relating to this activity. The MPEDA is publishing two journals namely MPEDA Newsletter' and Price Indicator for Marine Products Exports (PRIME). The MPEDA News Letter is a fortnightly publication that presents the national and international news relating to imports and exports, technological developments, political developments, legal developments and the opinions of the experts in the area. MPEDA has published fourteen books on various issues relating to fisheries sector.

MPEDA gave special attention to aquafarming as shrimp is the major exporting item. It has brought out 20 hand-books on aquafarming. In addition to the publication of books and journals, the MPEDA is printing and distributing huge volumes of extension material in the form of folders, book-lets and stickers since 1988-89. The material is being published not only in English and Hindi, but also in various regional languages of coastal India, such as, Telugu, Tamil, Gujarathi, Marathi, Malayalam, Kannada, Oriya, Bengali and

Konkani. The MPEDA failed to continue this exercise due to financial constraints since 1994.

Films and audiovisuals have also been produced by MPEDA for the purpose of exhibiting to the farmers, processors and exporters. The study revealed that there were in total seven films produced during 1986-87 to 1995-96. Out of them, four films were produced during the first two years (two each per year) and one film each was produced during the last three years. The production of audio-visuals started in 1988-89 and during the period 36 audio-visuals were produced. During the last two years, 28 audiovisuals were produced.

Seminars and workshops provide a common platform to exchange views, get clarifications and to develop plans and programmes to face the future. They play a key role in the development of inter-personal understanding and relationships. MPEDA is organising seminars and workshops in various places in the country on various issues of importance involving all sections of the society who are contributing for the growth and development of fisheries sector particularly the export of marine products. The study revealed, the MPEDA has organised 27 seminars and five workshops during 1986-87 to 1995-96.

MPEDA is organising promotional campaigns in the importing countries through publication of books, printing and distribution of folders, book-lets brochures, posters and catalogues and by releasing advertisements in various journals. Further, it campaigns in the selected importing countries, by participating in trade fairs and exhibitions and also by taking part in international seminars and conferences.

Regarding particulars relating to the folders, book-lets brochures, posters and catalogues printed and distributed by MPEDA during 1986-87 to 1995-96. The study revealed that two types of folders, 10 book-lets, none brochures, five posters and one catalogue were printed and distributed in different languages and in required number of copies.

The MPEDA has been actively taken part in trade fairs and exhibitions relating to fisheries sector within the country and outside the country. The study revealed during the period from 1986-87 to 1995-96, the MPEDA has participated in 95 trade fairs and exhibitions - (52 fairs and 43 exhibitions), among which 35 are within India and 60 are outside India. It has participated more in number of exhibitions with the country and when it comes to overseas market, the participation is more in number of fairs. MPEDA participated in a few international seminars and conference to rise the voice of Indian fisheries sector, and to develop marketing opportunities. During the decade of 1986-87 to 1995-96, MPEDA participated in five seminars and six conferences.

The MPEDA has been striving for exploring the new markets for the Indian Products. It has been encouraging the exporters who are on the look out of introducing new products to the international markets and introducing the existing products to the new markets. For the purpose, it has introduced financial assistance scheme for air freighting samples to the markets outside the country. However, due to financial constraints, it could offer only the maximum of Rs. 5,000 to each exporter and that too for a limited number.

EXPORTERS' PROFILE AND VIEWS

The age of 70 per cent of the units varied between five years and 15 years. Ten per cent of the units were established during the last five years while 3.3 per cent of the units had an experience of more than 25 years. As regards the age of the respondents, the study revealed, about 78 per cent of the total respondents are in the age group of 30 to 50 years. Fifty per cent of the respondents are graduates and 13.33 per cent are post-graduates. A little over 13 per cent of the respondents had technical qualification in fisheries while 23.34 per cent of the respondents had technical qualification in areas other than fisheries.

Locational advantage is the most influencing factor for entering into the business followed by high profitability and inheritance. The study revealed that out of the total, 36.67 per cent of the respondents had business experience before entering into the present line of activity. The study revealed that 80 per cent of the respondents got registered with MPEDA during the last ten years and others between 10 to 20 years.

An attempt has been made to know the break-up of various costs incured by the respondents. The study revealed that the share of cost of goods sold in the total cost of production was 94.02 per cent on an average. While the administrative and other overheads accounted for 3.16 per cent, marketing expenses were to the tune of 2.82 per cent. In the area of marketing, the expenditure is made under broad heads of advertising, packaging, transportation, storage and sales promotion. Among them packaging charges is the major expenditure item followed by storage and transportation.

As regards to the annual turnover of the respondents, the study revealed that during 1996-97 the turnover was varied between less than one crore rupees and Rs. 30 crores and above. As many as 43.33 per cent of the respondents had a turnover ranged from Rs. 10 crores to Rs. 20 crores. The turnover of 20 per cent of the respondents varied between one crore rupees and Rs. 10 crores. The turnover of 16.67 per cent of the respondents was in the range of Rs. 20 crores to Rs. 30 crores, while the same number of respondents achieved a turnover of Rs. 30 crores and above.

The study revealed that the total profit earned by all the concerns was Rs. 956 crores in 1995-96 which was increased to Rs. 14.07 crores in 1996-97 recording an increase of 47.17 per cent. In other words, the average profits earned by the units which was Rs. 31.87 lakhs in 1995-96 increased to Rs. 46.90 lakhs in 1996-97.

The fish and fish products exporters have varied forms of organisations. They include sole-proprietary, partnership, public limited company and private limited company. The majority of the respondents representing 52.33 per cent are having public limited companies. Out of the total, 30 per cent are private limited companies. Only 10 per cent preferred partnership form of organisation to derive the benefits of having services from friends relatives to carry out the business operations successfully. Out of the total, 6.67 per cent preferred to remain as sole-proprietors to have total freedom and control over business operations.

The units are engaging full-time employees and part-time employees to carry out the operations. The employees under managerial cadre are all full-time employees. Below the managerial cadre, there are two cadres such as technical staff and non-technical staff. The contract labour are engaged only in the category of technical staff. All non-technical staff are full-time employees. There are 170 employees under managerial cadre including ten female employees. On an average, each unit has three managerial personnel-one each in the categories of MD/ED, office manager and plant manager. The number of technical staff used by the sample units was 3,600, out of which 2,600 are contract labour and 1,000 are full-time workers. The full-time technical staff in all the oragnisations are male members while contract labour in all the organisations are women. The reason being the women are most suitable for certain technical processes and in such processes the requirement is only seasonal. In the category of nontechnical staff there are 730 employees comprising 604 men and 126 women. The study revealed that the respondents are experiencing shortage of skilled workers.

The study revealed, 60 per cent of the exporters are manufacturers cum exporters and the 40 per cent as merchant exporters. The manufacturer cum exporter will have his own plant and processing infrastructure for making ready the fish and fish products for export, while the merchant exporters do not have their own plant and the infrastructure facilities, but they take the facilities for lease or rent to carry out their operations. The study revealed during a year the period from August to December is the peak season and January to March is the moderate season. April to June is the off season and during this period they were forced to keep the plants idle.

The study revealed, 50 per cent of the units are working for 150 to 180 days with full capacity and 36.67 per cent of the units work for 180 to 240 days with full capacity. Ten per cent of the units work for 240 to 300 days with full capacity while 3.33 per cent of the units work for only 60 to 90 days with full capacity. It was also revealed, during non-season period they will take up other works such as repairs and maintenance of plant and machinery, buildings and other assets and the other developmental activities of business such as new market survey, attending training programmes, installation of new plant and machinery, etc. The units sponsor the employees for special training programmes being organised by the EIA,MPEDA,CIFT,etc.

An attempt was made to know the number of suppliers of raw shrimp and fish to the units during 1992-93 to 1996-97. The study revealed that the number of suppliers for the 60 units increased from 2,620 in 1992-93 to 7,950 in 1996-97 recording an increase of 203.4 per cent. The average number of suppliers per unit increased from 43.67 to 132.50. It can be infered that the units are building-up their supplier network over the years. The units are building-up supplier network mostly through company personnel. Existing suppliers are the second major source while the suppliers who came on their own are the third major source.

All the respondents are producing shrimp. Fish is also produced by a few respondents in limited quantities. The study revealed that more and more units are introducing fish as their new product line, as an expansion to their product mix.

Marketing information is the basic input for the organisations to become adaptable for the changes in the external environment. The study revealed agents and brokers are the major source for marketing information to the exporters followed by the association of the exporters. Apart from the two, the exporters are getting information by observing competitors and co-exporters, through trade journals and MPEDA. The MPEDA could not become a major source for the exporters as far as marketing information is concerned. It is unfortunate that the organisation though having supply of market information as one of the important objectives, could not turn to be useful source to the exporters. The findings of the study indicate that the information being supplied by the MPEDA is not been felt useful and important by the exporters for their business purposes. Therefore, there is a need for MPEDA to review the communication programmes and check their degree of effectiveness and usefulness to the target audience. It should include in its communication all such features of information which support the exporters effectively in their decision making process relating to various activities.

An attempt was made to know how the prices are being fixed in the business. The exporters have to arrive at pricing decisions in two different situations. First, when they buy raw-shrimp and fish from the suppliers, the exporter has to arrive at the pricing decision in the role of a buyer. Secondly, when the exporter offers it for sale to various importers he has to arrive at the pricing decision in the capacity of a seller. The pricing methods used for the purposes by the respondents include cost plus market price, negotiated price, negotiated price and the price suggested by the exporters association. They study revealed that the majority are purchasing the produce from suppliers at market price. A few are adopting negotiation price and some are following the price suggested by exporters association in purchasing the raw-shrimp/fish. In the case of pricing to the importers, the exporters are mostly adopting negotiated pricing method. Next to the negotiated price, mark-up pricing is followed by many. Market price and suggested price by exporters association are also being followed few. The respondents express that they are facing some problems with the suppliers as far as the fixation of price is concerned. They revealed, the suppliers are demanding for higher price every time and it has become very difficult for them to convince the suppliers on the changing situations in the market. The respondents also expressed that they are also facing problems with the importers too in pricing decisions. The major problem being language barrier in communication. The exporters are not eloquent with the foreign languages and as such they are unable to participate in the negotiations freely with confidence. Some exporters are of the view that the hospitality expenses are too heavy for them to continue the negotiations with foreign importers. The respondents are looking for the helping hand from MPEDA in this respect. The apex body can build-up a team of negotiations on behalf of the exporters of the country. These specialist negotiators shall take active part in arranging importer and exporter meets and facilitate for effective communication which yield fruitful negotiations.

The study revealed, 96 per cent of the respondents selling their produce to foreign agents while four per cent sell to customer companies directly. Regarding the criteria adopted by the respondents in selecting the agents and the customer companies, the study revealed that financial soundness is the major criteria followed by good will for selecting the foreign agents. In the selection of the customer companies also the financial soundness and the goodwill are the major influencing factors.

The study revealed personal selling and sales promotion are mostly used for promotion. All respondents are using personal selling and 80 per cent of the respondents are using sales promotion techniques for promotion. Advertising is not popular devise as considered by the respondents, only 10 per cent use advertising for promotion.

PERFORMANCE APPRAISAL

An attempt was made in the study to appraise the overall performance of The Marine Products Export Development Authority with the help of the analysis of capital, liabilities and assets and income and expenditure pattern and the opinions of the exporters on the role of the MPEDA in promoting export trade of fish and fish products.

The study revealed the capital fund of the MPEDA increased form Rs. 5.68 crores in 1986-87 to Rs. 12.07 crores in 1995-96 recording an increase of 112.50 per cent. The MPEDA also develops different funds for some specific purposes. The amount allocated to the specific funds for some specific purposes. The amount allocated to the specific funds which was Rs. 23.03 lakhs in 1986-87 rose to Rs. 1,162.73 lakhs in 1995-96 recording an increase of 4,948.76 per cent. The MPEDA has developed provident fund, terminal benefit of staff of MPEP Council, equity participation scheme investment fund account, bio-technology fund, and food processing fund.

The study revealed the MPEDA has surplus income over expenditure during 1986-87 to 1988-89. However, during 1989-90 and 1990-91 there was a deficit of Rs. 47.46 lakhs and Rs. 22.78

lakhs respectively. During 1991-92 the MPEDA had the surplus income of more than three crore rupees over expenditure and in the subsequent year also it had a surplus of more than Rs. 1.5 crores. In 1993-94, the surplus was reduced to Rs. 77.46 lakhs and during 1994-95 and 1995-96, the annual deficit raised to the tune of Rs. 231.00 lakhs and Rs. 175.23 lakhs respectively. The study observed that during the decade the MPEDA had surplus income over expenditure for six years and committed expenditure over income for four years. The expenditure over income was substantial during the last two years and there is a need to review the expenditure pattern in order to get the financial situation under control.

One of the important measures for the appraisal of the performance of a service organisation is to know the opinions, and the levels of satisfaction of the target market and to study their interaction with the organisation. Keeping this in view, an attempt is made in the study to know the interactions, views and opinions of the respondents on MPEDA. Regarding particulars relating to frequency of respondents contacts with MPEDA officials, the study revealed 53.33 per cent of the respondents do not have any pre-determined time schedule to contact the MPEDA officials. One third of the respondents revealed that they will contact the MPEDA officials once in a month regularly where as 13.34 per cent of the respondents revealed that they contact the MPEDA officials once in six months.

All the respondents revealed that the MPEDA officials visit their organisations to supervise how the activities are going on. One third of the respondents opined that the visits of the MPEDA personal are useful for the betterment of their organisations and they want greater frequency of the visits of the MPEDA personnel to their organisations.

Regarding the opinions of the respondents on the performance of the MPEDA in offering marketing services, the study revealed 90 per cent of the respondents rated the performance of MPEDA as satisfactory. While 6.67 per cent of the respondents rated the performance as very good, 3.33 per cent of the respondents rated the performance as excellent. None of the respondents rated the performance as poor or very poor. The study concluded that the MPEDA could establish a positive image through the efficient production and delivery of the services. However is has still to work hard with innovative schemes and greater involvement in the operations of the exporters to get an improved rating.

Sixty per cent of the respondents opined that the existence of the MPEDA is certainly resulting in promotion of export of fish and fish products from the country. While 13.33 per cent of the respondents are of the opinion that the existence of MPEDA hasn't promoted the export of marine products, the remaining 26.67 per cent said that they don't have any specific opinion on it.

As many as 76.67 per cent of the respondents opined that the MPEDA should supply accurate market information regularly and with greater frequency. Though the MPEDA is supplying market information it is not comprehensive and not representing the latest market position. The respondents are of the view that the information relating to what has happened is of little use for their business and they need such information that helps them in designing their future course of action. Out of the total, 56.67 per cent of the respondents are of the view that the number of training programmes being organised by the MPEDA is inadequate and as such the technical personnel of the exporters are following traditional methods in quality management. The respondents felt that there is a need to take up more number of training programmes for the technical personnel so as to improve and maintain quality of the exportable fish and fish products. As many as 46.67 of the respondents opined that the MPEDA should use its good offices to obtain grants of subsidies and licences from the concerned authorities of the Union Government and save delay in the execution of various programmes. As many as 40.00 per cent of the respondents opined that the MPEDA should take up publicity campaign in favour of Indian exporters in the markets abroad. Out of the total, 28.33 per cent of the respondents want that the MPEDA should publish the up-to-date list of importers and their current addresses.

Regarding the opinion of the respondents on the future prospects of marine products, the study revealed the vast majority of the respondents representing 73.33 per cent are hopeful of a bright future to this business activity. The remaining 26.67 per cent have not denied a bright future to this activity but preferred not to reveal their opinion. The study revealed that growing competition from other countries, difficulty in knowing the quality requirements of the consumers of the importing countries, increasing cost of production, political bans on import of Indian marine products in certain countries, frequent fluctuations in exchange rates, uncertainty and fluctuation in the supply of marine catch and excessive dependence on Japan for exporting marine products are the major challenges. Out of the total, 73.33 per cent of the respondents are of the view that the excessive dependence on Japan market for exporting Indian marine products is not good for the future of the industry as any changes in the market would collapse the business prospects. About 62 per cent of the respondents expressed that the frequent fluctuations in exchange rates are causing lot of problems to them and they are quite unsure of the returns due to the fluctuations. As much as 46.67 per cent of the respondents opined that the cost of production is going-up day by day. Since the market prices are not in their control, the increase in cost of production is eating away the margins. They fear that if the same trend continues the activity become unprofitable and discourages the new entrepreneurs to enter into the business. Some countries are creating problems for importing Indian marine products due to some political reasons or due to communication gaps. About 40.00 per cent of the respondents opined that such bans in any part of the world will de-moralise the Indian exporters and also damage the image of the Indian products in the other parts of the world.

The respondents suggested certain measures to be taken up by the Government of India for the development of export trade for fish products. Out of the total , 86.67 per cent of the respondents strongly feel that the government must take an active initiative and avoid political bans on Indian products in some countries. The Government of India should develop bi-lateral relations with the countries and enter into agreements that promote export and import trade in both the countries for mutual benefit. As many as 83.33 per cent of the respondents opined that the Government of India should take up market research programmes through the MPEDA and other market research organisations, to explore new markets for Indian marine products to avoid excessive dependency on Japan. The results of the research studies will be helpful in identifying the potential markets around the globe and as such to design a promotional programme to create demand for our products in the markets. Out of the total, 75 per cent of the respondents wanted the government to take up special programmes to avoid uncertainty and fluctuations in the supply of marine catch.

The strategic approach is not followed for the promotion of exports of fish and fish products in the country by the governmental as well as non-governmental organisations. The MPEDA, inspite of its existence for more than 25 years, has not achieved significant results. The abundant product resources of the country could not be used for the exploitation of market potential outside the country. In order to develop fisheries sector in India in general and promotion of exports of fisheries in particular it is necessary to develop strategies and orient organisational efforts towards the achievement of the objectives. The MPEDA should shoulder the major responsibility, since it is the only apex organisation looking after the exports of fish products from the country.

STRATEGIES FOR DEVELOPMENT

There are two different markets for which the MPEDA has to develop strategies. The first market being the exporters and fishermen of the country and the second market is the importers of various countries. The MPEDA should prepare the internal market to face and to win the markets outside. The study revealed that there are eight areas wherein the MPEDA should take proper steps for strengthening the internal market.

1. The exporters demand for up-to-date market information with projections for the future need to be satisfied. The MPEDA may purchase the services of the professional market research organisations to acquire the required information and should design the communication network which can pass on the information as quickly as possible to the exporters and fishermen in the country. It cannot be a difficult proposition for MPEDA in the era of information explosion.

2. The study revealed that the exporters are not equipped with the latest technology for quality processing and hygienic handling and they are also not able to find right technology and right source for the adoption in their plants. The international markets are becoming more and more sensitive as regards to the processing as well as hygiene factors are concerned. The had experiences the Indian marine products had in the recent years emphasises the need for greater care and concern over the issue. The MPEDA should get into collaborations with internationally reputed fisheries technological institutes for the supply of suitable technology as well as hygiene handing.

   There are a large number of exporters from the country exporting fish and fish products. The technical lapses in quality management by one or a few exporters will tarnish the image of the Indian products throughout the world. To minimise the risk of such happenings to the lowest point there is a need for the establishment of an independent agency for the issue of standardisation certificate to the exporters of the country. The agency will test the samples of the export of fish and fish products of each and every exporter and check whether the products satisfy the international standards or the standards expected by the respective markets to which the products are directed to. The Government of India should make the certificate as mandatory for all exporters from the country.
3. The personnel of the exporting organisations should be given training on latest developments in processing and hygiene factors. The MPEDA has already initiated programmes for training the fishermen and the employees of exporting organisations. There is a need to intensify these activities to cover larger groups.
4. The exporters of the country could not establish effective communication linkage with the importers of various countries due to problems mentioned already. The MPEDA should strengthen the liaison service offerings by supplying up-to-date list of importers to exporters and exporters to importers. It should build-up a team of facilitators who are experts in multiple languages to facilitate effective communication between the importers and exporters so that both the parties will have clarity and understanding on the proposed transaction. If the

communication between the importers and exporters is effective it may result in building-up good relationships.

5. The MPEDA has introduced a number of schemes for financial assistance to exporters and fishermen. The exporters revealed that the procedural complexities are very high and as a result they could not avail the benefits of the financial assistance and sometimes due to procedures, they could not get the assistance at the right time. In many of the cases, MPEDA is processing the applications and forwarding to the other governmental machineries for a grant of assistance. The Government of India should delegate the authority to MPEDA to decide the sanction of financial assistance and also release required amount of money to meet all these requirements. The MPEDA can adopt single window system for certain schemes.
6. Measures should be initiated to protect the Exclusive Economic Zone (EEZ).
7. The transport of exportable items has been one of the major problems faced by the exporters of the country. The fish and fish products are most perishable and as such any problem in transport may lead to disastrous consequences. Ocean transport is used mostly by the Indian exporters to reach overseas markets. Shipping space becoming scarce during the season periods and due to that the exports are getting delayed. The MPEDA should estimate the supply positions and take initiative for arranging shipping space to all the exporters.
8. Development of new products and value added products may have competitive edge in the overseas markets. The individual exporters cannot spend on research and development independently for the development of new products or value added products. Therefore, there is a need for promoting research laboratories on co-operative basis. A group of exporters may be encouraged to develop a co-operative research organisation. The exporters can share the benefits of the results of such organisations and strengthen their stand in the international markets.

In the overseas market lot of efforts need to be put into strengthen the marketability of Indian fish and fish products. The MPEDA should consider the following issues for the purpose:

1. The Indian exporters are depending upon the traditional markets particularly Japan. Serious attempts were not made so far for the identification of new markets. Fish is an universal product and the world statistics reveal that the markets for these products are spread throughout the globe. It is necessary to introduce the Indian products to the new markets so that the trade risk can be minimised and also new demand can be created. The MPEDA has to constitute a team of experts to study the potential markets for Indian products and the specific requirements of the markets. Based on the recommendations of the committee the supply can be arranged.
2. Competition became a universal phenomenon and the market for fish and fish products is not an exception. Even in the traditional markets India is facing severe competition from countries like China, Japan, Indonesia, Thailand, etc. No marketing organisation can ignore competition. Design such strategies that facilitate a run over on the competition to reach the market. The Indian exporters need strategic support to face competition from some countries. The MPEDA should extend a helping hand in this respect.
3. The influence of politics on international trade is always found significant. The bi-lateral relations between the countries are important for the import and export trade. The MPEDA, with the information that it has on various potential markets, should influence the Government to have bi-lateral relations for facilitating export trade of fish and fish products.
4. Communication plays predominant role in influencing the marketability of various products. The MPEDA has not directed its efforts significantly on this issue. Lack of proper communication campaign may be one of the major reasons for a number of problems for Indian products in the overseas markets. It is suggested therefore that the MPEDA should design promotional programmes on a regular basis for the established markets as well as the markets that are selected for entry. It should concentrate on building relationships with importers, maintaining relations with importers and also enhancing relationships. There is a need to replace the transaction oriented marketing by relationships marketing. The MPEDA should also establish communication linkage with the consumers directly, in such markets where the demand for Indian fish and

fish products is significant. It should take up mass communication campaign to build up a positive image to the Indian products. One important measure in this direction would be branding the Indian products. The MPEDA can promote some brands as the products of MPEDA and can use such brands for building-up image for Indian products.

To design the policies, programmes and strategies on various issues that are mentioned, there is a need for MPEDA to go for structural re-organisation as suggested in Chapter III. It is felt that such changes would certainly facilitate for the achievement of organisational objectives.

Bibliography

BOOKS AND REPORTS

AGARWALA, S.N., 'India's Population Problem', Tata Mc Graw-Hill Publishing Co. Ltd., New Delhi, 1974.

AMARCHAND, D., and Vardarajan, B., 'An Introduction to Marketing', Vikas Publishing House Private Ltd., New Delhi, 1979.

AMON, 'Report on the first Advisory Committee Meeting of the FAO/SIDA Centre for the Development of Traditional Fishing Communities in the Bay of Bengal', FAO Rome, 1976.

ANDERSON, Lee G., 'The Economics of Fisheries Management', John Hopkins, Baltimore, 1977.

ARORA, R.C., Fishery Development In : Development of Agriculture and Allied Sectors - An Integrated Area Approach', S. Chand and Co., (Pvt) Ltd., New Delhi, 1976.

ARUN MONAPPA, AND MIRZA S. SAIYADAIN, 'Personnel Management', Tata McGraw-Hill Publishing Company Limited, New Delhi, 1979.

BABAJI, U., Development of Marine Fisheries', Andhra University, Visakhapatnam, June, 1984.

BANSAL, M.P., Human Resource Development In Public Enterprises, RBSA Publishers, Jaipur, 1991.

Bearden, J.H., 'Personal Selling : Behavioural Science Readings and Cases', John Wiley and Sons Inc., New York, 1967.

BENNETT, 'Marketing', Tata Mc Graw-Hill Publishing Company Ltd., New Delhi, 1994.

BENSON, P. SHAPIRE, ROBERT J. DOLAN And JOHANA. Quilch, 'Marketing Management Readings from Theory and Practice', Vol.Iv, III,Irvin Inc., Illinois, 1985.

BHATTACHARYYA, B., Export Marketing, Strategies for success, Global Business Press, New Delhi, 1991.

BHATTACHARYA, S.N., 'Fisheries in Indian Economy', Metropolitan Book Company, New Delhi, 1965.

BOTTEMANNE, K.J., 'Principles of Fisheries Development', North Holland Publishing Co., Amsterdam, 1959.

BOVEE, 'Marketing', Tata Mc Graw-Hill Publishing Company Ltd., New Delhi, 1994.

CAVES, R.E., Trade and Economic Structure : Models and Methods, Harward University Press, Cambridge Mass, 1960.

CHAMBERS 20TH CENTURY DICTIONERY, W.R. Chambers Ltd., London, 1948.

CHARVAT, F.J., And WHITMAN, W.J., 'Marketing Management : A Questionnaire Approach', Boston (Massachusetts), D.C. Health and Company, 1964.

CHHABRA, T.N., And GROVER, S.K., 'Marketing Management', Dhanpatrai and Co. (Pvt.) Ltd., Delhi, 1997.

CHOPRA, B.N., Handbook of Indian fisheries, Ministry of Agriculture, Government of India, New Delhi, 1951.

CHUNAWALLA, S.A., 'Marketing Principles and Practice', Himalaya Publishing House, Mumbai, 1997.

CONVERSE, HUEGEY, MITCHELL, 'Elements of Marketing', Committee of Marketing Definitions, 'A Glossary of Marketing Terms', American Marketing Association, 1960.

CUISSY, W., And R. KAPLAN, 'Salesmanship : The Personal Force in Marketing', John Wiley and Sons Inc., New York, 1969.

DABLI, V.L., 'India's foreign Trade', Vora and Co., Bombay, 1973.

DEHADRAI, P.V., 'Creation of EEZ and Development of Marine Fisheries in India', Published in Trivedi, K.K., Fisheries Development 2000 A.D. Proceedings of an International Conference held at New Delhi, February 4-6, Oxford and IBH Publishing Co. New Delhi, 1986.

DESAI, M.B., and BAICHWAL, P.R., 'Economic Survey of Fishing Industry in Thane district', Maharashtra, Part 1, 1960.

DEVENDRA THAKUR, 'Export Marketing' (Trends in World Economy -3), Deep and Deep Publications, New Delhi, 1993.

DURAI RAJ, N., 'A study of Marwle Fishing Industry in Thanjavur District', Department of Economics, Madurai Kamaraju University, Tamilnadu, 1983.

ECONOMIC INTELLIGENCE SERVICE, Foreign Trade Statistics of India, May, 1996, Centre for Monitoring Indian Economy Pvt. Ltd. Bombay.

FOOD AND AGRICULTURAL ORGANISATION, 'Possibility of Increasing World Food Production', Basic Study, No.10, Rome, 1963.

——'Third World food Survey', Basic Study, No.11, Rome, 1963.

——'Fisheries in Food Economy', Basic Study, No. 19, Rome, 1968.

——'International Fish Marketing', Rome, 1954.

GANDHI, J.C., 'Marketing: A Managerial Introduction', Tata Mc Graw Hill Publishing Company Ltd., New Delhi, 1995.

GEORGE, P.C., ANTONY RAJA, B.T., AND GEORGE, K.C., Fishery Resources of the Indian Economic Zone', in souvenir issued on the occasion of Silver Jubilee Celebration of the Integrated Fisheries Project, Cochin, October, 1977.

GEORGE R. TERRY, STEPHEN G. FRANKLIN, 'Principles of Management', A.I.t.B.S. Publishers and Distributors (Regd.)., All India Traveller Bookseller, Delhi, 1994.

GEORGE T. MILKOVICH, And JOHN W. Boudreau, Personnel 'Human Resource Management, A Diagnostic Approach', All India Traveller Bookseller, Delhi, 1994.

GERALD M, MEIER., 'Problems of Trade Policy', Oxford university Press, 1973.

GLOBAL STRATEGIES FOR MARINE ENVIRONMENTAL PROTECTION, Reports and Studies No.5., IMO, London, 1991.

GOPALAN, C., RAMASASTRI, B.V., AND BALASUBRAHMANIAN, S.C., 'Nutritive value of Indian Foods', National Institute of Nutrition, Indian Council of Medical Research, Hyderabad, 1976.

GOPAL JI., 'Personal Management Through Cost and Ratios', Anmol Publications, New Delhi, 1988.

GOVERNMENT OF INDIA, Planning Commission, Planning Evaluation organisation, 'Evaluation of the programme of Mechanisation of Fishing Boats', New Delhi, 1971.

——Ministry of Agriculture and Cooperation, 'Handbook of Fishery Statistics', New Delhi, 1996.

GRANS, J.M., *et al.*, 'The Frontiers of Public Administration Code in Administration and Management of Electricity in India', Deep and Deep Publications, New Delhi, 1987.

HEINZ WEIHRICH, And HAROLD KOONTZ, 'Management, A Global Perspective', Mc Graw-Hill, Inc. New York, 1993.

INDIAN INSTITUTE OF FOREIGN TRADE, Survey of India's Export Potential of Marine Products, Indian Institute of Foreign Trade, New Delhi, March, 1970.

JAIN, P.K., 'International Marketing', Mrs. Kiran Gupta Printwell Publishers, Jaipur, 1988.

JHA, S.M., AND SINGH, L.P., 'Marketing Management in Indian Perspective', Himalaya Publishing House, Bombay, 1998.

JINGRAN, V.G., 'Fish and Fisheries of India', Hindustan Publishing Corporation, Delhi, 1991.

JOHN BERNARDIN, H., and JOYCE E.A. RUSSELL, Human Resource Management, An Experimental Approach, Mc Graw-Hill, Inc. New York, 1993.

JOHN CHILD, 'Organisation : A Guide to problems and practices', Harper and Rao Publishers, London, 1977.

JOHN FAYER WEATHER, 'International Marketing', Prentice-Hall of India Private Limited, New Delhi, 1976.

KULKARNI, G.R., And SRIVASTAVA, U,K., 'Systems frame work of the Marine food Industry in India', New Delhi, 1986.

KURIAN, C.V., And SEBASTIAN, V.O., 'Prawns and Prawn Fisheries of India', Hindustan Publishing Corporation, Delhi, 1986.

KURIAN, J., 'Technological Change in Fishing : Its Impact of Fishermen', Centre for Development Studies, Trivandrum, March, 1982.

LAKSHMINARAYANA RAI, M., 'Economics of Boat Building Yard in Mangalore', Central Institute of Fisheries Education, Bombay, 1977 (unpublished).

LANCASTER, 'Essentials of Marketing', Tata Mc Graw-Hill Publishing Company Ltd., New Delhi, 1994.

LUKAS, H.W., 'Fisheries of the Bombay Province', 1908-10, Bombay, 1911.

MAIZELS, A., Industrial Growth and World Trade', Cambridge University Press, London, 1963.

MAJUMDAR, D.C., 'Managing Marine Products Quality, Productivity', New Delhi, 1987.

MAJARO, 'The Essence of Marketing', Prentice- Hall of India Private Ltd., New Delhi, 1994.

MAMORIA, C.B., And Mamoria, S., 'Marketing Management', Kitab Mahal, Allahabad, 1997.

MARY CHANDY, 'Fishes', India- The Land and the People, National Book Trust, India, 1994.

MATHEW, M.J., 'Management of Export Marketing', RBSA Publishers, Jaipur, 1993.

MIRZA S. SAIYADAIN, 'Human Resources Management', Tata MC Graw-Hill Publishing Company Limited New Delhi, 1988.

MISRA, S.N., and BAYER, J., 'Cost-Benefit Analysis : A Case Study of the Ratnagiri Fisheries Project', Hindustan Publishing corporation, Delhi, 1976.

MITRA, G.N., 'Observations on the development of Fisheries in Orissa', 1961.

MOHAN, K.P., 'The Situation of Indian Fishing Industry and Indian Fishermen', 1950.

MOOKERJEE, S.S., 'Theory and Practice of Management', Surjeet Publications, Delhi, 1993.

MONK, 'Go International : Your Guide to Marketing and Business Development', Tata Mc Graw-Hill Publishing Company Ltd., New Delhi, 1994.

NCAER, Techno-Economic Survey of Madras, National Council of Applied Economic Research, New Delhi, 1961.

——Techno-Economic Survey of Andhra Pradesh, National Council of Applied Economic Research, New Delhi, 1962.

——Techno-Economic Survey of Kerala, National Council of Applied Economic Research, New Delhi, 1972.

——Techno-Economic Survey of Orissa, National Council of Applied Economic Research, New Delhi, 1972.

——Techno-Economic Survey of West Bengal, National Council of Applied Economic Research, New Delhi, 1962.

——Techno-Economic Survey of Gujarat, National Council of Economic Research, New Delhi, 1963.

—Techno-Economic Survey of Maharashtra, National Council of Applied Economic Research, New Delhi, 1963.

—Techno-Economic survey of Goa, Daman and Diu, National Council of Applied Economic Research, New Delhi, 1964.

—Techno-Economic Survey of Mysore, National Council of Applied Economic Research, new Delhi, 1964.

NCAER, Demand for fish and its transportation and storage in selected cities, Publications Division, National Council of Applied Economic Research, New Delhi, 1980.

NCAER, Export Prospects of Fish and Fish Products, National Council of Applied Economic Research, New Delhi, 1965.

NEELAMEGHAN, S., (Ed.,), ' Marketing Management and Indian Economy', Vikas Publishing House, New Delhi, 1987.

ORGANISATION AND MANAGERIAL PROBLEMS OF APEX CO-OPERATIVE ORGANISATION, with Special Reference to Markeeed, Co-operative perspective, vol, II, No,1, 1977.

PRASAD, B., 'Post-war Development of Indian Fisheries : Memorandum', Government of India Press, New Delhi, 1943.

PERUMAL, M.C., 'Operation of Training Vessels, Proc.symp. On the need for a Techno-Economic Survey of the Deepsea fishing Resources', Agricultural Finance Corporation Ltd., Bombay, 1973.

PETER, F. DRUCKER, 'Marketing for Results', Allied Publishers, Bombay, 1975.

PHILIP KOTLER, 'Marketing Management : Analysis Planning, Implementation and Control', Printice Hall of India, New Delhi, 1994.

PHILIP KOTLER, And ARMSTRONG, 'Principles of Marketing', Prentice-Hall of India Private Ltd., New Delhi, 1994.

PILLAI, T.V.R., 'Socio-Economic Development of Fishermen Communities in India-Progress of Fisheries Development in India', The first All India Fisheries Exhibition, Cuttack, 1956.

PLANNING COMMISSION 'First Five Year Plan', Ministry of Information and Broadcasting Government of India, Delhi, 1952.

PLANNING COMMISSION 'Second Five Year Plan', Government of India, New Delhi, 1956.

PLANNING COMMISSION 'Third Five Year Plan', Government of India, New Delhi, 1961.

PLANNING COMMISSION 'Third Five Year Plan', A Draft Outline, Government of India, New Delhi, 1960.

PLANNING COMMISSION 'Fourth Five Year Plan', Government of India, New Delhi, 1969.

PLANNING COMMISSION 'Fifth Five Year Plan', Government of India, New Delhi, 1976.

PLANNING COMMISSION 'Sixth Five Year Plan', Government of India, New Delhi, 1981.

PLANNING COMMISSION 'Seventh Five year Plan', Government of India, New Delhi, 1985.

PLANNING COMMISSION 'Eighth Five Year Plan', Government of India, New Delhi, 1993.

RAJAN SEXENA, 'Marketing Management', Tata Mc-Graw Hill Publishing Company Ltd., New Delhi, 1997.

RAMESH BABU, S, 'India's Foreign Trade-Some Trends', Chugh Publications, Allahabad, 1988.

RAMI REDDY, S., 'Study of fisheries Development in the Coastal Districts of Andhra Pradesh', Technical Cell, Andhra University, Waltair, December, 1978 (Mimeo).

RAO, P.S., 'Fishery Economics and Management in India', Pioneers Publishers and Distributors, Bombay, 1983.

RAO, T.V., VERMA, K., ANIL K. KHANDELWAL And E. ABRAHAM S.J., 'Alternative Approach and Strategies of Human Resources Development', Rawat Publications, Jaipur, 1989.

RANDALL B. DUNHAM, And JON L. PIERCE, 'Management', Scott, Foreman and Company, Glenview, Illinois, London, 1989.

RATHOR, B.S., and RATHOR, J.S., 'Export Marketing', Himalaya Publishing House, Delhi, 1993.

RAVI SHANKAR, 'Services Marketing-The Indian Experience', Manas Publications, Delhi, 1993.

RICHARD HACON., 'Personal and Organisational Effectiveness', McGraw-Hill Book Company (UK) Limited, Maidenhead, 1972.

RICHARD R. STILL, EDWARD W. CUNDIFF, and NORMAN A.P. GOVONI, 'Sales Management Decisions, Strategies and Cases', Printice-Hall of India Private Limited, New Delhi, 1996.

RICKY W.GRIFFIN, 'Management', A.I.T.B.S. Publishers and distributors (regd.), Delhi, 197.

SANJEEVA RAO, M.S., 'Export of Indian Marine Products - A study of the Trends and Prospects for Product and Market Diversification', Ph.D. thesis, Andhra University, Waltair 1980 (unpublished).

SATISH KUMAR., 'Developing Countries in International Trade Relations', Chugh Publications, Allahabad, 1987.

SILAS, E.G., Indian Fisheries 1947-1977', The Marine Products Export Development Authority, Cochin, 1977.

SINGH, S.B., Hon. Minister for Agriculture and Rural Development At International Conference- 'Fisheries Development : 2000 A.D.' held at New Delhi, February 4-6, 1985.

SINHA, P.K., and SAHOO, S.C., 'Services Marketing', Himalaya Delhi, 1992.

SREEDHARAN, V.P., 'Industrial and Commercial Prospects of Fish and Fish products in India with Special Reference to Kerala', Kerala University, 1989 (unpublished thesis).

SRIVASTAVA, K.R., Report on the fishing Industry, Kutch, Government of India, Bhuj Kutch, 1951.

SRIVASTAVA, U.K., BAKUL DHOLAKIA, H., Vathsal, S., And Chidambaram, K., Fishery Sector of India', Oxford and IBH Publishing Co., New Delhi, 1991.

SRIVASTAVA, U,K., BAKUL DHOLAKIA, H., VATHSAL, S., AND CHIDAMBARAM, K., 'Fishery Sector of India', Oxford and IBH Publishing Co., New Delhi, 1991.

SRIVASTAVA, U,K., DHARMA REDDY, M., and GUPTA, V.K., 'Management of Marine Fishing Industry', An Analysis of Problems in harvesting and Processing, Oxford and IBH Publishing Co. New Delhi, 1982.

STANTON, W.J., 'Fundamentals of Marketing', Mc Graw Hills, New York, 1980.

STEVEN W. HAYS, And Zane Reeves, T., 'Personal Management in the Public Sector', Allen and Bacon, Inc. Boston, 1984.

SUBBA RAO, N., 'Economics of Fisheries : A case study of Andhra Pradesh', Daya Publishing House, New Delhi, 1986.

—'Mechanisation and Marine Fishermen : A case study of Visakhapatnam', Northern Book Centre, New Delhi, 1988.

TALWAN, P.K., And KACKER, R.K., 'Commercial sea fishes of India', Zoological Survey of India, Calcutta, 1984.

THE MARINE PRODUCTS EXPORT DEVELOPMENT AUTHORITY, Act, Rules and Regulations, The Author, Cochin, 1972.

THE MARINE PRODUCTS EXPORT DEVELOPMENT AUTHORITY, MPEDA-An Overview, Cochin, 1994 and 1995.

THE MARINE PRODUCTS EXPORT DEVELOPMENT AUTHORITY, Marine Products Export Reviews 1986-87 to 1995-96, Cochin.

——Annual Reports, 1986-87 to 1995-96, Cochin.

TOM CANNON, Basic Marketing Principles and Practice, A.I.T.B.S. Publishers and Distributors, Delhi, 1997.

TRIVEDI, K.K., 'Fisheries Development : 2000 A.D., Oxford and IBH Publishing Co. New Delhi, 1986.

TRIPATHI, P.C., And REDDY, P.N., 'Principles of Management', Tata McGraw-Hill Publishing Company Limited, New Delhi, 1994.

VARSHNEY, R.L., And BHATTACHARYA, B., 'International Marketing management: An Indian Perspective', Sultan Chand and Sones, New Delhi, 1996.

VERGHESE, C.P., and JOY, P.S., 'Development of Marine fisheries for higher Productivity and Export', Central Institute of Fisheries Nautical and Engineering Training, Cochin, 1993.

VERN TERPSTRA, 'International Marketing', Dryden Press, Hinsdale, Illinois, 1972.

VIJAYA PRAKASH, D., 'Problems and Prospects of fishermen: A Study of Socio-Economic, Marketing and financial Aspects of the Marine Fishermen in Visakhapatnam District', Andhra University, 1992 (unpublished M. Phil. Thesis).

WADHAVA, C.D., 'Some Problems of India's Economic Policy', Tat McGraw-Hill, New Delhi, 1973.

WILLIAM B, Cornell, 'Organisation and Management in Industry and Business', The Ronald Press Company, U.S.A., 1947.

Articles and Papers

AGNELL, R.J., 'Prices and Property Right in Fisheries', *Southern Economics Journal*, Vol. 42, 1975.

AJITH THOMAS JOHN AND SHAHUL HAMEED, M., 'Fisheries Development in India During the plan period - part - 1, Objectives, Outlays and Achievements till the end of Seventh Five Year Plan', *Seafood Export Journal*, Vol. XXVI No. 3, March, 1995.

BABY JACOB, 'Upgradation of Processing Facilities, Sea Food Units' *Seafood Export Journal*, Vol. XXIII, No.90, November 1991.

BAPUJI, M., AND PANDIT, J.V.K.V., 'The socio-Economic Conditions of the Fisheries of Bheemunipatnam', Andhra Pradesh, 22 (7) may 1978.

BASIC FACTS, *Fishing Chimes*, Vol. 11, No.10, January, 1992.

BHADRY, S.K., 'Marine Fisheries Development', *Fishing Chimes*, Vol. 10, No.6, September 1990.

BHASKARAN NAIR, P., 'ISO 9000 For Marine Products Industry Requirements of ISO 900s : Quality system', *Seafood Export Journal*, Vol. XXV, No. 22, December 1994.

BHASKARAN NAIR, P., 'ISO 9000 For Marine Products Industry Requirements of ISO 9002: Document and Data Control '*Seafood Export Journal*, Vol, XXVI, No.3, March 1995.

BHASKARAN NAIR, P., 'ISO 9000 For Marine Products Industry Requirements of ISO 9000 : Purchasing', *Seafood Export Journal*, Vol. XXVI, No. 5, May 1995.

BHASKARAN PILLAI, N., 'The Economics of Operation: Mechanised Boats', The *Economic Times*, September 10, 1983.

BHATIA, K., 'Deep Sea Fishing Scheme Evoking Little Response', *Fishing Chimes*, Vol.9, No.7, October 1989.

BHULLAR, K.S., 'Credit for Fishing Industry', *Seafood Export Journal*. Vol. 4, No. 11, January 1972.

BUSINESS STANDARD, 'Fishing Industry: Problems and Prospects of Development', March 1, 1976.

CHAUHAN, D.P.S., 'Present Status of Fisheries in India with Suggested Measures for Development', *Fishing Chimes*, Vol. 11, No. 5, August 1991.

CHELLAPPA, S., 'Fisheries Development in Andhra Pradesh', *Fishing Chimes*, Vol. 11, No. 1, April, 1991.

DASARADHARAMI REDDI, B., and Sundaraiah, O., 'Credit Structure in an Andhra Pradesh Village', *The Economic Times*, September 10, 1983.

DEVARAJ, M., 'A Programme for Deepsea Fisheries Development in the Indian Exclusive Economic Zone', *Fishing Chimes*, Vol. 7, No. 6, September, 1987.

DEY, V.K., 'World Shrimp Market - Changing Trends', *Seafood Export Journal*, Vol. XXVI, No. 7, July 1995.

ELIAS SAIT, 'Overview of the Marine Products Industry in India', *Seafood Export Journal*, Vol. XXV, No. 12, February, 1994.

FISHERY BULLETIN, U.S. Department of Commerce, Vol. 90, No. 1, January, 1992.

FISHING CHIMES, 'World Catch', Vol. 11, No.10, January, 1992.

FISHING CHIMES', Larger Role of MPEDA in Fishery Development', Vol.9, No.4, July, 1989.

——'Chrosome Manipulation in fish', Vol.8, No.10, January, 1989.

——'Fish Production in India', Vol. 11, No. 10, January, 1992.

GEORGE, C.S., 'Global Fish Production Trends', *Fishing Chimes*, Vol. 10. No.4, July, 1990.

GOKHALE, S.V., 'Marine Fisheries Research and Survey in India', *Seafood Export Journal*, Vol. XXII, No.4, April, 1990.

GOPUKUMAR, K., 'Packaging for Fresh and Processed Marine Products, *Seafood Export Journal*, Vol. XXVII, No.2, February, 1996.

JACOB J., TALIA, 'Domestic Marketing of Fishery Products as support to Export Industry', *Seafood Export Journal*, Vol. XXIII, No. 8, September, 1991.

JAMES, P.S.B.R., 'Marine Fisheries Research: Impact on Fisheries Development', *Fishing Chimes*, Vol. 8, No. 10, October, 1973.

JOHN, K.J., 'Electronics for Deepsea fishing', *Fishing Chimes*, Vol. 15, No. 11, February, 1996.

MUKUNDAN, M.K., And KURIYAN, G.K., 'Fisheries in India', *Yojana*, Vol. 24, No. 19, October, 1980.

NAMBIAR, K.P.P., 'Food fish Scarcity - An impending Reality ? *Seafood Export Journal*, Vol. XXVII, No.2, February, 1996.

PARA, 'Management of Marine commercial Fisheries in India', *Fishing Chimes*, vol. 10. No. 3, June, 1990.

PERIGREEN, P.A., and GOVINDAN, T.K., 'General Transportation of Fish in India : Problems and Prospects', *Fish Technology*, Vol. 15, No. 6, May, 1991.

PRANAB MUKHERJEE, 'Raise India's Share in Seafood Exports', *Fisheries World*, Vol 1, Issue: 7, March 1994.

PURUSHAN, K.S., 'Challenging Scenario of Scientific Shrimp Farming in India - An Overview', *Seafood Export Journal*, Vol. XXV, No. 7, July 1993.

RAJA GOPAL, S., LYLA, P.S., And AJMAL KHAN, S., Seafood the Nutritional Insurance', *Seafood Export Journal*, Vol. XXV, No. 7, July 1993.

RANGA RAO, I.V., 'Is Blue Revolution in the Offing', *The Economic Times*, September 10, 1983.

RAO, K.V.R., 'Some Suggestions for the Betterment of Indian Fishing Industry and Fishermen', *Seafood Export Journal*, Vol. 3, No.9, September, 1973.

RON BAYNES, 'Market Information on Fish', International Trade Forum, Internal Trade Forum, International Trade Centre, UNCTAD/GATT, Vol. XIX, 3/1983.

SEAFOOD EXPORT JOURNAL, 'New Deep-sea Fishing Policy to Boost Exports of Marine Products', Vol. XXII, No. 7-8, July-August 1990.

SIVASHANKAR, A., A., and YOGAMOORTHI, A., 'India's Seafood Export Trend and Its Future Prospects by 2000 A.D., '*Seafood Export Journal*, Vol. XXV, No. 11, January, 1994.

SRINIVASULU REDDY, M., 'Shrimp Pond and Water Management', *Seafood Export Journal*, vol. 15, No. 6, September, 1995.

SUDARSAN, D., 'Marine Fishery Resources in the Exclusive Economic Zone of India with Special Reference to Deepsea Fishing', *Seafood Export Journal,* Vol. XXIII, No. 7, August., 1991.

The Economics Times, 'EU Ban on Indian Seafood Exports' comes into effect, Hyderabad Edition, Saturday 2, august, 1997.

——'EU bans Indian Seafood Exports from August 15', Hyderabad Edition, Thursday 31, July, 1997.

THE HINDU, 'European Union lifts ban on Marine Products', Friday, December, 19, 1997.

•••